THE ROVER V8 ENGINE

THE ROVER V8 ENGINE

2ND EDITION

David Hardcastle

Haynes Publishing

THIS BOOK IS DEDICATED TO MY WIFE SANDRA

First published in 1990
Reprinted 1991 and 1993
Second edition published in 1995
Reprinted 2002 and 2004

A catalogue record for this book is available from the British Library

ISBN 0 85429 961 0

Library of Congress catalog card no. 94-79679

G. T. Foulis is an imprint of
Haynes Publishing, Sparkford,
Yeovil, Somerset BA22 7JJ, UK

Tel: 01963 442030 Fax 01963 440001
Int. tel: +44 1963 442030 Fax +44 1963 440001
E-mail: sales@haynes.co.uk
Website: www.haynes.co.uk

Haynes North America, Inc.,
861 Lawrence Drive, Newbury Park,
California 91320, USA

Printed and bound in England by J. H. Haynes & Co. Ltd, Sparkford

**Jurisdictions which have strict emission control laws may consider
any modifications to a vehicle to be an infringement of those laws.
You are advised to check with the appropriate body or authority
whether your proposed modification complies fully with the law. The
author and publishers accept no liability in this regard.**

**While every effort is taken to ensure the accuracy of the information
given in this book, no liability can be accepted by the author or
publishers for any loss, damage or injury caused by errors in, or
omissions from the information given.**

Contents

Acknowledgements

Preparing this 2nd edition enabled me to renew many acquaintances made when this book was originally written, and meet still more interesting and helpful people connected in some way with the engine.

My thanks for their cooperation and support goes to John Eales of J. E. Developments, Ron Hall and all the staff at J. E. Engineering in Coventry, Ray Webb of Rovertec, Kevin Jones of Rover Group External Affairs, whose help and interest has never faltered, Mike Creswick, Mike Trzcinski, Dave Wall, Don Groves, Simon Maris and Nick Argent at Land Rover in Solihull. To Tony Pond goes my sincere thanks for his interest and for providing the Foreword.

Organisations that have given their assistance include Real Steel, The Patrick Collection, Vandervell Ltd, the V8 Register (part of the MGOC), the Austin Rover Heritage Trust, John Woolfe Racing, TVR Sports Cars, RS Engineering, S & S Preparations, Tom Walkinshaw Racing, Industrial Control Services, Grinnall Cars, Janspeed and F. G. Rallying.

Individuals who have given freely of their time and in many cases encouraged me with their interest are Andy Rouse, Peter and Yvonne Nott, John Ward, Bill Price, Don Moore, Dave Angel (of the Angel Collection), Nic Mann, Mike Gibbon, Andrew Massey, Mark Grinnall, Reg and Ray Woodcock, Dennis Leech, Steve Trice, Dennis Chick, David Jenkins, Mick Moore, Don Pither, David Wood, Cliff Humphries, Alvin Smith, Roger Bywater, Geoff Mortimer, Chris Schirle, Ben Samuelson, and Noel Palmer.

Additional photographs were contributed by Stefan Piasecki, John Colley, Bill Mantovani, Chris Harvey, Ian Messanger and the Haymarket Photo Library.

I would also like to acknowledge the influence of the work of Graham Robson The Rover Story and Land Rover/Range Rover), Hot Rod Magazine, The Autocourse History of the Grand Prix Car by Doug Nye, Autocar and Autosport.

Foreword

Throughout my rallying and racing career I have been fortunate in not only having the opportunity to compete with a variety of vehicles in various types of motor sport but also to enjoy sampling many different road cars, too. It was in the latter context that I first drove a pre-production Triumph TR8 and was impressed by the quantum leap forward of the Rover V8-engined over the four-cylinder version.

When the Triumph TR7 V8 rallying programme got under way, an enormous effort was put into developing the car for its appointed task. Tuning the Rover V8 was completely new territory in those days, but even in its early twin-Weber form it was superbly powerful over a wide, if somewhat lowly, rev range. But it still possessed considerable potential which was really unleashed later in quadruple-Weber form, and by the end of 1980 the car had evolved into a first class rallying contender, untouchable on tarmac and getting the measure of the Escort in the forests. I had high hopes for the 1981 European Championship, confident that the TR7 V8 could take on, and beat, the dominant Porsches, but the programme was cancelled as TR7/TR8 production was phased out.

Attention then switched to the Rover 3500/SD1 saloon and I began testing a version being developed for long distance events such as the intended Paris-Peking rally. The specification of the engines we used was carried over from the TR7 V8 and, despite its physical size, the big saloon

complemented the smooth, immensely powerful V8 perfectly. So good was it, in fact, that the Rover's circuit racing potential was quickly recognised and before long I was behind the wheel of one of Tom Walkinshaw's magnificent Group A Rover Vitesses. The Rover V8 which had proved itself as a rallying engine was equally magnificent in fuel injected form for racing, a graphic illustration of its amazing versatility.

We even rallied TWR-prepared Group A Rover Vitesses, probably best remembered as the Computervision cars, with virtually race spec engines and Getrag gearboxes. Those gearboxes and the homologated ratios, especially those for the rear axle, were hardly ideal but this didn't detract from the car's superb and very competitive performance.

Progress marches on and the increasing sophistication of cars in the rallying world meant that, as part of the Austin Rover Motorsport team, I had my part to play in developing the MG Metro 6R4 as

our Group B contender. So too did the Rover V8, albeit chopped down from eight to six cylinders, to give us an engine to enable serious testing to get underway. It could still deliver enough power to propel one extremely quick motor car. I'm pleased to see that someone has at last had a good look 'under the bonnet' at an engine whose glorious sound and effortless power I shall always look back on with relish.

Tony Pond

Introduction

The Rover V8 engine has been in continuous mass production for over 20 years and with a planned production life to the end of the nineties, looks like being part of the British motor industry for some time to come.

It is a remarkable power unit. When the rights to manufacture it were bought from General Motors in 1965 the then Buick/Oldsmobile 215 had only had three years of manufacture (1961-63), at a time when V8 engine production for a particular design was normally measured in decades. It had been dropped from GM's engine line-up, not because it was no good (far from it) but because they had lost faith in the dream of 'exotic' lightweight materials and the problems they created. The American motorist, used to the sheer indestructibility of a 'good 'ole' cast-iron engine, could not get used to giving it the extra attention it needed for trouble-free, high mileage operation and the advancing 'technology' of thin-wall cast-iron engine production went some way towards negating the weight advantage of the aluminium alternative. In short, the aluminium V8 was a luxury they decided they did not want to afford.

So Rover brought the engine to the UK, where engines of V8 configuration were not entirely unknown, but unlike in North America, where the V8 once reigned supreme, it had never, and now probably never will be, considered suitable for lower and mid-range mass produced cars. The higher manufacturing costs of multi-cylinder (in this context meaning six or more) engines makes them better suited to lower volume, higher priced production applications.

There have been British-designed and manufactured V8 engines – the Daimler 2.5-/4.5-litre V8 and the ill-fated Triumph sohc V8 being two well known examples. Both these engines were compact and innovative in design, but they were not particularly powerful and with cast-iron blocks were heavy, too (the Daimler weighed over 400lb dry).

The Rover V8 was originally perceived by its new manufacturers as a smooth, refined powerplant ideal for their range of luxury cars. In its pre-Rover days the design had seen one branch of its family tree blossom in Formula One competition with the Brabham team. This performance precedent was repeated years later in the arena of British and European touring car racing where the Rover SD1 enjoyed a truly magnificent eight-year career, achieving success which even now has never been fully honoured or appreciated. The engine's power and the sound of its bellowing exhaust also created an international rallying legend and was even once the heart of a brave attempt at the classic Le Mans 24 Hour race.

There is nothing high-tech or exotic about the Rover engine. To anyone with an understanding of standard American V8s and an appreciation of their simplicity this little beauty will hold no mysteries except that it is made from aluminium and therefore weighs little more than a cast-iron four-cylinder engine.

Whereas an American cast-iron V8 would sorely test the structure and suspension of any car originally designed for half as many cylinders, the Rover V8 can reside with ease and safety.

This engine's performance potential is astounding; as well as being the basis of a powerplant for one of the fastest road-driven cars ever built it is proving versatile enough and capable enough to power a number of exciting and impressive specialist sports cars with performance guaranteed to increase the pulse rate. For a few hundred pounds one of these engines can be picked up from any number of breakers' yards the length and breadth of the country. With some basic mechanical knowledge and a further few hundred pounds the Rover V8 can be turned into a very respectable powerplant for any number of road and competition vehicles. For the owners of Rover V8-engined cars there is ample potential under their vehicles' bonnets to unleash considerably more power and torque for greater performance both on and off road, as well as enhanced towing ability and even economy.

It may be American in origin but in years to come, when the Rover V8 ceases production, this light but strong, powerful but docile, simple but refined now all-British classic engine will be sorely missed. Enjoy it while you can!

Chapter One

From Transatlantic Origins . . . .

The United States automobile industry has been responsible for the design and production of vast numbers of V8 engines, which have proved powerful, dependable and cheap to manufacture without being particularly efficient. Their weight has often been excessive and their fuel consumption, by European standards (and judged in later years by ecological standards) little short of irresponsible. Henry Ford brought the luxury of eight-cylinder power and torque to the 'average' American motorist in 1932 with his flathead V8, a cast-iron lump of 3.6 litres which produced a healthy 65 bhp and weighed in at 616 lb complete with clutch and gearbox. This milestone of mass production remained in production until 1954 when it was replaced by a new overhead valve V8. Rival manufacturers too, had not been slow to take the V8 engine away from the luxury car and into the family car market.

In 1955 Chevrolet launched what has now become a legend, the ubiquitous 'small-block' Chevy. Originally available as a 265 cu in (4342 cc) engine this relatively light and compact (by contemporary standards) overhead valve cast-iron V8 revolutionised engine design. Although 575 lb in weight (or 450 lb with aluminium heads) and producing around 200 bhp in production form it could easily be tuned to one bhp per cubic inch; in fact this was offered in production from the 350 cubic inch version. The one bhp per cubic inch milestone was first achieved in a production engine by the Chrysler 300B of 1956 and it was

equalled by the small-block Chevrolet with the classic 283 cu in (4637 cc) fuel-injected version in the '57 Chevy. Still in production today, the Chevrolet 'mouse' has total production exceeding 35 million units.

It was in the late Fifties that the American automobile industry first began to feel the bite of imported European cars, of which the Volkswagen Beetle is probably the most obvious example. This was perceived as a threat but it also created a potential new market. It was then a matter of producing a product to meet the needs of that market, for which the industry planned a new range of 'compacts'; smaller, lighter and more efficient than those being currently manufactured but still identifiable as pure American. An essential element in this scaling-down process was the powerplant and for the Buick division of General Motors this did not mean a four-cylinder engine. The V8 would prevail.

The 1961 Buick Special represented one manufacturer's reply to the intrusion by imported cars into their territory and the engine chosen to power it represented an equally radical departure from the established norm.

Building an engine in aluminium was not a totally new concept, indeed just about every brave new advance in automotive engineering generally has its roots in earlier experiments which were, perhaps, abandoned because the technology was not available to make them a feasible, cost-effective proposition. Aluminium engines, at least in the United States, went back to 1916 and the Marmon 34, this same company producing an aluminium V16 in 1930. But this was low-volume production. The Aluminium Company of America (Alcoa), keen to promote the widespread use of their product in industry, began experimenting with an aluminium V8 in 1917, going on to commission the Englishman L.H. Pomeroy, later to achieve renown as Chief Engineer of Vauxhall during the Vintage period, to design and build a number of all-aluminium automobiles. In 1942 Alcoa revealed an all-aluminium six-cylinder engine, based on a Pontiac design. Buick too had been busy, particularly in the post-war years. In 1951 they unveiled the Le Sabre and XP-300 experimental cars both of which had an all-aluminium engine with bore and stroke of 3.25 inches giving 231.7 cu in (3798 cc), with hemispherical combustion chambers and a Roots-type supercharger; power output was very healthy 300 bhp. General Motors designed and built an aluminium V6 in 1955 with a single overhead camshaft on each cylinder head which led in 1958 to a more conventional 253 cu in (4145 cc) V8. In was from this 1958 experiment that the Buick-Oldsmobile production V8 developed but it was Buick engineers who designed it.

The all new aluminium Buick engine was a V8 of 215.5 cu in (3531 cc), having a bore of 3.5" and a stroke of 2.8" Taken from this design was the Oldsmobile version, offered in the Oldsmobile F85 of the same year, 1961, but Divisional autonomy within the GM empire meant their engineers were able to put their own stamp of individuality on the engine by making several changes. They designed their own cylinder heads which had a six-bolt pattern around each combustion chamber instead of the Buick's five-bolt, made changes to the valve gear and used different pistons. Although both Buick and Oldsmobile used the same basic wedge-shaped combustion chamber, Buick opted for relatively small-volume chambers in the head and dished-top pistons, while Oldsmobile had a larger chamber in the cylinder head with a flat-top piston. The Buick heads also had the valves more offset from the centre of the chamber with the spark plug nearly in the centre, striving for a squish effect across the whole chamber. Compression ratio was 8.8:1 on the Buick and 8.75:1 on the Oldsmobile versions of the engine. Of greater significance was that the Oldsmobile had bigger ports and valves, although the rated power of both engines was the same.

Engine compartment of the 1961 Buick Special with 215 cu. in. aluminium V8 engine.

'Aluminum Fireball V8' – 155 bhp at 4600 rpm and 220 ft/lb of torque at 2400 rpm.

The design of the engine, even by contemporary standards was not remarkable; similar engines were being manufactured in cast iron up to 400 cubic inches capacity. But the bigger the engine the heavier they were. The little Buick V8, weighing in at a mere 318 lb, represented a significant advance, not only in material – Reynolds 356 silicone aluminium alloy instead of cast iron – but in manufacturing methods. Not that using this material was new to GM, but building large numbers of relatively expensive engines with an acceptable casting scrap rate and a good standard of reliability in use was not an easy task.

Although to all intents and purposes a die-cast engine the Buick V8 was not fully so; this would have required tooling expenditure far in excess of the norm for even a mass-produced engine. In this instance the system used was of a semi-permanent mould type; that is external steel moulds with all the internal passages made from sand cores which were then shaken or blown out of the finished casting. The molten aluminium was gravity fed, instead of being introduced by the high pressure feed a full die-casting process would have required, and there was no bonding in the head or block castings. Such a system was even thought at the time to be superior to the conventional sand casting of cast-iron engine parts. Had the whole process proved a success it could even have led to the demise of the cast-iron engine but, as we shall see, such methods had their problems.

At the design stage one problem to be overcome was the selection of material for the actual cylinder bores. Aluminium alloys were available that could endure the rubbing of piston and rings, but there were problems with the piston ring scuffing of the bores immediately after cold starts. Chrome plating or metal spraying the bores would have overcome the problem but was too expensive. Added to this, these harder silicon alloys were also more difficult to cast or machine. Cast-iron *dry* cylinder liners were the answer – not *wet* liners, where coolant is actually in contact with the outer surface of the liner. Buick engineers did not consider that the high precision machining involved would be cost effective and had grave misgivings about coolant leakage between liner and block. The cost of inserting cast-iron cylinder liners into the aluminium blocks was also considered prohibitive so a clever method was devised to locate pre-heated iron liners in the mould and pour the molten aluminium around them, the outside of the liners having rough corrugations machined into the outer surface to lock them firmly into place once the aluminium had solidified. The block with liners in place was then heat treated to condition -T6; this was one area of the manufacturing process which caused serious problems. It could result in the displacement of liners which then meant rejection of the entire blockcasting; the rejection rate at times exceeded 90 per cent.

The block had plenty of material below the centre line of the crankshaft, providing strength and support to the crankshaft and its cast-iron main bearing caps. Cast iron was used for greater rigidity and more constant bearing clearances under varying temperatures. The crankshaft itself was a perfectly conventional two-plane design, precision cast in Pearlitic ductile iron. It had five main bearings with the centre (No 3) bearing being the thrust bearing, locating the crank in the block. In a cast-iron engine it is usually the No 5 or end bearing that does the job but the different expansion rates between iron and aluminium make this impractical. Main bearing journals were of 2.3 " and rod journals 2.0 " diameter. The connecting rods on the Buick were conventional too, manufactured in SAE 1141 steel, weighing around 17.5 ounces and having a centre-to-centre length of 5.66 in. As previously stated, there was a significant difference in pistons between the Buick and Oldsmobile engines, Oldsmobile going for a flat-top design and Buick having a shallow circular depression, but they were both cast, with two compression and one oil ring per piston. The 0.875 " diameter gudgeon pin was a push-fit in the unbushed upper rod end.

The aluminium cylinder heads were cast from the same alloy as the block and by the same semi-permanent mould process with sintered iron valve seats shrunk into place and pressed-in cast-iron valve guides. The combustion chambers were machined into the heads (unlike the Rover V8 which are cast). Both Buick and Oldsmobile versions of the cylinder head used the same spacing for the intake and exhaust ports (although they did not share the same intake and exhaust manifolds) but the Oldsmobile heads had less restricted ports. The water jacketing inside the heads was ample, especially in the critical areas around the spark plugs and exhaust valves but the superior heat conductivity properties of aluminium allowed simpler water jacket coring in certain areas, in particular above the inlet ports.

Both versions of the engine had the same camshaft and hydraulic lifters. Timing was: intake opens 22 degrees BTC, closes 58 degrees ABC (260 degrees duration); exhaust opens 60 degrees BBC, closes 20 degrees ATC (260 degrees duration and 42 degrees overlap). Total lift for intake and exhaust valves was 0.384". Solid forged pushrods differed in length slightly between Buick and Oldsmobile engines because of differences in valve gear design and valve length. Both designs used 1.6:1 ratio rocker arms, but those on the Buick were forged aluminium with pressed-in steel buttons on the valve end and sockets on the pushrod end. The Buick rocker shaft stand assemblies bolted into the cylinder head casting. This differed from the Oldsmobile, in which the aluminium rocker shaft stands were held in place by long cap screws which went right through the head and located in the block, thus helping to hold down the cylinder head. The Oldsmobile also used steel rocker arms. Lubrication for the valve gear also differed slightly between the two designs but basically the oil flowed from the main oil galleries, one on each side of the lifter chamber, intersecting the lifter bores, with passages drilled to camshaft and crankshaft main bearings. Rocker oil travelled up a passage to the top of the block, into the front rocker stand and the hollow rocker shaft.

The valves themselves were not interchangeable between Buick and Oldsmobile engines. The Oldsmobile intake valves at 1.522 " diameter were slightly larger than the Buick which were of 1.500 in diameter; similarly the exhaust valves were 1.353 in against 1.313 in. The Oldsmobile valves were also slightly larger in stem diameter (by 0.002 ") and 0.25 in longer. Valve shape and stem taper also varied slightly. The Buick engine used single, straight valve springs while the Oldsmobile had conical springs, tapering near the valve cap; spring load was 168 lb.

One aspect of the engines which was unusual, by contemporary V8 engine design standards, was the positioning of the oil pump driveshaft/distributor driveshaft ahead of the timing chain in an extended cast-aluminium timing chain cover. This put the distributor well forward on the engine, clear of the inlet manifold and any other induction equipment, with the oil pump also mounted forward of the engine to the right and on the bottom of the cover with the oil filter pointing down from below the pump. Oil pressure was set by the relief valve at 33 psi. The water pump then sat even further forward of the timing chain cover. The generator sat on the left of the engine (looking from the front) at crankshaft level.

Although the inlet manifolds were interchangeable, they were not the same. The Oldsmobile version had a cast 'dam'

around the centrally mounted single car-burettor, on to which fitted a larger-than-normal stamped steel air cleaner box which completely enclosed the carburettor, caus-ing air to be drawn into the engine from beneath the inlet manifold. The idea of this unique arrangement was to cool the car-burettor, reduce intake noise and keep the linkages clean. The Buick engine used a more conventional air cleaner arrangement mounted on top of the Rochester carb, with its two 1" venturis fed by a mechan-ical fuel pump mounted on the left-hand side of the timing cover. Rocker covers were of stamped aluminium. The exhaust manifolds, again interchangeable between

Buick and Oldsmobile versions of the engine, were of cast iron.

Having being introduced in the autumn of 1960 the all-new aluminium V8 was made available to the American motoring public in the 1961 Buick Special and Oldsmobile F85, and as an option (Buick version) in the Pontiac Tempest. The all-new Buick Special sat on a 112" wheel-base, weighed under 23 cwt and was com-petitively priced at around $2500 – 3000 depending on specification; a price, incidentally, on par in the US with the first Rover 2000s on sale there. Performance was lively with 0-60 mph capability of less than 11 seconds and 25 mpg could be

Hugely American from this angle, the 1961 Buick Special was sur-prisingly compact by American standards.

Two views of the 1961 Buick Special in which the all-new 215 aluminium engine was debuted. *(The Angel Collection)*

achieved if the car was driven with economy in mind. As standard, 6.50-13 bias ply tubeless tyres were fitted but 6.00-15 tyres were an optional extra. It had worm and sector power steering and drum brakes only although US manufacturers had learned a lot about stopping their big heavy sedans without discs, even in the extreme conditions of NASCAR racing. The engine was heralded as 'The incredible new power team – Aluminum Fireball V8 and Dual-Path Turbine transmission'. In fact a three-speed manual transmission was standard, the two-speed automatic (weighing a commendable 95 lb) being an extra cost option, as was a four-barrel Rochester carburettor. Buick offered a two-barrel Rochester as standard, with 8.8:1 compression ratio, 155 bhp at 4600 rpm and 220 ft/lb of torque at 2400 rpm. The four-barrel Rochester option with a 10.25:1 compression ratio boasted 185 bhp at 4800 rpm and 230 ft/lb of torque at 2800 rpm.

The Oldsmobile offering with the new engine (dubbed the Rockette) was called the F85 to give the impression of having descended from the F88 show car. It used the same floor pan as the Buick Special but had its own distinctive style. It was the least successful of the trio. In May 1961 Oldsmobile introduced the F85 Cutlass coupé and convertible which, being sporty models, widened the appeal of the range to younger buyers. The Pontiac Tempest was unique in having independent rear suspension, incorporating the transmission and floor pan of the rear-engined Corvair, fitted as standard with a front mounted four-cylinder engine.

The new engine was enthusiastically received and the prospect of a new generation of aluminium V8s had tremendous appeal. Cylinder blocks and heads cast in such an exotic material were, and still are, highly prized, particularly by those with an eye to performance, although in this case the rather small capacity of the engine was a limiting factor.

For the buying public and General Motors, however, the reality of long-term customer ownership and mass-production were beginning to turn a little sour. Mention has already been made of the difficulties encountered in production with which, quite rightly, GM persevered, aware no doubt that the product was unquestionably a good one and that new methods often needed patience and development. But the fickle American motorist was unfamiliar with the special needs of an aluminium engine, which had a particularly large capacity cooling system (around 4 gallons of coolant) requiring special antifreeze, this being long before the days of siliconized antifreezes. Available only from GM outlets and therefore not generally available the special antifreeze was also expensive. Using incorrect coolant caused a reaction within the engine, releasing an aluminium-silicone oxide which clogged the radiator leading to engine overheating and eventual warping of the engine in critical areas such as the cylinder heads.

By 1963 production of the engine was halted and from the design and tooling was developed a cast-iron V6 of 198 cu in (3244 cc) which replaced the aluminium V8 in the same range of GM compacts.

This V6 remained in production from 1962 to 1967 (by which time it had grown to 225 cu in) (3687 cc) after which the tooling was sold to Jeep who wanted a smaller/cheaper engine in their range. By the mid-Seventies the accent was once again very firmly on economy and GM bought their V6 tooling back from AMC (who by then owned Jeep) and in 1975 introduced a 231 cu in (3785 cc) version. These V8-derived V6s had a very odd firing sequence, simply because the crankshaft was essentially a V8 design less two cylinders. The V6 gradually became a more important part of the GM engine line-up and needed refinement so in 1977 it was endowed with an even-firing V6 crankshaft, with improved cylinder heads; a turbocharged version followed in 1978. The legendary Smokey Yunick applied his skills to this extremely potent V6 and McLaren took it to Indianapolis. By 1985, racing specification turbocharged engines were producing 800 bhp, once again using special aluminium blocks for lightness. It is worth noting that, by this stage, new 'thin-wall' casting techniques had been developed for the cast-iron production engine, significantly reducing the weight penalty with, of course, none of the earlier difficulties encountered with aluminium. Cast-iron had far fewer mysteries, and in fact the aluminium V8 design was evolved into a cast-iron V8 too, known as the Buick 300 and 340.

But for the Buick/Oldsmobile aluminium V8 1963 was the end of the line after some three-quarters of a million units.

The bench seat, column gear selector and chrome trim are typical of the Sixties American automobile.

Chapter Two

The Power Race

The performance potential of the aluminium General Motors V8 had not gone unnoticed or unexploited. Many of America's leading aftermarket performance part manufacturers had examined the engine and begun marketing camshafts, high compression pistons, improved inlet manifolds for single or multiple carburettors and tubular steel exhaust manifolds. *Hot Rod* magazine wasted no time in getting both versions of the engine on to a dynamometer and applying a variety of standard tuning techniques to them. With step-by-step changes to ignition timing, carburation, compression, camshaft, valve springs, inlet and exhaust manifolding, they easily exceeded 1 bhp per cubic inch, revving the engines to 7000 rpm. Problems were encountered only in two areas: stripping of some threads in the aluminium despite careful use of the torque wrench, and excessive wear in the distributor drive gears. More of that anon.

A leading name in V8 tuning in the States is Traco (Travers & Coons) of Culver City, California and this company too wasted no time in applying itself to the little aluminium V8, being one of the first to increase the engine's capacity beyond 215 cubic inches. Even the GM factories had time to dabble, particularly Oldsmobile who released a turbocharged version of their engine in April 1962 at the New York International Auto Show. This produced 215 bhp at 4600 rpm (and 300 lb/ft of torque at 3200 rpm). The car into which the engine was fitted was

known as the Oldsmobile F85 Jetfire (based on the Cutlass hardtop coupé body) and not only was this their first turbocharged offering in a production car but it achieved the significant advertised figure of one horsepower per cubic inch, enough to urge the new car from 0-60 mph in 8.9 seconds.

Oldsmobile wanted a high-performance version of the aluminium engine for the F85 but felt the engine had limitations for raising power output. The conventional methods of carb, cam and port work were estimated to yield only about 30 per cent more output, and this with unacceptable alterations to the engine's characteristics. GM Research had done much assessment work on turbocharging between 1953 and 1956, remaining unconvinced of its value in production engines. Oldsmobile began their own experiments, centred around the idea that lowering the compression ratio, which was the accepted practice for turbocharger installations, meant poor economy and poor driveability in general road use. They did in fact raise the compression ratio to 10.25:1 and devised a special Rochester carburettor, combined with an injection system which used 'Turbo Rocket Fluid'; actually an innocuous 50/50 mix of distilled water and methyl alcohol, which was injected into the cylinders during boost and had the effect of suppressing detonation and raising power output. The turbocharger was a Garrett AiResearch unit, limited to 5 psi boost.

ROVER V8

It was mainly the Oldsmobile version which, suitably tuned for racing by people like Traco, appeared in a variety of racing cars. In 1958 the Cooper racing concern introduced what was to be their last two-seater sports racing car, the Monaco, usually powered by a 2-or 2.5-litre Climax FPF engine. By the early sixties, however, Briggs Cunningham was competing in one using a Buick engine following the even earlier example of Sy Kaback (Lotus Fifteen). By 1962 Roger Penske was racing the rather special Cooper-Zerex built around a Cooper F1 chassis with two-seater bodywork. This same car was bought by one Bruce McLaren and with Oldsmobile power, became the first McLaren sports racing car. By September of that same year he had designed and built his own McLaren M1A, based on the Zerex and powered by a Traco-Oldsmobile engine producing over 350 bhp. This proved very successful, winning the *Daily Express* meeting at Silverstone, with McLaren trying a Ferguson-developed automatic transmission. The M1A and its lighter successor, the Mk 2, continued to be successful through to 1965, but by now the Oldsmobile units were being superseded by Chevrolet.

Scarab, the racing car project of American Lance Reventlow, used Buick engines in a single-seater and a sports racing car in the early Sixties. The Scarab works subsequently became the basis for Carroll Shelby's Cobra operation; Cobra replica builders in the UK who are using the Rover V8 might be interested to know that the Buick aluminium engine was one of the units considered for adoption by Shelby in the early days of creating the Cobra.

1965 was the last year of the 1.5-litre formula, the following year seeing the introduction of the 3.0-litre (normally aspirated) Formula 1 regulations which have continued until very recently, Coventry-Climax were a major long-term engine-supplier to Formula 1 during the time it required 1.5-litre engines, rather like Cosworth more recently, except that the Climax company did so on a totally commercial basis. They had no major motor manufacturer backing them as a prestige venture and no team (with the possible exception of Lotus) were being supplied with engines unless they paid for them in full. As well as for Formula 1. Coventry-Climax engines were being used extensively for the Tasman Series, a 2.5-litre single-seater formula very well supported in Australia and New Zealand.

With the advent of the new 3.0-litre Formula 1, Coventry-Climax lost interest in racing and returned to their main business of manufacturing materials handling equipment. In Australia a major customer for the Climax FPF engine in 2.5-litre Tasman guise was Repco (Geoffrey Russell's Replacement Parts Pty Ltd of Melbourne) an automotive parts and equipment company with considerable resources. They realized that parts for the Climax FPF could cease to be readily available while the 2.5-litre Tasman formula was still current so set about designing a new engine. Repco had long been a supplier to Jack Brabham's racing team in England and Brabham was now commissioning cars from Motor Racing Developments in Surbiton built by fellow Australian Ron Tauranac. MRD were also supplying 'Repco-Brabham' Tasman cars to Repco in Australia.

Repco gave their engineers Frank Hallam and Phil Irving a design brief to build a new 2.5-litre engine that would fit into existing Tasman chassis, but the budget allocated did not allow for the design of a completely new engine from scratch. They therefore designed a V8 around the Oldsmobile F85 production cylinder block which they concluded could be built in a range of capacities from 2.5-litre for the Tasman Series version to 4.4-litres for Group 7 sports car racing. The design parameters also called for a minimum engine frontal area and an overall width falling within that of existing spaceframe chassis. The prototype of this new engine first ran in March 1965,

The 21 year old Repco Brabham engine installed in Pilbeam MP47HRB. It powered Charles Wardle to the 1988 Guyson USA British Hillclimb Championship.

This Marsh Special of Tony Marsh, with its Buick 3.5-litre engine was a hill climb winner in 1965. Now it's back and still a strong performer.

slightly less than a year after design work began and Jack Brabham reached agreement with Repco to build a 3.0-litre version for the new Formula 1.

The result of their endeavours and a triumph of compromise and expediency was a production-derived engine which won the 1966 Formula 1 World Championship for Jack Brabham. Indeed a further development of the engine which abandoned the Oldsmobile block won the 1967 World Championship for Denny Hulme, despite the introduction in that year of the Cosworth V8. It must be made clear that the Repco-Brabham 3.0-litre engine was not the fastest, not the most sophisticated, nor indeed the most powerful, amongst its contemporaries but it proved the best combination at the time; and it won.

In the past, many successful Formula 2 and 3 engines had been based on production pushrod engines, so this was not entirely new territory. As in such cases only the GM V8 cylinder block was retained, and that required stiffening by filling up all the unwanted holes and spaces normally used for the now redun-

dant centre camshaft, pushrod valve gear and oil supply to the hydraulic lifters. A steel stiffening plate was bolted to the sump flange and a three inch deep cast magnesium dry sump added below. The new steel single-plane crankshaft, weighing 45 lb and manufactured by Laystall, was exceptionally rigid. Main and big-end bearing journals were unchanged in size, but featured Repco-designed new main bearing caps held down by longer bolts and using Repco plain bearings. Connecting rods were production items, (taken from the Daimler Majestic 4.5-litre V8) and were 6.3″ long. The stroke of 2.37″ with the retained standard bore size of 3.5″ gave 183 cu.in. (2994cc) and an extremely low bore to stroke ratio. Such a low ratio would encourage high rpm but the long con-rods would reduce maximum piston acceleration and ease bearing and parts stress within the engine. Pistons were special Repco items cast in aluminium silicon alloy with shallow indents in the crown for valve clearance, running in bores reamed out to accept 0.010″ thick cast-iron Repco liners.

19

ROVER V8

Single overhead camshaft cylinder heads were decided upon mainly because a twin-cam head would have made the engine too bulky for the intended chassis. It also kept the chain drive to the camshafts compact, beneath a Repco cast magnesium Y-shaped cover bolted to the front of the block. The cylinder heads were of straightforward design, common to left- or right-hand cylinder banks to keep down production costs and reduce the spares requirements to customers. It had in-line valves, inclined at 10 degrees, and a wedge-shaped combustion chamber; of the type used on the original Buick-Oldsmobile cylinder heads but unheard of in Grand Prix engines. Repco made adaptors for Lucas fuel injection as well as for Weber carburettors for customers looking to use the engines outside Formula 1 and also made their own oil and water pumps. Lucas Opus ignition was used. The complete engine weighed 340 lb; light by Formula 1 standards.

Light, too, was the Brabham BT19 rolling chassis into which the engine went. The spaceframe BT19 was built for the stillborn Climax Flat-16 1.5-litre engine and with the new V8 became the lightest 1966 F1 competitor. Being very economical (around 8 mpg) it had the added advantage of starting a Grand Prix with only 35 gallons of fuel on board. But the Repco V8 was not the most powerful F1 engine by any means, beginning with 285 bhp at 8000 rpm (later rising to 300 bhp), while both Ferrari and BRM had nearer 400 bhp. However, it produced good torque from 3500 rpm, peaking at 6500 rpm with 230 lb/ft but still strong at 8000 rpm (after 8200 rpm cylinder head design became the limiting factor) and this typical V8 attribute gave the car plenty of urge out of the slow-and medium-speed corners found on two-thirds of the GP circuits then in use.

Jack Brabham and the people behind the Repco-Brabham V8 engine had not gone for the expense of ultimate top-end power, instead settling for reliability and practicality. The car proved the worth of those qualities, dominating the 1966 season by winning four GPs in a row and continuing to win as the later BT20. The full potential of 300 bhp was developed with the help of John Judd, who had joined Brabham from Coventry-Climax, following replacement of the lowly GM production block. The Oldsmobile F85 based-engines were designated Type 620 with an RB prefix, 600 denoting the block and 20 the sohc cylinder head thus commencing with engine RB620-E1.

It is at this point that we leave the story because once the basic design had proved sound Repco pressed ahead with the 30 lb lighter Type 700 block which, with improved cylinder heads, meant the ancestry was all but gone. It was the Type 700 which won the 1967 Championship for Denny Hulme (in 1969 Brabham went over to the Cosworth V8). Customers were still offered the Type 620 in 2.5-litre Tasman form (bores sleeved down to 3.34" and a stroke of 2.16"), 3.0-litre and 4.4-litre capacities. In 1968 John Woolfe had a very special Chevron B8 built, so special in fact that it was redesignated a 'B12'. The wheelbase was lengthened by 2.5" to make room in the engine compartment for a 3-litre sohc per cylinder head Repco V8 but the car was not a success. It was entered for Le Mans that same year, co-driven by Digby Martland, but lasted only two hours before retiring with head gasket failure.

Chapter Three

Renaissance At Rover

After a production run of only three-quarters of a million units (paltry by General Motors standards) over a scant three years, manufacture of the Buick/Oldsmobile aluminium V8 ceased. And there the story might have ended – an unimportant footnote in motoring history, had fate and chance not intervened.

The story of how Rover acquired the GM aluminium engine involves three people – William Martin-Hurst of the Rover Company, Karl Kiekhaefer of Mercury Marine and J. Bruce McWilliams, who joined Rover in 1962 as President of its North American operations.

Prior to joining Rover, J. Bruce McWilliams had been Vice-President for Sales & Marketing of Mercedes in the United States whose distribution was at that time owned by the Studebaker company. McWilliams was eager that Studebaker should distribute other imported automobiles and was given the go-ahead to begin negotiations with target companies, one of which was the Rover Company.

McWilliams was impressed with the motivation and interest shown by William F. F. Martin-Hurst, the Managing Director of Rover at that time, and during a meeting in the UK McWilliams was offered the position with Rover, with a brief to pick a team and establish Rover in the US as well as enhance the distribution package of Rover cars with other franchises.

McWilliams set about revitalising the North American organisation, which he had initially found unprofitable and inade-quate, but, most importantly, had a product range that was simply not attractive, at least to American buyers. The losses were especially worrying, but with the organisation revitalised, improving the product range was now the key issue.

From a North American market perspective the Land Rover, good as it was, was underpowered, and the Rover 3-litre 'stodgy'. The Rover 2000 was imminent, but it would have a four-cylinder engine. In this modern era of manufacturers possessing wide vehicle ranges, it is hard to imagine a company existing with such a limited product line-up!

McWilliams began to push for product line improvement, the first step being a six-cylinder engine for the Land Rover 109, although he felt that a small V8 would be more appropriate. That conviction led him to call Martin-Hurst in January 1964, proposing that they should seek out an American V8 for the purpose, there being no prospect of an adequate Rover engine. Martin-Hurst agreed and asked McWilliams to start looking, and so the search began.

McWilliams first approached Chrysler, who had good engines, had supplied others in similar engine deals, and, because they needed funds, would perhaps be more amenable than Ford or General Motors. A suitable Chrysler engine was identified and Martin-Hurst visited New York for further negotiations. During that visit he called on Karl Kiekhaefer, with whom he had become acquainted during a joint gas turbine test programme with

ROVER V8

Mercury. It was during this visit that he noticed the Buick aluminium V8 in Keikhaefer's workshop, learned that it had been withdrawn from production by GM and, with Keikhaefer's prodigious knowledge of engines, learned that the tooling might still be available and that the engine was worth pursuing.

It was at this point that the charm and dash of William Martin-Hurst took over, and his energy and determination made things happen. General Motors were not in the habit of selling the manufacturing rights to an engine, and he had to work hard to convince them that he was serious. With great haste he made a point of meeting with any GM executive that might have influence over the deal, and met with, amongst others, Edward Collert, head of Buick, Philip Copelin, head of GM overseas, and ultimately John Gordon and Frederick Donner, President and Chairman of GM respectively, before the deal was done.

Not everyone within the Rover Company was charmed by the news that an American V8 engine was to be crammed into a Rover; indeed, there was a fair amount of consternation at the news, but it was a *fait accompli* and the practical work got under way almost immediately.

Eventually, though, a generous (to Rover) licence was negotiated and the much needed background technical information on the engine began to flow from Detroit, along with a batch of engines which Rover could immediately begin working on. GM were not going to supply Rover with engines; after all, they had ceased production of them some time before. It was left to Rover to take the design, some American tooling and what production information was available, interpret it and begin manufacturing the engine at Solihull. The interpretation was a major problem. They had the original GM drawings but because of various alterations made during manufacture to solve emerging problems and to improve the product, the drawings did not necessarily conform to the definitive engine. Rover were fortunate in being able to retain the services of Joe Turley, Buick's chief engine designer, who was nearing retirement and generously allowed by GM to move to Solihull as a consultant. During his stay his contribution, although not extensive, was absolutely vital not only in providing detailed information not on the record but also assisting Rover in adapting the design to their own needs.

Rover acquired the licence to manufac-ture the engine from GM in January 1965. Actually producing it involved considerable fresh thinking. Although die-casting gives better metallurgical properties to the finished casting, the techniques involved were virtually unknown in the UK in the early 1960s, certainly for anything as complex as a V8 cylinder block. It was decided to sand-cast the block, which Birmingham Aluminium of Smethwick succeeded in doing with few problems. Centrifugally cast iron cylinder liners were designed to press into the block after it had been heated in an induction furnace to 160°C. Final machining was then carried out. Shrink-fitting the dry liners in this way also improved the torsional rigidity of the block. The cylinder heads were die-cast, with the combustion chamber cast in (as opposed to machined) but as with the Buick, water passages were formed by sand cores.

The original Rochester carburettor was not considered satisfactory; no UK dealers had experience of servicing such a unit and the particular model used was about to go out of production. So Dave Wall at Rover designed a new inlet manifold, loosely based on a contemporary Rolls-Royce

The big, bold Rover 3.5-litre, the first Rover production car to benefit from the new Rover aluminium V8.

The Rover 3500 (P6B) was launched in April 1968 as a refined performance touring car.

design, with a 'pitched-roof' mounting for a pair of SU carburettors. Lucas designed their first V8 distributor for this engine, and Hobourn-Eaton supplied the oil pump. The camshaft blanks, timing chain and gears and the hydraulic tappets were supplied from the States – as indeed they still are today. The Diesel Equipment Co. of Grand Rapids can produce them so cheaply, and to such high standards that an alternative source was never necessary. Hydraulic tappets are now widely used in the motor industry but in the early days of the Rover V8 they were most commonly used on American V8 engines. With the aluminium engine they were useful, not only for their service-free operation, but because they compensated for the different material expansion rates within the engine.

But now Rover experienced excessive rocker shaft and rocker arm wear which a modified oil feed failed to cure. Joe Turley, with his experience of American engines,

was unconcerned. The hydraulic tappet again compensated and by the time wear became serious the engine would be in a scrap yard anyway! Rover engineers were not so sanguine about the problem, which resulted in the underside of the rocker arm cutting into the shaft. Eventually nickel plating of the rocker shaft effected a cure. There were also problems with the Buick-designed pistons cracking which was easily solved by a change of design. Pistons are supplied today by Aeroplane & Motor Aluminium of Erdington and machined by Rover in house.

The Rover V8 engine made its public debut in September 1967 at the Earls Court Motor Show, as the new powerplant for the ageing Rover P5 saloon, which was relaunched there as the Rover 3.5-litre. The new Rover engine was now a production reality. It represented an enormous capital outlay which Rover intended to utilise in the fullest possible way and this meant further research

ROVER V8

and development, not only on the new engine itself but also its production applications.

In March 1967 Rover merged with Leyland, putting Rover and Triumph under the same corporate banner. The Triumph Stag was by this time a running prototype, but its unique 2.5-litre V8 was not. A prototype was running with a Rover V8 by 1968, but the Triumph engine eventually held sway. However, some were built using Rover V8s and 5-speed gearboxes, using the specification intended for the Triumph TR8, but body/chassis retooling was needed and, with the emergence of the bigger Rover V8-powered 2 + 2 TR7, dubbed the Lynx, the idea was not sanctioned.

Rover were not an established sports car manufacturer but when in 1965 they took over Alvis, stylist David Bache was asked to propose a replacement for the current Alvis model, the TF21. The result was an attractive 2-door coupé built around a P6 floorpan and running gear which was built during the winter of 1966-67. Stifled by the Leyland merger in '67, the car never got beyond this single prototype and Alvis never again produced motor cars.

Rover quickly perceived the performance potential of the Rover V8 engine themselves and in keeping with their 'feel' for innovative and advanced automobile engineering produced a mid-engined sports car prototype known as the P6BS.

Rover's own performance project, known at the Works as 'BS' was the brainchild of Spen King and Gordon Bashford and built outside the scheduled programme of the experimental department. Having been designed in 1966, the prototype was ready after the Leyland merger of '67 and thereby its fate was almost sealed.

Much of the work of the first prototype was done by Alvis in great secrecy. The Rover V8 engine, with tubular exhausts, was mid-mounted and De Dion rear suspension was used. Transmission and engine accessibility for servicing was a problem as was the gearchange linkage although development work later made things easier. The prototype was exhibited at the New York Motor Show in the spring of 1968 and at the request of Bruce McWilliams (of Rover North America) Rover did some styling drawings for a production version. The original body, although not unattractive had been designed by Chief Engineer Spen King, with assistance from Geoff Crompton, simply to clothe the mechanical package. Mid-engined cars are notoriously difficult to style satisfactorily and it is to their credit that the full-size clay model production pro-

posal produced for viewing in 1969 closely followed the original prototype shape. After a stop-start period in which the car was given a great deal of favourable publicity. It was finally cancelled.

In 1969-70 Rover engineers were given a brief to produce a Rover V8 engine with the largest possible capacity in anticipation of it being used as the powerplant for the proposed P8 saloon. The stroke *only* was increased within the limits of connecting-rod/camshaft clearance, resulting in a 'square' 4404cc engine. This required the manufacture of a new crankshaft, new main bearing caps for bigger bearings, new con-rods, and new longer cylinder liners to match the $^{11}\!/_{16}$" increase in block deck height. There were one or two detailed changes too, for instance the rocker arm layout was changed to that of the former American Oldsmobile with pairs of stamped steel rockers joined by an aluminium bridge and top end oiling via hollow pushrods. Only about a dozen complete engines were made and they produced hardly any extra bhp, but a massive 260 lb/ft of torque which was far too much for existing transmissions and then available tyres. The project involved much capital outlay but was cancelled along with the P8 saloon.

The Rover P8, with its 4.4-litre V8 engine would have been quite a car, prestigious and technically advanced in a way that had become expected of Rover. Development work began with CXC 838G, a P6B 'hack', retaining its original front suspension but using a P8 version of the De Dion rear suspension and the P8 self levelling system. From there a P7 (actually P7-C) was converted to full P8 running gear,

The Leyland P76, made in Australia, used a 4.4-litre version of the Rover V8 engine originally developed for the Rover P8 saloon.

Rover V8 dressed up for display purposes in the original 1976 cutaway Rover SD1 exhibition car.

'Exploded' Rover V8 (SD1 type) engine with Borg Warner Type 65 automatic transmission.

unit is probably best known for its use in the Leyland P76 saloon (and a fastback spin-off) but was also used in Leyland Australia's Terrier trucks, too.

In 1975 British Leyland came under close scrutiny by Lord Ryder and his team. Amongst the many recommendations of the Ryder Report was the suggestion that the individual identities of the various manufacturers making up Leyland should be merged into one giant corporation. Jaguar was fortunate in being considered worth saving, at least in name, but from the early 1970s British Leyland tried to exercise considerable influence on the future shape and mechanical specification of the new Jaguar saloon destined to replace the XJ6. It was during these 'dark days' that BL put forward the suggestion that the Rover V8 should be used as the power unit for this new car. Bob Knight of Jaguar, graciously and quite rightly, conceded that the Rover V8 was excellent but even GM thought the idea patently misguided and Jaguar ultimately got the AJ6 unit. But Jaguar had considered building their own V8, in fact they actually built a 3.5-litre 60° V8, derived from their V12 and using the same sohc cylinder heads. It produced 200 bhp but was abandoned in 1972.

The Rover V8 engine, although manufactured at the corporate Austin Rover facility at Acocks Green, was the technical responsibility of Rover at Lode Lane, Solihull. The application of the engine to the MGB GT V8 had involved the MG staff at Abingdon and BL (later Austin Rover) Motorsport had undertaken much development work on the engine themselves, but always the fount of all engine knowledge was based at Solihull. When a new requirement was put forward for a version of the engine suitable for a specific application it was to Solihull that the task of providing the right version of the engine fell. And so it was that when the P10 project evolved rapidly into the SD1, the engine was yet again developed.

The version of the Rover V8 engine fitted to the SD1 retained the 88.9 mm bore and 71.1 mm stroke for a capacity of 3528cc but power output was up from 143 bhp at 5000 rpm to 155 bhp at 5250 rpm. Torque was actually down slightly from 202 lb/ft at 2700 rpm to 198 lb/ft at 2500 rpm but overall engine flexibility was improved. The camshaft remained unchanged but the valving of the hydraulic tappets was altered to enable the engine to operate at slightly higher

with a V8 engine, before a complete P8 prototype was built. The self-levelling suspension system developed as a possible option for the P8 was fitted to this P7. The idea was to have a car which did not roll when cornering but which retained normal suspension action over uneven surfaces – an early form of 'active' suspension. It was an hydraulic system, using Lockheed hardware, controlled by lead pendulums in boxes and first tested on a Citroën slave vehicle.

After the project was cancelled the engine design was sold to Leyland Australia who altered it in detail and planned even bigger capacity versions. The 4.4-litre rpm and the inlet and exhaust valves, now with single valve springs, were increased in size. Inlet valves went from 38 mm head diameter to 40 mm and exhaust from 33 mm to 34 mm. Porting in the cylinder heads was not altered other than to improve airflow behind the larger valves and the compression ratio went down to 9.35:1. The most significant change was in the cast iron exhaust manifolds which now had twin outlets and were very well designed, allowing the engine to breath more freely at higher rpm. New Lucas electronic, contact-less ignition was part of the improvement package too, which included a new oil pump giving higher output at lower rpm and an improved water pump.

When Rover bought production rights for the aluminium V8 from General Motors they also acquired a good deal of tooling. This machinery had within its scope the ability to handle the precision machining of a 4-cylinder engine that was to all intents and purposes half the V8. Rover, as part of their many development projects asked BL Motorsport, sometime in the late 1970s/early 1980s to build them a prototype engine because their own engineering department did not have the capacity to undertake the work at that time. It was in fact a 'cut' 4.4-litre 'Australian' engine to produce a 2.2-litre slant-4, running with a single SU carburettor. 'It is rumoured that this makeshift engine is still 'running around in a Land Rover somewhere' but whether it had any serious production possibilities remains to be seen. Land Rover themselves insist that the engine was a Motorsport project but such is the blanket of security surrounding such matters that the real truth may never be revealed. Likewise the same V8 engine tooling has the capability to produce a V6 and this too has been part of research and development carried out at Rover. Although no working prototypes have been revealed to the public such an engine certainly exists.

Not all research and development work reaches a successful conclusion. One such example was the ill-fated 'Iceberg' project undertaken by Rover in collaboration with the Perkins diesel engine company and HM Government to produce a diesel engine based on the Rover V8. The project became a development 'blind alley' which was cancelled in 1984. It did leave a legacy though, which has been of great benefit to those seeking more performance from their Rover V8. The crankshafts manufactured for 'Iceberg' had bigger overlaps and larger big end bearing diameters which could be machined back to standard Rover petrol engine size to produce a crankshaft with a longer stroke (see J E Motors of Coventry, Chapter 5). Every cloud . . .?

The concept of a 'sporting executive express' had been formulated as early as 1980, at the time of BL Motorsport's first, tentative steps towards making the SD1 a successful racing touring car. An appraisal car (XON 742T), dubbed the HPD or 'High Performance Derivative' was built to assess product viability, featuring as it did all the trappings of high performance motoring – a Rover engine with four twin choke IDF Webers, Recaro seats, Minilite wheels and lowered, stiffened suspension and a limited-slip differential. It was dubbed the 'Rover Rapide V8', but Aston Martin had rights to the Rapide name so Vitesse was chosen from the company's archives.

The quadruple Webers were a problem for production, particularly in view of the car's intended refinement. There was no possibility of an automatic choke, the Weber carburettors would take a long time to set up as each car rolled off the production line and servicing at dealers garages would require special training. In short, they were too complicated. Petrol injection was the answer, so on 23rd October 1981 Rover engineers were given the green light to develop what was to become the Vitesse engine, a new version of the Rover V8 'giving maximum torque, maximum performance'. It was ready 12 months later. The Lucas 'L' electronically controlled fuel injection system that was applied to the engine had been fitted to V8 Rovers for the Australian market (built at Cowley) as early as 1977 to enable the engine to meet emission control regulations. In fact an earlier Brico-built electronic fuel injection system had been tried on some P6Bs for the American market. North American Triumph TR8s had also used the Australian 'emission' version of the system and 100 TR8 fuel injection engines had been sanctioned for the UK market shortly before the sports car ceased production. But for the Vitesse, the Lucas 'L' system was fitted to produce more power. It uses solenoid injectors with pulsed operation to inject fuel under low pressure into the inlet ports. The air intake has an air meter, which together with engine speed information from the ignition system, provides primary control for the quantity of fuel injected. There are also sensors monitoring engine coolant temperature, inlet air temperature and the position of the throt-

The Rover V8-derived V6 engine (the V62V) used to good effect in the prototype MG Metro 6R4 Group B rally car.

tle and this data enables the engine's electronic control unit (ECU) to control the optimum fuel/air ratio for any given conditions. The ECU produces electrical pulses of varying duration which regulate the injectors. The application of the 'L' system to the Vitesse engine required a new air flow meter, new ECU and altered ignition curve for the distributor but further work on the engine itself was needed to take full advantage of these developments.

The inlet manifold was designed specifically for the Vitesse engine by Richard Twist at Rover, Solihull with eight distinct inlet tracts, culminating in eight flared tubular steel 'trumpets' inside the plenum chamber, a totally enclosed cast alloy body with single throttle butterfly. The cylinder heads of the Vitesse engine are standard SD1 type but the inlet and exhaust valves are machined behind the heads for better gas flow. The compression ratio is increased slightly to 9.75:1 by using standard SD1 pistons with slightly shallower depressions in the crown. The exhaust system on the Rover Vitesse, which used the standard SD1 manifolds, was increased from 54mm to 60mm bore. The remainder of the engine is unchanged from the SD1 and after the Rover Vitesse ceased production at the end of 1986 the engine became the standard power unit of the Range Rover EFi and Vogue but the valves were changed back to standard SD1 type.

Not all the work undertaken by the engineers at Land Rover on behalf of British Leyland/Austin Rover involved such extensive engineering development. They

were called upon to produce a Rover V8 engine for a specific application and had to ensure that the engine specification satisfied certain criteria. For instance, fitting the Rover V8 engine in the Triumph TR7 to produce the Triumph TR8 presented its own set of problems. It was the first application of the engine to use two separate air cleaners (on the carburetted version), a design used for a short time on the Range Rover, and it had unique exhaust manifolds, too. The fan was mounted on the end of the crankshaft, instead of on the water pump because of the lower radiator and the inlet manifold was lower by $\frac{11}{16}$" for bonnet clearance, because not only did the vehicle production people want to maintain a sleek bonnet line, but to raise it any further would have meant that the car would not conform to EEC sight Lines for forward vision!

When the Metro 6R4 prototype was unveiled to a startled public in February 1984 its power unit was seen to be the trusty Rover V8, with two cylinders 'sliced off the block'. When work had started on the Metro 6R4 in 1981 its intended power unit was a competition version of the Honda V6 now used in the Rover 800 series saloon. AR Motorsport needed to give their new rally car motive power during initial development and testing and of course they already had rallying experience of the Rover V8 with the TR7 V8. But because the intended power unit was a V6 they could not use the Rover V8 as it was. The bulk and balance of the V8 was all wrong and their findings during testing would not have been relevant. So they cut out one pitch of the V8 block, welded the block together and then did all the necessary machining. They had to make a shorter crankshaft (67 mm stroke), camshaft and rocker shafts. The bore remained standard Rover 88.9 mm giving a capacity of 2495 cc. With a pair of triple-choke downdraught IDA Webers and dry-sump lubrication the engine gave 240 bhp. This engine, known as the V62V, was never developed and eventually AR Motorsport engineer David Wood designed the V64V engine for the Metro 6R4 Group B rally car, which in 'Clubman' tune used Group A Rover Vitesse conrods.

At the end of 1983 Land Rover made the decision to bring together all its manufacturing facilities on one site at Lode Lane, Solihull, which by 1985 would be 100% Land Rover. This major undertaking took a little over two years and required the closure of 14 outlying 'satellite' facto-

ROVER V8

ries, including the Rover V8 engine plant at Acocks Green, and resulting in a massive reduction of operational costs.

Land Rover took this opportunity to review engine manufacture, looking closely at the current methods employed by rivals throughout Europe and introducing new manufacturing technology where appropriate. This enormous undertaking involved assessment of future production needs, examination of five major options and consultation with staff from many different areas of production from engineering to safety. The company opted for AGVs (automated guided vehicles) which are battery-powered trucks guided by an automatic, computer controlled system. Land Rover designed the layout of the AGVs in house, building mock-ups to achieve the correct working height and access. Also quite radical is the mounting of the cylinder block on the AGV – for instance for the fitting of such major components as the crankshaft and camshaft the block is mounted so that it can be rotated 360° about a point on the side face. The engine is then lifted off the AGV and remounted so that it rotates 360° around the crankshaft axis for fitting the cylinder heads, etc. So from a bare cylinder block mounted on an AGV the engine is assembled as it travels around the large assembly area, going through various stages with the assembly operator on board, passing component stations where he collects conrod and piston sets, cylinder heads, manifolds and all the other sub-assemblies and components that constitute a complete engine. As he moves slowly along, the pneumatic tools needed by the operator hang down from an overhead track and smaller nuts and bolts are close at hand in storage bins. Engines complete a 'short engine build' and from then on can be assembled to varying specification and delivered to the engine balancing station, all the time guided automatically around 'loops' in the AGV track guidance system. The entire system is fed by an automated warehouse facility which supplies the machine shops with raw materials and feeds the production line with a constant stream of parts.

Every Rover V8 engine manufactured is carried by overhead conveyor to the test facility where it is mounted on a dynamometer and put through a pre-programmed acceleration and deceleration pattern, resulting in a computer printout for that particular engine. In this way, consistent power output can be maintained and monitored and any customer/dealer

complaints of poor engine power output verified by the dynamometer results. In addition, one engine per day is taken at random from despatch and disassembled to look for any component or assembly problems. This highly advanced system, which was the first in the industry to use AGVs for assembling complete engines, can handle up to 1000 per week, has raised production standards, while minimising component damage and reducing assembly-operator fatigue as it allows Rover V8 engines of consistent high quality to roll off the production line.

Late in November 1988 news broke in the motoring press of a significant development in the Rover engine, probably the biggest change in specification since the introduction of the 'Vitesse' injected unit in 1982. Rumours had been rife throughout the industry of a larger capacity Rover V8 engine, and those with American connections were insisting that 3.9-litre Range Rovers were already on sale in that market. Few who attended the 1986 Motor Show are aware that a 3.9-litre Rover V8 engine was under the bonnet of the 2-door Range Rover 'Olympic' on display there.

Engines built to North American specification had always had the internal

Bodyshells descend on to pre-assembled running gear.

Every one of the fuel injected Rover V8 engines coming off the production line at Land Rover is tested on a dynamometer.

Rover SD1 production at the purpose built Solihull plant. Engines are being lowered on to front cross members.

An AGV carrying a cylinder block prior to assembly. The mounting for the block and the axis on which it is rotated can clearly be seen.

working code-name of *Eagle* while the new, larger capacity replacement is known as *Osprey*. There was a need to restore some of the power loss associated with North American emission regulations and the necessity to run on unleaded petrol in this very successful and prestigious market. The engine retains the standard stroke of 71.1 mm but the bore is increased to 94 mm, giving a capacity of 3948 cc. Maximum power is increased to 178 bhp at 4750 rpm and torque to 220 lb/ft at 3250 rpm. This gives the North American Range Rover a 0-60 mph time of 10.9 seconds and a top speed of 100 mph.

Although the new 3.9-litre Rover V8 replaces the 3.5-litre version in the North American Range Rover and is available in Austria, Germany, Switzerland and the Netherlands, Land Rover stated that only the 3.5-litre unit would be available in the UK.

Chapter Four
Production Applications

The Rover V8 engine has proved its versatility time and time again, firstly by being part of the Rover vehicle range and then by moving into wider spheres as a corporate powerplant after Rover became part of the British Leyland/Austin Rover organisation. However, only two vehicles were actually launched with Rover V8 power, the Range Rover and the Rover 3500 (SD1). Certainly the Triumph TR7 sports car was built in prototype form with a Rover V8 engine at the same time as the 4-cylinder version but the TR8 was eventually added to the range long after the TR7 appeared. Had the TR8 been launched simultaneously, or soon after the TR7 perhaps more sales and a longer production life could have done justice to this grossly underrated sports car. As for the 2 + 2 development of the Triumph TR7/TR8, the Rover V8 powered 'Lynx', its full story has yet to be revealed. This more substantial coupé and the convertible which mirrored the Lynx's styling improvements over the TR7/TR8 could have moved the model further upmarket and made the range more appealing and profitable. Now we shall never know.

The Range Rover is the vehicle with which the Rover V8 engine has become synonymous, the two being paired so perfectly it is difficult to imagine that the Range Rover could ever have been as successful with any other engine. The new Rover 3500 of 1976, the SD1, was designed around the Rover V8 and much of its appeal and success is due to the refinement and performance of the V8 powerplant. It is indeed unfortunate that the Rover V8 engine is no longer available in any volume car, but for those who still feel that a real engine has to have at least eight cylinders we have been left a legacy. There are now thousands of second hand Rover V8-engined vehicles on the roads waiting for those who can appreciate them.

THE ROVER 3.5 Litre (P5B)

This portly and substantial vehicle first appeared in 1958 as the Rover 3 Litre (P5), showing a distinct family resemblance to the Rover P4 'Auntie' which preceded it, but actually being derived from a fixed head coupé design exercise by Pininfarina, built in 1953 on a P4 chassis. Unlike the P4 however, the new car was a monocoque design, with engine, transmission and front suspension carried on a detachable subframe. The all-steel (as opposed to part aluminium) body was styled by David Bache, who had joined Rover in 1954, and in 1963 a coupé version appeared, still retaining four doors but having a lower roofline and a more steeply angled rear window.

This was the car in which the new Rover V8 engine made its public début, at the Earls Court Motor Show in September 1967. Available only as an automatic, with

The Rover V8 gave an extended lease of life to this solid saloon by adding refinement and performance.

the Borg Warner Type 35 transmission, it was an altogether more refined automobile, giving greater performance in astonishing silence. The V8 weighed 200 lb less than the 6-cylinder engine it replaced, while adding 40 bhp and 50 lb/ft of torque, but offering equal fuel consumption. The lighter engine also altered the handling somewhat, by all accounts removing what little feel there was from the standard power steering. Mechanically it was basically P5 with subtle development; suspension was by laminated torsion bars at the front and semi-elliptic, variable rate leaf springs at the rear. Brakes were Girling disc at the front and drums at the rear, aided by a Lockhead servo. The rear axle ratio was 3.54:1. Visually the car differed little from the 3-litre except for fog lights sunk into the front wings below the headlights, rubber faced overriders and chromed Rostyle wheels with 6.70 x 15 Dunlop RS5 or Avon Turbospeed tyres. Production ceased in May 1973 after

20627 had been built of which most were sold on the UK market.

In 3-litre form this car personified the Rover image of solid durability, high standards of engineering and outstanding quality of construction. In V8 form speed and performance could now be added to the list. Although a conservative but sound car, often seen on television bringing politicians to No 10 Downing Street, it was a car which heralded a new era for Rover. The 2000TC 'performance' version of the smaller P6 was already available at the time of the P5B's launch and was quite an improvement over the Rover 2000, but there was still much more to come.

THE ROVER 3500 (P6B)

Like the P5, the sleeker P6 was styled by David Bache and aimed squarely at the

ROVER V8

young executive buyer. The V8 version of the car was launched in April 1968 as the Rover 3500 but whereas the P5B had been given the V8 as a means of extending its production life, a larger-engined P6 had always been part of the model's development programme. It was not intended as a replacement for the 2-litre four, itself not a bad engine within its class, but rather as a means of extending the car's attraction to a wealthier clientele by offering a car that was more expensive (with better equipment), quieter, smoother and more flexible, if a little less economical. It is interesting to note that a Rover P6 (code-named P7) with an experimental 6 cylinder engine derived from the 2-litre four, was the original course considered. This engine weighed 460 lb, produced over 180 bhp at 5250 rpm and 185 lb/ft of torque at 4000 rpm, but not only was it a long engine for the P6 bodyshell but its weight and unfavourable weight distribution detracted from the 4-cylinder car's inherently good handling. Installing the V8 maintained the balance, however.

The Rover 3500's début in April 1968 (the original 2000 P6 shape dating from October 1963) as a refined high speed touring car was the culmination of a considerable development programme, integrating the new V8 into the car's overall design to a much greater extent than in the big P5B. The car weighed 60 lb more with the V8 installed, some of this extra weight coming from the use of the BW Type 35 heavy duty automatic gear box, there being no manual version at this

The North American specification air cleaner which connected with the centre scoop for cold air induction.

The North American specification bonnet. Fresh air for the engine via the centre scoop and cooling air for the engine bay via the two smaller ones.

HUE 877L

The Rover 3500 (P6B) was a very successful car, quiet V8 performance in a more compact, better handling package. *(Patrick Collection)*

The Rover V8 engine installed in the Rover 3500 (P6B)

stage. The suspension was uprated; at the front spring rates went up from 150 to 170 lb/in. with larger bore dampers while at the rear spring rates went up from 230 lb/in. to 265-lb/in., supporting a beefed-up De Dion rear axle fitted with a final drive ratio of 3.08:1 instead of 3.54:1. Avon collaborated with Rover in developing special 185 x HR14 tyres. The steering was slightly lower geared and the brakes up-rated, although they were already discs all round. The battery went into the boot (RH wing valance) and the 12 gallon petrol tank was replaced with one holding 15 gallons.

The engine was mounted on the front cross-member which was moved forward slightly, unlike the 4 cylinder original. The engine itself now had 2 SU HS6 $1\frac{3}{4}$ " carburettors, a 10.5:1 compression ratio and exhaust manifolds exiting from the centre, instead of from the rear as on the P5B. It was also restrained by a torque stay attached to the nearside inner wing. The result was a gross output of 184 bhp (nett 160 bhp), peaking at 5200 rpm but safe up to 6000 rpm and plenty of torque, 210 lb/ft at 2600 rpm. Externally the car was altered very little. The panel beneath the front bumper now had a large air intake and there were, of course, new badges bearing the Rover 3500 legend. The new V8 had 75 bhp more than the 2000 automatic but only 46 bhp more than the 2000TC which with its manual gearbox had more closely comparable performance. This was even more so with the North American version, despite its sporty looking 'ram-air hood', which included three scoops on the bonnet. The centre scoop fed directly into the air cleaner box while the outer two vented air into the underbonnet area. Much has been made over the years of direct cold air induction but it didn't seem to help the Rover, probably because it carried 330 lb more weight in power accessories than the European model. When it went on sale in the USA in 1969, it was marketed as the 'Rover 3500S' despite having the standard 3-Speed automatic transmission. Sales there virtually ceased by 1972.

It was September 1971 before Europe got the 3500S and the S designation was

33

ROVER V8

considered appropriate in view of the performance improvement brought about by the cheaper 4-speed manual option. The gearbox was in fact an uprated version of the 4-speed used originally in the 2000TC. It was strengthened with a new finned casing, had increased oil capacity (2 more pints) and an internal oil pump for positive lubrication of the mainshaft gears and bearings. The needle roller and ball bearings on the layshaft were replaced by tapered roller type, with larger bearing area and more positive location. The gears were now shot-peened, but the ratios and the final drive remained unchanged. A 9 " diameter clutch was deemed adequate for the V8's torque. The V8 had already made the Rover P6 a far more refined automobile but of the Rover 3500S testers spoke excitedly of the startling transformation, rocket-like acceleration and remarkable top gear flexibility. The new manual gearbox absorbed less power than the automatic transmission and improved fuel consumption, but also the more compact manual gearbox made room for a more efficient exhaust system, with large diameter pipes meeting just behind the gearbox instead of behind the engine. This helped increase bhp and torque slightly. At the same time the automatic version got new HIF 6 (annular float) SU carburettors.

Throughout its production life the Rover 3500 was altered very little, except in detail. For instance, the two bonnet bulges which seemed to be moulded on

the shape of the rocker covers of the engine beneath (but were not needed for clearance) first appeared in September 1970, as did the black plastic grille and new fascia with circular instruments. This did not stop outside companies making their own derivation of the V8 saloon; the same year the model appeared the Swiss coachbuilder Graber built a one-off two door coupé and estate versions were also available from Crayford. In October 1973 a more compact BW Type 65 automatic transmission was used and in 1974 the V8 engines had new lower compression pistons of 9.25:1 to suit the 97 octane (4 star) petrol which was increasingly becoming the best available. The resultant power loss was hardly noticeable. Production finally ceased in 1976.

RANGE ROVER

Not only has the Range Rover been in production since June 1970 with (until recently) no other engine but the very qualities of the V8 have contributed enormously to its capabilities and upheld Rover's reputation for producing distinctive vehicles. The concept was conceived in the early 1950s, long before the V8 engine was a possibility as a bridge between the P4, which was then the current Rover saloon, and the Land Rover which was

The 1967 prototype Range Rover shows how little the shape of the original concept had to be re-styled for production.

then of a very utilitarian nature. Ideas matured slowly through the early Sixties as a '100 " Station Wagon', with smooth power being supplied by the P5's 3-litre, 6-cylinder engine and four-wheel drive being added as an essential element to the concept, but with a more sophisticated suspension system than the Land Rover for greater comfort and payload. And who is to say whether this package might not have achieved adequate success had not the new V8 been inserted into the equation by 1966 and work begun on the first prototype?

At this stage it was decided that the transmission was of paramount importance, Rover designers opting for permanent 4-wheel drive and a 4-speed manual gearbox capable of handling the V8's power and torque. In the early days of Rover using the V8 in any application, developing transmissions (and indeed the availability of tyres) capable of transmitting that kind of power was a problem. It is also worth remembering that at the time the Range Rover was being developed there was no clearly defined market for such a concept, so Rover were uncertain of its reception by the motoring public and what kind of price level to aim for.

In 1967 came the Leyland-Rover merger but any fears for the future of new projects were unfounded as Leyland, under Sir Donald Stokes, the dominant influence, approved production of the new V8 and the Range Rover with great enthusiasm.

The prototype Range Rover had been styled originally by Spen King and Gordon Bashford but was hardly found wanting when examined by David Bache's Leyland styling team, so production development moved swiftly. The main problems encountered were in finding adequate production capacity, and despite the Range Rover being strictly for the home market when introduced, demand exceeded supply for some considerable time.

The Range Rover as revealed to eager new buyers was a safe and solid multi-purpose vehicle, offering spacious internal dimensions, a commanding view of the road with outstanding performance for such a heavy, un-aerodynamic shape, despite considerable power losses through the transmission. It was also thirsty, but the enormous variety of buyers it attracted were not put off by its fuel consumption. In addition to considerable interest from private buyers from all walks of life its performance and ruggedness made it the workhorse of all sorts of organizations; fast motorway patrol work for the police force in all weathers, carrying a full payload of essential equipment; for vehicle recovery duties needing towing and passenger capacity and specialized fire-fighting either needing quick response or rough terrain ability – or both! In addition to its considerable load-carrying and off-road capabilities it was a vehicle of luxury and refinement, capable of nearly 100 mph (at a time when Land-Rovers only managed

The original 2-door Range Rover was quick to create its own market niche, but makes up a very small percentage of current production.

Rover V8 in the Range Rover, this early Zenith/Stromberg induction setup has been largely replaced by fuel injection.

60-70 mph) and acceleration from 0-60 in 14 seconds. Not bad for a versatile people/load carrier weighing 3900 lb ready to go. It made a great towing vehicle too. It became like the Mini, but in a different market sector, very 'trendy'.

The V8 as built for the Range Rover application was detuned by having a lower compression ratio (8.5:1) and two Zenith-Stromberg carburettors. Power was 135 bhp (DIN) at 4750 rpm, torque 205 lb/ft at 3000 rpm but this was altered in July 1981, with the compression ratio going up to 9.35:1, power down to 125 bhp (DIN) at 4000 rpm and torque down to 185 lb/ft at 2500 rpm which although reducing peak power actually made the engine more flexible in use. The success of the Range Rover continued unabated; in 1973 the standard of interior equipment and appointment was raised and by 1975 two-thirds of production was being exported, although still not yet to North America. The versatile chassis was lengthened and adapted for all manner of tasks such as ambulances and fire-tenders which made full use of the V8's power and torque.

In 1978 BL under Sir Michael Edwardes created a more autonomous Land-Rover Ltd to develop and exploit the success of their specialized 4-wheel drive products and the investment included in the plan provided finance for more Range Rover variants. Four-door Range Rovers had, for some time, been available from specialist converters, often including a lengthened chassis. In 1981 four-doors became available as a factory option on the standard 100 " chassis, but demand quickly exceeded that for the 2-door (by

over 90%!) which is now only available in a basic Fleetline model. In August 1982 came an automatic transmission option by a Chrysler Torqueflite A727 three speed unit, again a much and long demanded option. Then in 1983 the corporate five-speed as used in the Rover 3500 (SD1) Saloon became standard. 1984 saw the first total interior facelift and an In Vogue Limited Edition (1000) trim pack produced in conjunction with Wood & Pickett, the London coachbuilders. Demand was such that it was quickly made a specific Range Rover model.

Throughout all these changes the performance of the Range Rover had changed little but even that aspect was not being neglected by the engineers and planners. In the autumn of 1985 they revealed the fuel injected version of the aluminium V8 which was to become the standard power unit of the Vogue by the end of 1986. Although superficially a Vitesse engine it was in fact detuned, having 165 bhp instead of 190 bhp, but still giving 30% more power than the previous carburetted unit and the Range Rover, for the first time offered a top speed of over 100 mph and a 0-60 mph time of under 12 seconds. Fuel consumption remained unchanged. Eventually the smooth but inefficient (by today's standards) Chrysler automatic was replaced by a German ZF 4-speed 4HP22 unit and bowing to the demands of fashion and aerodynamic efficiency, the Range Rover acquired a front spoiler.

Remarkably, it was the 'Federalising' of the V8 engine (of American birth ...) to meet the demands of North American emission regulations that was the major obstacle to marketing the Range Rover in

Left The 'hose-out' interior of the original Range Rover contrasts strongly . . .

. . . with the opulent luxury of the current Range Rover Vogue SE.

Range Rover chassis has massive strength which contributes enormously to the vehicle's rugged durability.

ROVER V8

North America. The vehicle itself was up to the task, both in terms of competing in this tough marketplace and in its ability to meet all the impact and passenger protection requirements. But it was an expensive and, for Rover, a time consuming business when the company was already fully occupied by buoyant sales in the UK and established export markets. But by the mid-Eighties production capacity had been increased and experience gained in 'Federalising' the V8 for sales of the SD1 and TR8 in North America, so in December 1985 Land-Rover Ltd made the final decision to tackle a major market they had neglected for the first 17 years of the Range Rover's production life. Range Rovers had before then found their way into the USA but not through official channels.

Range Rover of North America was set up with a network of prestige car dealers and the Range Rover marketed successfully as one of the most luxurious, or as they say in the States 'fully loaded', 4x4 vehicles available. That success continues. In late 1988 the North American Range Rovers were the first to receive Land Rover's new 3.9-litre fuel injected Rover V8.

LAND-ROVER – THE 101 in FORWARD CONTROL

The first Land-Rover to be fitted with the Rover V8 was the 101 ″ wheelbase model – the standard long wheelbase for Land-Rover – forward control, denoting a two seater cab sitting astride the engine, which was in the standard position, with virtually no bonnet. This type of Land-Rover had already been in production since 1962 for the Army, although many eventually found their way into private hands. As is the way of the Armed Forces, they issued a 'requirement' for a 4x4 vehicle with 1 ton payload and a 4000 lb towing capability. Also it had to weigh 3500 lb in stripped condition for lifting by helicopter. This called for a development of the forward control concept, using a 101 ″ wheelbase chassis, Range Rover engine (V8 of course), gearbox and transfer box but big Salisbury axles with semi-elliptic springs mounted above them to give a full 10 inches of ground clearance.

Announced in 1972, it was manufactured between 1975 and 1978. Less than 2000 were produced.

For 1988 the Range Rover became available with the newly developed 3.9-litre unit.

The V8 badge – guaranteed to give any mediocre sports car a new lease of life.

THE MGB GT V8

At the 1967 Earls Court Motor Show Rover unveiled the new 3.5 litre (P5B) and at that same show MG chose to reveal their new big-engined version of the MGB sports car, with a 6-cylinder engine, the MGC. It was destined not to be the only big-engined version of this enduring car from the hallowed ground of Abingdon.

The body shape which is now universally known, went into production in July 1962, closely followed by the coupé in 1965 and was in styling and engineering a product of MG Abingdon. There also was built the ageing Austin Healey 3000, itself in need of replacement and it was the intention, from very early in the MGB's life that a bigger-engined version of the new car would serve to replace the Healey. Although the MGB was never engineered for anything other than a 1798 cc 'B' Series 4-cylinder engine, it did fortunately have plenty of space under the bonnet.

Accepting that the Healey's big six was obsolete, a new six-cylinder engine was designed and built, but as it transpired, had little to recommend it over the old. It was both heavy and not particularly powerful. The poor MGB had to be considerably re-engineered to accommodate this 'lump', including replacement of the coil spring suspension by a torsion bar system (to make room), plus a change of gearbox and back axle. The resulting new car, the MGC, was somewhat controversial. There is no doubt that the engine chosen was not *sporting* and that its weight and length did not endow the car with good weight distribution, nor did the torsion bar front suspension contribute anything to handling. The question of whether the MGC was a success or a failure is not relevant here but the car remained in production until 1969, not a long time, although far more were sold than the next big-engined MGB derivative, the MGB GT V8.

In 1970, one Ken Costello completed his first installation of a Rover V8 engine into an MGB Roadster, using the standard MGB gearbox (with a bell-housing adapter), flywheel, rear axle and non-standard, specially fabricated tubular exhaust manifolds. The second car to be converted was a MGB GT, but with a higher-geared MGC back axle and MGC radiator. The standard brakes were considered adequate. Costello's conversions, of which he

The now classic MGB GT V8, in original chrome bumper guise, with only discreet badging and special wheels to denote its bigger engine.

did many over a period of years, resulted in a very potent sports car package, although considerably more expensive than a standard MGB which at the time cost around £1400. The Costello, depending on specification could cost £1000 more. In 1971 he demonstrated one of his creations to British Leyland and while at the time he seemingly made little impression, a Works prototype was running at Abingdon (whose own new MG EX234 and AD021 projects had been cancelled) very shortly afterwards and Costello found it more and more difficult to obtain supplies of engines. Whether these events were, or were not connected is not recorded and will not be speculated upon here. There was now an opportunity for MG to re-engineer the ageing sports car and perhaps inject new interest into the model range with a V8 coupé. The MGB GT V8 made its bow in August 1973 and from the beginning a decision was taken to market the car in Great Britain only and only as a coupé.

As will be seen in the story of the new Rover 3500 (SD1), at the time the MGB GT V8 was under development BL did not have large sums of money to invest in advanced new engineering, especially not for a car well past its prime, and the approach to 'converting' the MGB to V8 power reflects this. As already stated, the engine compartment was already quite roomy but nevertheless the inner wheel arches and chassis side members were reshaped to give more space around the new engine. The then current MGB back axle, with 3.07:1 final drive and drum brakes, was used as was the 4-speed (with overdrive) manual gearbox, although with a new bellhousing/casting and altered intermediate gears. The V8 car used the MGB coil-spring front suspension, with different rate springs, and thicker brake discs. The new car was given unique wheels with cast-alloy centres and steel rims carrying 175 – 14 HR tyres.

The Rover V8 engine fitted to the MGB was not a high power sports specification engine, in fact it was slightly milder in tune that the engine then fitted to the saloons, but it was 40 lb lighter than the 1.8-litre unit it replaced. It had a low compression ratio of 8.25:1, produced 137 bhp at 5000 rpm and 193 lb/ft of torque at 2900 rpm. The two SU HIF6 carburettors were not the same as fitted to the saloons and were mounted on a two-piece manifold specially made for this particular application. The main part of the manifold was similar to the saloon type with a rear facing 'adaptor' which mounted both carburettors side by side facing the main bulkhead, and allowed the use of the standard bonnet with no bulge. Costello had encountered the problem of the carburettor's being too high and had fitted a distinctive bulged bonnet, but eventually adopted a similar system to that of the MGB GT V8. On the production car, this required a unique air cleaner box. There were also unique 'MG' cast rocker covers. All the special MG engine parts were sent to Rover at Solihull, fitted to the engines during assembly and then sent back to Abingdon on complete engines. There was no room in the engine compartment for an engine-driven cooling fan so a pair of electric fans were standard as was an oil cooler. A unique sump was not needed.

There is no doubt that the MGB GT V8 was a classic even while in production. It was produced in limited numbers (but not for 'exclusive' reasons) at a time when the whole classic car movement was gathering momentum. It was and still is out of the ordinary and is mechanically an excellent combination if somewhat 'vintage' in character. It was expensive, because offered with a full specification and high equipment level as standard, but nonetheless very well received. The press at the time could not avoid comparing it with the old MGC and the comparisons were favourable. The new car was over 200 lb lighter (than the MGC) and the balance of the original MGB was retained. They also raved about the engine's characteristics; its performance, smoothness, refinement and even fuel consumption when compared with the 4-cylinder MGB. The majority of the negative points were directed at the areas carried over from the original MGB; its ride, interior trim, wind noise and its ageing structure. Why the engine of the car was thus 'de-tuned' and why it was never officially exported (some were sent to the US for assessment) can only be speculated upon, but it was nonetheless a fine performer capable of accelerating from 0-60 mph in 8.3 seconds and tested to a top speed of 138 mph (while officially only being capable of 121.8 mph).

Production of the MGB GT V8 was steady, rising to a peak from the middle of 1973 to mid 1974 and it was in 1974 that the whole MGB range went black bumpered and had the ride height increased to enable the cars to meet new US construction regulations. These seem-

ingly simple changes actually involved fairly extensive alterations to certain body pressings, the cost of which meant no more chrome bumper models even for the home market. It was also at this time that many of the alterations made to the MGB's body to allow for the fitting of the V8 engine were, for reasons of simplicity, adopted on all 4-cylinder MGBs too. From mid 1974, production of the MGB GT V8 (it was never offered as a roadster) declined steadily to the point of simply fading away in July 1976 after a total of just 2591 had been produced. This was much fewer than the MGC (which was offered as a coupé or roadster) and a long way short of the MGB's half million!

THE ROVER 3500 (SD1)

The replacement for the successful and

The factory installation of the Rover V8 in the MGB GT V8 was very neat. The rear facing carburettors were essential for bonnet clearance.

Interior of the MGB GT V8 differed very little from the original 4-cylinder model. Classic and tasteful understatement.

long-running Rover 3500 (P6B) was not a Rover project, although they had been working on their own projects before coming under the BL umbrella. It was the first Leyland car to be designed for the new V8, as opposed to being altered or adapted either during design or in actual metal to take the engine. Because of this, the Rover 2000 and 2000TC stayed in production for some time after the new Rover 3500 (SD1) became available, while the SD1 itself was developed further into 6-cylinder form with new engines.

In the days of an independent Rover company it had already been recognized that because of the enormous development costs involved for any new model they needed a single replacement for the P5 and P6 and with it a range of 4, 6 and even 8-cylinder engines. After the 1967 merger, the decision to develop a new large, roomier, high performance saloon became part of the overall BL corporate as was the requirement for launch in 1971. This first concept was the P8. Encouraged by the success of the previous V8 saloons Rover, quite naturally, wanted to create a bigger, bolder flagship but the result was too similar in size, performance and target market to the product of another Leyland company, Jaguar. It was also a bad time for the Leyland group as a whole; sales were booming but profits were not and the P8 was not going to be cheap to manufacture. Rover, after all, knew how to engineer a quality product and that cannot be done on the cheap. The P8 project, to the eternal dismay of many at Rover and the astonishment of many more

outsiders, was cancelled early in 1971.

One aspect of the Leyland merger that had not been resolved during this period was the duplication of some model types within the total Leyland range, exemplified by the Rover 2000/Triumph 2000 clash. The P10 project (P9 being the productionised version of the mid-engined sports car prototype) compounded this problem, being a parallel model to the also authorised Triumph 2000 saloon replacement. It was a blessing that both projects were cancelled before they had progressed too far. So RT1 was born, under Spen King (Leyland Cars Director of Engineering) and David Bache (Leyland Cars Director of Styling). But the brief given to them was not an easy one. Leyland wanted a quality product but at lower production cost and this required a much simpler approach to the engineering of the new car. By this time it was well into 1971 and the new model, by now redesignated SD1 (Special Derivative One) was needed urgently. David Bache's five-door styling concept was, for such a big, quality car, very radical but it had been unreservedly approved by February 1972. Development work began with a P6B (JXC 820D) lightened to the projected weight of an SD1, which included fitting Minilite wheels and a Vauxhall Victor 'live' rear axle but retaining the original P6B front suspension. Prototypes were prepared by the end of 1972 and the first 'off-tools' bodyshells were available by April 1975. The new car represented a £95 million investment, with £27 million of that going into a new purpose-built factory at Rover's Solihull plant. Production of the P6B Rover 3500 would cease at the end of 1975 and the new SD1 was planned to reach an ambitious 3000 units per week.

The SD1 was finally announced on 30th June 1976, a little late, as Rover's first all-new saloon since 1963. It was also the first Rover saloon to use rack & pinion steering (Burman power rack), but there was not anything particularly innovative about its engineering. Gone was its predeccesor's De Dion rear axle, to be replaced by a simple live rear axle with torque tube, on coil springs, located by trailing arms and lateral Watts linkage. It had Boge self-levelling dampers too. At the front, suspension was by McPherson strut, the upper mount swivelling in ball-bearing mountings. Brakes were solid 10.15" discs on the front and 9 inch drums on the rear assisted by a servo. Transmissions were either an all-new standard 5-speed manual

The *new* Rover 3500, universally referred to as the 'SD1' was powered by a considerably developed Rover V8 engine.

or optional BW Type 65 (a development of the Type 35) automatic. At the time of its unveiling the car was available with only one engine specification, the aluminium V8 which had been comprehensively uprated for the new application.

The new Rover 3500 SD1 was very well received and rightly so. It was an excellent car and a credit to the engineering team which had managed to refine such a simple mechanical package to such a high standard of ride, handling and performance. Its overall styling was, and still remains somewhat controversial, not for its radical interpretation of the executive saloon concept but because to some it incorporates elements of other cars including the Ferrari Daytona. But such matters did not detract from the initial success of the SD1, which suffered from deficiencies in build quality far more than basic design, but endures as a fast, handsome and refined 'executive' saloon.

In 1982 the SD1 received a major facelift which included a larger rear window and a deep chin spoiler on all models from the 2300S upwards. These changes coincided with the closing of the purpose-built Solihull SD1 Plant and the transfer of production to the original Morris plant at Cowley. On 19th October

1982, at the British Motor Show in Birmingham the Rover Vitesse was launched. The Vitesse name had first appeared on the 1914 Austin 20 hp Vitesse Tourer and pre-war sporting Triumph, then later on a six-cylinder derivative of the Sixties Triumph Herald saloon. Now it was to gain new prestige as Rover's high performance flagship. Available only to special order at first, such was the demand that it was soon a regular part of the range which by now included the 3500S, which appeared in

The Rover Vitesse – circa 1984. Executive jet for flying with all four wheels firmly on the ground.

The Rover Vitesse with deep front spoiler which appeared in production in 1985. The racing version had to wait till 1986.

44

1979 as a high specification model with alloy wheels, 3500SE and Vanden Plas which inherited the fuel-injected Vitesse engine. The Vitesse was a potent package and a strong performer, giving 0-60 mph in just 7.1 seconds and 0-100 mph in 21 seconds. It had the usual five speed manual gearbox, beefed up with stronger bearings and shot-peened gears (as was done to the Jaguar version of the same gearbox), ventilated 10.15 inch diameter front discs with four-pot callipers, lowered (by 1") and stiffened suspension with Pirelli 205/60VR-15 P6 tyres on alloy wheels. Aerodynamic efficiency at high speed was assisted by a large black spoiler across the rear edge of the tailgate which added over 80 lb of downforce to the rear of the car at 100 mph.

Two prototype SD1 estates, of especially handsome proportions were built but never reached the showroom and production of the SD1 ceased altogether in the autumn of 1986, except for a few special Vitesses to fulfil motorsport requirements in 1987.

LAND-ROVER V8

Introduced at the Geneva Motor Show in the spring of 1979, the Land Rover V8 heralded a new phase in the development of a tough utilitarian vehicle which had been a British success story since 1948. But it was beginning to show its age and with BL intent on investing millions to increase production of both Land-Rover and Range Rover it was vital that the range be updated. Installing the V8 in the basically unaltered Land-Rover chassis was to be Stage One.

Land-Rover (and BL) recognised that the 4x4 market was becoming increasingly sophisticated. Indeed their very own Range Rover had been instrumental in widening the demand for off-road vehicles which the Japanese in particular were ready and able to exploit. But mindful of the Land-Rover's handling limitations , the V8 engine in this application was de-tuned to 91 bhp (DIN) at 3500 rpm and torque to 166 lb/ft at 2000 rpm compared with the previously most powerful power unit (a 6-cylinder) having 86 bhp and 132 lb/ft. The low-speed torque of the V8 ideally suited the need for easier off-road ability while acknowledging the limitations of the old chassis suspension, steering and brakes at high speed over rough terrain. Mechani-

cally, the Land-Rover V8 was given the gearbox and transfer case of the Range Rover, hence incorporating permanent 4-wheel drive, with slightly higher axle ratios, in 109 " wheelbase configuration only. Externally the need for more under-bonnet space meant a change to flush front styling, soon to be seen on the new One Ten Land-Rover, and black deformable plastic wheel arch extensions. Production ceased with the introduction of new V8 engined Land-Rover models.

TRIUMPH TR8

The Triumph TR7, as it was first introduced, was probably the most controversial sports car ever made by a major UK manufacturer, certainly in terms of styling. It upheld the TR tradition of straightforward engineering with saloon car derived powerplants but broke new ground with its radical styling and 'unsporty' refinement. It was also a very comprehensively equipped motor car. Initially too, it was only available as a coupé thanks to the prevailing safety regulations of the dominant North American market, which was also responsible for its massive black bumpers and generous boot. In 2-litre form the TR7 was launched in January 1975 and sold exclusively and well in the North American market for which it had been tailored.

The TR7 was launched in the UK in May 1976 and proved a fair and refined performer. The 4-cylinder 1998 cc engine producing 105 bhp at 5500 rpm and 119 lb/ft of torque powered the car from 0-60 mph in 9.0 seconds and gave a top speed of 110 mph with an average fuel consumption of 28 mpg.

The TR7 may have broken new styling ground but it was very straightforward mechanically. Perched on a short 85 " wheelbase it was 160" long overall and 66.5" wide. Front suspension was by McPherson struts, with front brakes by solid discs and a solid rear axle and drum brakes at the rear, suspended on coil springs and located by trailing arms.

Production began at Speke in Liverpool but in October 1977 this plant was closed and production transferred to Canley, recommencing October 1978, a one year gap of lost production. About this time too the Rover SD1 5-speed gearbox was standardised and the Dolomite-based rear axle dropped in favour of one derived

The Triumph TR8 at its launch in the United States. Note the bulkier front bumper and 'TR8' legend.

Triumph TR8 - rear view. Note the larger North American specification rear bumper with over-riders moulded in.

from the SD1 unit with the bonus of slightly bigger rear drum brakes. When SD1 production ceased at Solihull and moved to Cowley, production of the TR7 was transferred to Solihull (in 1980), by which time a drophead derivative had been introduced, commencing production for the American market in June 1979 and the UK market in February 1980. An extra 2 cwt added weight to the claims of excellent rigidity for a drophead and it answered many of the criticisms about the car's styling. A projected 16-valve Dolomite

Sprint-engined TR7 Sprint came very close to, but never reached, full production.

The Rover V8 engine was destined for use in the TR7 bodyshell from the very beginning but it took until May 1980 for that combination to emerge as the TR8. Again North America got all the initial production, after 202 TR8 coupés had gone there for pre-production testing prior to the model's launch. The coupés however were not that popular and 90% of the cars sold in the USA were dropheads. The Rover V8 in this application had twin Zenith/Stromberg carburettors, producing 133 bhp at 5000 rpm and 174 lb/ft of torque at 3000 rpm, but California got Lucas L injection which yielded 137 bhp at 5000 rpm and 165 lb/ft of torque. Compression ratio in both cases was 8.8:1. In the TR8 the rear axle ratio was 3.08:1 instead of the 4-cylinder's 3.45:1 and the battery went into the boot for better weight distribu-

Interior of the North American Triumph TR8, the genuine article, was little changed from the TR7 except for steering wheel and glove box badge.

Homologation picture of a Rover V8 production specification engine. Note the TR7 Sprint decal.

A Triumph TR8 coupe? actually a TR7 V8 homologation photo showing '3.5 LITRE' on the front wing and 'TR7 SPRINT' and 'SPRINT' elsewhere. Rover V8 under the bonnet, nevertheless. tion. The TR8 was never sold in the UK although about 20 pre-production examples did escape BL captivity and are now highly prized. The Rover V8 engine specified for the British market would have been a 152 bhp (at 4750 rpm) unit with a pair of Zenith/Stromberg 175CD side-draught carburettors (manual choke). Production ceased, regretfully, in October 1981 after just 2815 TR8s had rolled off the production line.

ROVER V8

LAND-ROVER ONE TEN/NINETY

The new range of One Ten Land-Rovers was launched at the Geneva Motor Show in March 1983 and heralded as the most significant development of the Land-Rover since its launch 35 years earlier. Within the One Ten range were V8 variants, although the new designations involved a development of the complete Land-Rover range.

A completely new chassis of 110 inch wheelbase had been developed, with vertical coil-springs and drastically increased wheel travel. Self-levelling struts were stan-

The Land-Rover One Ten set new standards of ride and refinement for the Land-Rover range.

The Land-Rover Ninety soon followed its One Ten stable mate into production. Both are available with a 134 bhp Rover V8.

Freight Rover created a commercial vehicle with real punch. Built originally for the police, they have found use with emergency services and even freight companies.

ROVER V8

dard on the County Station Wagons, optional on others and the V8 versions got permanent 4-wheel drive. Front disc brakes had servo assistance. A wider track meant wheel arch extensions. The Rover V8 engine, with twin Zenith/Stromberg carburettors, was rated at 114 bhp and retained the Range Rover gearbox of the old V8 Land-Rover rather than the LT77 5-speed of the SD1 and Vitesse which was available in the non-V8 One Tens. It was thought that the 5-speed was not up to rough off-road V8 motoring although by this time Range Rover was using the LT77 box too.

The Ninety Land-Rover followed on in June 1984, the 'Ninety' designation actually coming from the prototype, which had a 90 inch wheelbase although the production version was of 92.9 inch wheelbase. At the time the four-cylinder Ninety was launched a V8 option was not available, but by the spring of 1985 a V8 with LT85 5-speed gearbox was part of the range. These new long (One Ten) and short (Ninety) wheelbase Land-Rovers replaced the traditional semi-elliptically-sprung Land-Rover completely. In 1987 the V8 used in the range was up-rated to 134 bhp at 5000 rpm.

FREIGHT ROVER – SHERPA

Late in 1984, Freight Rover Vans, (now Leyland DAF), were approached by the Metropolitan Police who had a requirement for a rapid intervention minibus (personnel carrier). The vehicle was to be based on a Sherpa 350 long wheelbase/high roof van but was required to have automatic transmission, a V8 engine, and uprated front axle.

With the delivery of a batch of vehicles required by August 1985, the engineering team assigned to the project had little time for extensive redevelopment and their task was made more difficult by subsequent revisions to the specification which included reinforced high roof, special safety tanks, ZF automatic transmission, heavy duty electrics, bullet proof windscreens and side windows and safety-banded wheel and tyre assemblies.

A Rover V8 engine was obtained from Land-Rover and 'shoe-horned' into the engine compartment of a Sherpa. The dash panel had to be extensively modified to clear the inlet manifold, but because of the time scale could not be retooled, so hand-worked blister panels were fitted. Finding room for the larger radiator needed was also a problem. Firstly, Freight Rover had to design a more compact water pump and viscous fan assembly, reducing the overall length of the engine, and the radiator was moved forward from its normal chassis mounting to the front bumper armature. A fluid cooler for the automatic transmission was also mounted up front. At the time Land-Rover were developing the ZF automatic transmission for use on their own vehicles and Freight Rover were allowed to draw freely on their pool of knowledge and components. The front suspension was changed from single to multi-leaf springs so that there was adequate clearance between the torque converter housing and the steering components. The engines themselves are a Saudi specification using twin SU carburettors, with slightly modified air cleaners, producing over 130 bhp and giving the Sherpa V8 a top speed, fully laden, of 92 mph.

After the production of that initial batch for the Police, the Sherpa V8 was further refined and now the Rover V8 engine is an option in the Sherpa range, being used to good effect by ambulance services and certain freight companies.

Rover V8 in Sherpa engine compartment. Note the clever positioning of the air cleaner box.

V8

Chapter Five

Specialist Applications

The Rover V8 engine was used as a sports car power unit by British Leyland/Austin Rover in only two instances and only one of those, the MGB GT V8, was made available in the UK market. The Triumph TR8 nearly made it. Instead it has been left to our imaginative specialist manufacturers to fully exploit the engine's performance potential in a variety of 2-seater and 2+2 seater sports cars and they have made an excellent job of it. Morgan were the first to fully appreciate the potential of the Rover V8, and in fact it was probably in a Morgan Plus 8 that the engine first saw real sporting (ie. competition) use. But Marcos and TVR have both done justice to the engine with sleek interpretations of the V8 sports car which must surely rank as some of the swiftest and most capable available today. The blossoming component car industry too has grown to offer a mouth-watering selection of competent chassis and sleek well finished bodyshells within which a Rover V8, along with other readily-available components can be assembled to produce dream cars within the means of many enthusiasts who might not otherwise have been able to afford such a high level of performance and style.

MORGAN PLUS 8

The Morgan Motor Company Ltd of Malvern Link entered the Rover V8 engine story at a very early stage, in fact there was

at one time the possibility that Morgan might become part of the Rover group. In 1966 Peter Wilks of Rover approached Peter Morgan about a take-over, but this was respectfully declined. From this amicable dialogue came discussions about the new Rover V8 engine and the possibility that Morgan might be allowed to use it as a much needed replacement power-plant for their Plus 4. Peter Morgan was quick to recognize the potential of this combination and enrolled Maurice Wilks, a local racing engineer, to take on the development of a prototype in the modest workshop marked Research & Development. By the end of 1966 work was under way, using at first a mock-up of the new engine and later a Buick engine, obtained by Morgan and brought up to Rover specification.

Fitting the engine into what was then the Plus 4 was not a straightforward swap. The prototype, which was ready by February 1967, had a widened and lengthened chassis, widened (by 2 inches) body, new steering column and a bigger fuel tank. There was insufficient room for an engine-driven fan so an electric one was necessary. The traditional Morgan suspension was left virtually standard, and a Salisbury rear axle with a 3.58:1 final drive and unique 15 x 5.5 inch wheels fitted. The gearbox was a problem, as it was at the time for Rover, except that Morgan could hardly use an automatic! So the usual Moss gearbox was retained, this being mounted in a rather unusual (not so for

Left The Morgan Plus 8 – announced in August 1968.

Morgan) manner. The gearbox was centrally positioned in the chassis, connected to the engine by a short propellor shaft, within an especially long bell-housing, inside which was the clutch and flywheel. The 4-speed Moss gearbox actually ceased volume production in the late 1960s when Jaguar phased out its use but Moss very helpfully continued to produce it for Morgan until a suitable replacement could be found.

Changes at Rover (the BL takeover in January '67) meant that Morgan might have to look again at a power unit for their new car as supplies of the new engine were for some time in doubt. It was during this time that the Triumph V8 engine, destined for the Stag, was offered as an alternative but Peter Morgan patiently waited to see what transpired with the Rover. He was rewarded with the heartening news in mid 1968 that engine supplies would be assured.

In August 1968 the new Morgan Plus 8 was announced. It was enthusiastically received, retaining as it did all the traditional Morgan virtues, but with 54% more power it also offered a healthy dose of exhilaration. Its success owed much to its fine power unit and not a little to the inspired act of bringing the car and engine together.

Road cars make equally good weekend competitors. This is Doug Pond's Plus 8 at Prescott.

Left Ever since its introduction the Morgan Plus 8 has been raced. this is Graham Bryant's Plus 8 at Oulton Park.
(Chris Harvey)

Rover V8 in the Morgan Plus 8. The Vitesse fuel-injected unit is now the standard powerplant.

ROVER V8

An inspired combination perhaps, but the Morgan Motor Company has a long history of independence and imagination. The company was founded by Harry Morgan and first produced a three-wheeler in 1908-9. It was Harry who designed the 'advanced' sliding pillar independent front suspension first seen on those early three-wheelers and still in use on the Morgan Plus 8 today. The first four-wheeled Morgan was shown at the 1936 Motor Show. By the Fifties the Morgan sports car was already being seen as 'old fashioned', leading in 1953-54 to styling changes that introduced the curved cowl with vertical grille bars and headlights faired into the wings, resulting in the Morgan 'look' we know today. But for all its traditional qualities the Morgan Plus 8 has not stood still throughout its production life. Being at the mercy of major manufacturers for components has meant that as well as improving the model, changes have sometimes had to be made as parts ceased to be available.

In the Spring of 1969 an aluminium body (over 100 lb lighter), became an option for those with competition aspirations and minor lighting changes became necessary both in 1970 and again in 1976. In 1972, the availability of a Rover 4-speed manual gearbox ended uncertainty about the Moss gearbox but installing it, now in the 'normal' position on the back of the engine, required chassis alterations. More chassis (and some body) modifications were required when Salisbury introduced a new, lower 3.31:1 rear axle which was 1.5" wider too.

Exhaust system development had eventually seen the replacement of the cast Rover manifolds with four-branch tubular steel manifolds with a twin system connected by a balance pipe. Engine power output dropped slightly in 1975 as Rover made subtle alterations to the engine to meet emission regulations but power soon rose again in 1976 when the Morgan Plus 8 got the new SD1 engine with all its improvements. The new 5-speed Rover gearbox that went with it meant yet more chassis modifications and a specially modified Rover bellhousing. With the new 5-speed transmission came standard 14x6 alloy wheels which had first appeared as options on the 1975 aluminium-bodied Special Edition but in 1982 bigger brakes meant the return of the original unique 15" Plus 8 alloy wheels, but with 6.5J rims. Also in 1982 came Stromberg carburettors, which replaced the SUs as Rover

again worked to meet European emission regulations calling for automatic chokes controlled by water temperature. The engine in this form produced 155 bhp

In 1983 the Morgan Plus 8 got some extra 'plus' with the introduction of the Vitesse 3.5-litre fuel injected engine, which with the Morgan tubular exhaust manifolds and system produced 205 bhp, making the Plus 8 capable of 0-60 mph in a brutish 5.2 seconds.

In line with many other specialist manufacturers, Morgan were quick to adopt the 3.9-litre EFi Rover V8 once production of the engine at Land Rover had been geared up sufficiently to meet demand. However, emission requirements had taken their toll and, with 190 bhp to offer, the bigger capacity only maintained the performance, although the Morgan Plus 8 surely has enough of that for anyone?

THE V8 TVRs

The original Trevcar Motors was founded in 1946 by Trevor Wilkinson, a 23 year old budding entrepreneur, in Blackpool. A name change the following year resulted in TVR (TreVorR) Engineering and from the start car building was to be their business, although series production did not begin in earnest until 1954, after which rapid development and evolution resulted in a number of individual cars emerging from the factory.

The model that established the character of the TVR sports car was the Grantura Mk1 which appeared in 1958, but again fairly rapid evolution through Mk2, then Mk2A and Mk3 led to the first V8 engined model. TVR had established a modest export trade to North America through Ray Saidel, an American car dealer, whose steady demand for cars had helped TVR through the occasional unsteady period. It was during just such a particularly low spell in TVR's business fortunes that the Americans, for no particular reason other than perhaps, curiosity, transplanted a 4.7-litre Ford V8 from a Cobra into a Grantura Mk 3. The result impressed Jack Griffith, a Ford dealer in Long Island and after development the Grantura V8 found itself in demand, enjoying successful production between 1963 and 1965 and providing a welcome boost to TVR fortunes in Blackpool.

In 1965 Martin Lilley became the new owner of TVR and briefly resurrected the Grantura V8 as the Tuscan V8 although

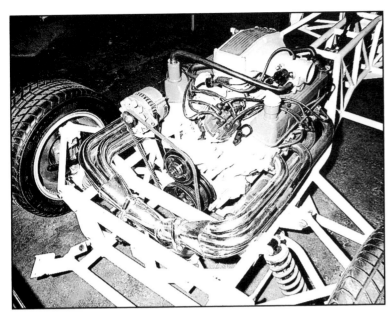

The exhibition chassis of the TVR Tuscan. Note the unusual forward-running tubular exhaust manifolds.

The TVR Tuscan – ready for the TVR Tuscan Challenge, a one make series for these specially produced Rover V8 engined cars.

As Wheeler gradually took control of his new company so his ideas on the direction TVR should take in the future began to be seen in new projects. At the Birmingham International Motor Show TVR had exhibited a Tasmin Fixed head coupé powered by a Ford V6, with intercooled turbocharger and fuel injection. This had been intended to become the new top of the range model for TVR, who once again wanted to see their sports cars endowed with real power. But this route presented problems and following the arrival from Rover-Triumph in March 1982 of John Box as TVR's chief engineer the Rover V8 was looked at as a possible powerplant. Initially they took delivery of an engine with twin SU carburettors and automatic transmission and also a manual, injected Vitesse unit (the Rover Vitesse having been launched late 1982). A prototype Tasmin V8 was built using the Vitesse engine. To suit the TVR application the engine used Land-Rover cast exhaust manifolds, a remote oil filter (with cooler on some models) and a slightly different alternator because of bonnet clearance problems. Interestingly, the carburetted engine with the automatic gearbox did eventually find its way into a one-off TVR 350.

production of this very fast car faded out in 1970. TVR sports cars continued with the M series, the most powerful of which had a Ford V6 engine and in January 1980 the Tasmin appeared, styled by Oliver Winterbottom, with its distinctive sharp edged wedge shape, first as a coupé and later and more successfully as a convertible. Control of the company was sold in 1981 to present chairman Peter Wheeler, although at first the running of the company was left to MD Stewart Halstead.

The result of combining Tasmin with fuel injected Rover V8 was announced on August 23rd 1983 as the TVR 350i. It differed visually from the V6 Tasmin (or TVR

280i, as it had become known) by having bigger 15 inch wheels, new front air dam and a bonnet with a large but unobtrusive centre bulge to clear the V8's plenum chamber. The TVR 350i was very well received by motoring press and customer alike, who were equally enthusiastic about this open top two seater that could accelerate from 0-60 mph in 6 seconds or 0-100 in 16.5, and with a maximum speed of 120 mph while managing 22+ mpg.

Development of the 350i centred around the exhaust system which, in its original form, was contributing nothing to the engine's power output, and a four branch manifold/ single tailpipe system was eventually adopted. During 1984 TVR began consulting various Rover V8 specialists seeking ways of tuning the 3.5-litre, but found that with more power came reduced reliability, which could not be tolerated in a production car. 1984 was also the year that Andy Rouse of Andy Rouse Engineering in Coventry won the British Touring Car Championship in the ICS Rover Vitesse, so TVR turned to him for help in developing the engine for their application.

The result of the TVR/Rouse collaboration was the TVR 390SE Convertible, introduced at the 1984 Birmingham Motor Show. Externally it followed closely the TVR 350i, but the fully blueprinted Rover V8 had a bigger 93.5 mm bore with the standard 71 mm stroke, Cosworth pistons, gas flowed

cylinder heads, Vitesse valves with special valve springs, 10.5:1 compression ratio and 'TVR' camshaft. The exhaust system was the same as that designed for the 350i, but, with bigger diameter pipes and with some tweaks to the Vitesse fuel injection system,

Above The TVR Chimera introduced in 1992 with a choice of 4.0 or 5.0-litre Rover V8 engines.

Inset Rover Vitesse fuel-injected V8 installed in the engine compartment of the TVR 350i.

Above left TVR Challenge powerplant – 4.4 litres of full race prepared Rover V8 producing 420 bhp.

the engine produced 275 bhp at 5500 rpm with 270 lb/ft of torque at 3500 rpm.

Rapid, on-going development is a way of life at TVR, and the 1986 Birmingham Motor Show saw the launch of the fearsome TVR 420 S.E.A.C. (Special Equipment Aramid Composite) Convertible, officially the TVR flagship model. Through 1985 the factory had supported two 390SEs in production sports car racing, partly to enhance the company's growing reputation for producing a new breed of high performance sports cars and partly to assist in overall product development. This programme culminated in the 420 S.E.A.C. race car, a one-off powered by a 4.2-litre Rover V8 engine.

Built around a factory cross-bolt mains cylinder block with dry sump lubrication,

the 93.5 mm bore of the 390SE was used in conjunction with a 77 mm stroke crank-shaft, resulting in a capacity of 4228 cc. The full race prepared engine was fitted with one of the rare 'twin plenum' racing fuel injection systems, actually a twin throttle body plenum chamber over a slightly enlarged Vitesse type manifold as used on the TWR racing Rover Vitesses. Additional modifications included 12:1 compression ratio, Cosworth pistons, Group A con-rods, Group A large diameter rocker shafts and pillars with Volvo adjustable rockers, fully gas flowed cylinder heads and a studded block using larger diameter aircraft quality fasteners to hold down the cylinder heads. With 330 bhp, the race car, driven by Steve

57

Cole, was very successful, so much so that it was eventually banned!

Proved on the race track, the TVR 420 S.E.A.C. went into production, its composite bodyshell saving 200 lbs without loss of strength and its chassis fully developed with the aid of racing experience. The production engine was still 4.2 litres, but used a standard 2-bolt mains block, single throttle body injection with a larger airflow meter and upgraded wet-sump lubrication system. Power was still 300 bhp at 5500 rpm with 290 lb/ft of torque at 4500 rpm.

Development of the model range continued, as did that of the Rover V8 engine at TVR Power in Coventry to produce power and torque in abundance. The TVR 350i was available with a high output 225 bhp 3.5-litre engine, and a new TVR Tuscan, based on the TVR S (Ford V6-powered), was restyled and fitted with the same 225 bhp 3.5-litre engine as standard. The TVR 390SE, with a bigger 94 mm bore, became the TVR 400SE, and an even bigger engined TVR 450SE was added to the range, which used the enlarged version of the TVR 420 S.E.A.C. engine, but with an 80 mm stroke crank for a capacity of 4.5 litres and producing 320 bhp at 5700 rpm and 310 lb/ft of torque. By virtue of the same engine the 420 S.E.A.C. became the 450 S.E.A.C.!

The TVR V8S was introduced in 1986, with production beginning the following year. The S-Series closely resembled the M-Series, but was a totally new model under the skin and represented the 'entry level' model of the TVR range as well as excellent value for money. Available as either a V6 (Ford) or a V8 (Rover 3.9-litre), sales have been good, with production continuing very successfully right up until 1994, with 2,500 examples made.

The new flagship of the range was the Griffith, introduced in 1991 with a 4.3-litre Rover V8 using the 94 mm bore of the 3.9-litre combined with a 77 mm stroke crankshaft, actually the same dimensions as the Land Rover 4.2-litre engine, but seriously rebuilt by TVR Power to produce no less than 280 bhp and 305 lb/ft of torque. Performance was excellent, with a standing quarter mile time of 13.3 seconds and a terminal speed of 109 mph. The 0-60 mph time was 4.8 seconds, 0-100 mph in 11.2 seconds, and the top speed a blistering 155 mph!

The Griffith was soon to be replaced in July 1993 by what will probably go down in the history books as the pinnacle of Rover V8 road going performance. The Griffith

500 took the concept one serious step forward with a bigger 5-litre engine, using a 90 mm stroke crankshaft combined with the 94 mm bore, producing 340 bhp and 360 lb/ft of torque, enough grunt to propel this 1,060-kilo machine to 60 mph in 4.1 seconds or 100 mph in 10.5 seconds from a standing start. Top speed was nudged still higher to 160 mph.

Styling had become a major strength of the TVR range, none more so than with the pretty Chimera models introduced in 1992 and commencing production in February 1993. The body clearly mirrors TVR's familiar styling cues, polished to perfection in the Griffith, on which the Chimera is based, while a range of Rover V8 engines completes the picture. The engines begin with a 240 bhp 3.9-litre version called the 4.0, then there is a 4.0 HC (hi-output version) producing 275 bhp, and, for the power crazy, there is the same fire breathing 5.0-litre, 340 bhp engine found in the Griffith 500. Rover V8 power endows the Chimera with all the power it needs to fulfil its dual role of Grand Tourer and sports car.

The future for TVR features strongly their brilliant AJP8 engine, which is destined for immortality as a Le Mans powerplant as part of TVR's Cerbera challenge. But the Rover V8 too has had an illustrious competition career perpetuated by TVR's racing programme. It began in the 'eighties with V8 Tasmins and the highly successful 420 S.E.A.C., but for the past six years the TVR Tuscan Challenge has treated race fans to the glorious thunder of race prepared 420 bhp Rover V8 engines in these short, squat open sports cars bellowing around Britain's racing circuits. This highly successful one make series has attracted some top driving talent and provided yet another competition arena for the Rover V8 to exhibit the excitement and spectacle of the engine unleashed.

GINETTA

Anyone who saw the racing driver Tiff Needell put a Ginetta G33 through its paces on BBC's *Top Gear* programme cannot fail to have been impressed. The car, powered by a fuel injected 3.9-litre Rover V8, had an animal presence and radiated excitement worthy of the best in British sports cars.

The Ginetta lineage goes all the way

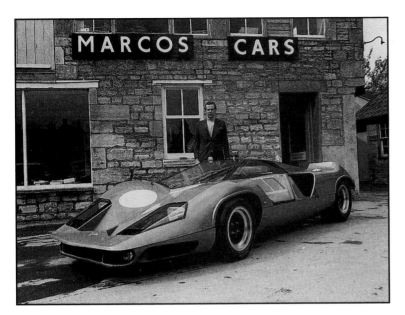

Marcos boss Jem Marsh with his Repco-Brabham powered Mantis. It was renamed Marcos XP when the Mantis name was given to a new 4-seater model.

A Marcos Mantis 4-seater undergoing restoration and the installation of a Rover V8 in place of the usual 6-cylinder Triumph engine.

tious and muscular G33 can be bought as a partly assembled 'Super Kit', and a Rover V8, tuned or standard, will put the icing on a very delicious cake.

MARCOS

Jem Marsh entered the automobile business in 1958 by establishing the Speedex specialist parts company in Luton. He later formed a business partnership with Frank Costin, an expert aerodynamicist who was enthusiastic to use wood in automobile construction. Marsh shared his conviction about the potential of the material and their collaboration produced the first Ford 100E-engined Marcos sports car in 1959. When Costin withdrew, Dennis Adams, who had designed a spaceframe for Lister Jaguar became involved and development of the Marcos company and cars continued throughout the Sixties supplying customers direct from the new Bradford-on-Avon works following reconstruction of the original company.

back to 1957, and while the name has survived it has not flourished, which is a great injustice to the marque. Resurrected by the kit car boom and enjoying healthy if conservative growth, the range developed with a vengeance, projecting the Ginetta name as never before, and they have ventured tentatively into turn-key territory.

But the recession has forced the company to once again draw in its horns and revert in part to the kit car market. Now the Ginetta G27 and G33, both able to utilise the Rover V8, are available again as kits, which is good news for anyone with a hot engine that needs a capable and attractive home. The exquisite G27 uses more modest mechanical hardware, such as Triumph based front suspension and a Ford Capri or Morris Marina rear axle. The more ambi-

The shape of the current Marcos sports car designed by Adams, first appeared in October 1963 as the Marcos GT, with wooden chassis and glassfibre panels. Its beautiful, low shape was a sensation, the Volvo powertrain supplied excellent performance and the independent front/De Dion rear suspension endowed the car with superb handling. The costly De Dion rear suspension was eventually dropped in favour of a 'live' rear axle on coil springs and a Ford Cortina engine was offered as an option.

A Buick aluminium V8 engine was first tried in the car (with wooden chassis) in 1966 and proved a very promising combination but at the time Jem Marsh could not obtain supplies of the engine from Rover. That same year a Mini Marcos had been the only British-made finisher (although last) at Le Mans (driven by two Frenchmen) and this achievement prompted an unsuccessful attempt by Jem Marsh and Chris Lawrence the following year. They tried again in 1968 with a Marcos GT but were frustrated by engine problems so Jem embarked on a more ambitious project to take to Le Mans in 1969.

This was the Marcos Mantis, a dramatically styled (again by Dennis Adams) wedge shaped 3-litre prototype sports racing car with a wooden chassis. Mid-engined, its suspension was essentially Formula 1 Cooper, with a Hewland gearbox

The Marcos Mantula V8 and the timeless shape that first appeared in 1963.

The Marcos LM500 BRDC GT Challenge success story destined for the Le Mans race.

The Marcos LM500 Coupé – race bred road car.

models and the continuous need to meet ever more stringent emission and safety regulations meant heavy investment and consequently, cash flow problems. By 1971 Marcos had again ceased trading as a car manufacturer, but Jem Marsh continued to supply spare parts, carry out servicing, repairs and restorations.

Ten years later demand for the Marcos GT was such that Jem Marsh decided to put the car back into production. For a design that had originally seen the light of day in 1963 it could easily have been a case of selling a 'classic' for its nostalgic qualities but this is definitely not the case. The car is as modern and appealing now as it was then.

The biggest step in its evolution was the introduction in 1984 of a new model, the Mantula. The Marcos Mantula is powered by the Rover V8 and because the car is sold in component form to the UK market, that can mean a secondhand engine or a brand new fuel injected Vitesse unit supplied by Marcos, which nowadays they are able to obtain from Land-Rover at Solihull. The exhaust manifolds have to be from a Rover 3500S (P6B), which are now becoming increasingly difficult to obtain, or Marcos 4-branch tubular manifolds which also give a slight horse-power boost. No alterations are needed to the engine for this application except for slight alterations to the inlet manifold flange to allow the carburettors to clear

and power was a 3-litre Repco-Brabham engine. The car raced only once, at the very wet Spa 1000 Km in 1968 from which it retired. The Mantis was later converted to a road car by the insertion of a Buick aluminium V8, and sold to an American enthusiast who still owns it.

In 1969 the Marcos GT road car lost its wooden chassis in favour of a more conventional, cheaper tubular steel spaceframe and a new Marcos Mantis 4-seater road car was introduced with Triumph 2.5-litre six cylinder engine. But the demands of expansion, developing new

The Rover Vitesse fuel-injection engine installed in the Marcos Mantula.

ROVER V8

the underside of the bonnet and a pair of K&N air filters. Cars fitted with an injected engine have a K&N filter on the end of the intake pipe. Standard Rover engine mountings are used as is the engine steady bar (slightly lengthened). The engine is used with the standard Austin Rover 77mm 5-speed gearbox, fitted with the Jaguar remote control to bring the gearstick forward and there has to be a protective plate for the sump because of limited ground clearance. Future engine plans include the availability of a 3.9-litre unit.

The next step in its evolution was the introduction in 1984 of a new model, the Mantula, which still retained the timeless styling, though subtly altered, by Dennis Adams of course, to open up the front air intake, and with a front spoiler to improve the aerodynamics. The Mantula was available with a brand new 3.5-litre Rover V8 EFi, which enabled it to accelerate from 0-60 mph in just 7 seconds and reach nearly 140 mph, or it could be bought ready to accept the new owner's Rover V8 engine if so desired. In 1986 a truly beau-

The Westfield SEight in '330' form does 0-60 mph in 3.4 seconds and 0-100 mph in 7.9 seconds.

Rover V8 power for the big, bad Sebring MX classic.

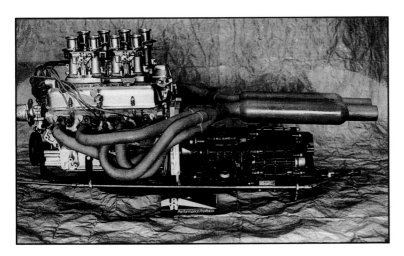

A Rover V8 mounted on a transaxle, ready for installation in a mid-engined sports or racing car. *(UVA)*

tiful Spyder version was added to complement the coupé.

Marcos continued the forward pace both in development and performance with the even more powerful Mantara. Styling was handsome and distinctive but clearly evolutionary, retaining all the original shape with extended wheel arches, accommodating at the rear an independent suspension system using unequal length wishbones and spring struts. Available in coupé and Spyder form, the Mantara is available with the 3.9-litre EFi Rover V8 (190 bhp), and for performance can offer a 0-60 mph time of just 5.4 seconds and a top speed of 140 mph. However, for those who consider that this is not enough, the Mantara Sport comes with a specially built 5.0-litre Rover V8 producing 300 bhp (at 5500 rpm) and 280 lb/ft of torque. The quarter mile standing start dash is over in just 12.5 seconds!

Marcos Cars have a Le Mans tradition, albeit a modest one, and the magic of the Sarthe circuit has once again beckoned. Competing in this classic race can create a mystique about a marque that can last for decades, and when Marcos once again decided to embark on a Le Mans project they called upon Dominic Smith to develop the aerodynamics of the Mantara for serious competition. Shown first in 1993, the car responsible for the Le Mans effort will be entered as soon as possible, but in the meantime the company have developed from that project the Marcos LM500, powered by a full 5-litre producing 350 bhp at 6000 rpm and 318 lb/ft of torque at 4500 rpm. Acceleration from 0-60 mph takes just 4.3 seconds and the top speed is 155 mph. Truly a Rover V8-engined supercar. The LM500 found success on the race track in the BRDC National Sports GT championship in 1994 and a one make series is planned in 1995.

KIT CARS

The kit car industry has flourished in the past decade and although hit by the recent downturn in economic prosperity, a number of companies have continued to prosper and still others have emerged to replace those that scaled down their production facilities. The industry provides the enthusiast with a wide range of relatively inexpensive performance vehicles, many of which accept the Rover V8 as a powerplant. At the time of writing there are over 30 different kit cars available that either use the Rover V8 engine, or list it as an optional powerplant. There are an additional ten vehicles that could accept the engine if so

The Rover V8 sits confidently in the engine bay of a Ford GT40 replica.

No prizes for guessing the inspiration behind the Hawke kit car. The Rover V8 is a big 'plus'.

The rugged Dakar 4x4 is based on the Range Rover chassis. Lighter weight equals performance!

required.

These can be divided into two categories, those that use the engine in its usual, front mounted position where it can utilise the well-known Rover 77 mm 5-speed gearbox (or the new Land Rover R380 5-speed?), and those with a mid-mounted engine, which require the Rover V8 to be mated to a suitable transaxle that has the gearbox and final drive in one unit. Because the Rover V8 has never been mid-mounted in any production application, there is no Rover transaxle available and the engine's torque requires units of some strength. The better known are Volkswagen, Porsche, Renault and Hewland. Styling ranges from the replica, such as the Cobra or Countach, the off-road/utility vehicle, historic sports and pre-war sports cars.

Cobra replicas are a very popular choice for those wishing to build a car that combines a strong image and relative simplicity of construction. The Rover V8 excels in such an application, being light, powerful, inexpensive and, most importantly for a Cobra, possessing that superb V8 sound.

Berido Replica Automobiles have been producing their neat BRA 289 Mk11 for over ten years. It is a replica of the original and very pretty 289 Cobra. The kit is not based on a specific donor vehicle, but does utilise MGB steering, suspension and axle. *Hawke Cars,* of Frant, East Sussex, also offer a Cobra 289 replica, which is also based on an MGB donor car, with a Rover V8 option.

Other Cobra replicas suitable for receipt of Rover V8 power include the Cobretti Viper V8, by *Cobretti Engineering*

of Morden, Surrey, the KF Premier, by *AK Sportscars* of Peterborough, the GD427, by *Gardner Douglas* of Bottesford, Leicestershire, the Ram SC, by *Ram Automotive* of Witham, Essex, the SR V8 Roadster, by *Southern Roadcraft* of Lancing, West Sussex, the Viper, by *Classic Replicas* of Bournemouth, and the Pilgrim Sumo, by *Pilgrim Cars* of Henfield, Sussex. The Sumo is especially interesting because it represents probably the cheapest route to getting a Rover V8-engined Cobra replica on the road. It began life as a budget Cobra replica, with the emphasis very much on low building cost and low running cost, to the point that the earliest offerings were based on Ford Cortina mechanical components, including the engine! An increasing interest from customers in more powerful variants saw the Sumo evolve into the Ford Granada-based Sumo MkII, which accepts either a Ford V6 or Rover V8 engine. Accomplishing this evolution involved redesigning the chassis, with a longer wheelbase, 91.75 inches (up from 90 inches), and mounting the Rover V8 lower and further back for 50/50 weight distribution. It also allows the use of the standard oil filter location. While lacking the sophistication (and cost) of the more prestigious Jaguar-based Cobra replica kits, the Sumo MkII is exceptional value for money and capable of handling any Rover V8 up to 300 bhp.

The superb DAX Tojeiro by *DJ Sportscars International* is without doubt one of the best Cobra replica kits available. It was first introduced in 1982 and its development was furthered by the collaboration of John Tojeiro, designer of the AC Ace. The

Ford GT40 replicas like this Tornado TS40 have been built using Rover V8 power – a lighter and more practical alternative to the real Ford V8.

The current proliferation of Cobra replicas such as the beautiful Cobretti Viper V8 are ideally suited to raw Rover V8 power.

Tojeiro has two chassis options: the ladder/platform chassis and the 'Supertube', which is both stiffer and lighter, although either chassis would handle power far in excess of anything a Rover V8 could produce. This company also have in their range the DAX Rush, a car designed along similar lines to the Lotus 7, which can be built using a Rover V8, and the magnificent DAX 40, a replica of the mighty Ford GT40. Introduced to the range in 1988, their own demonstrator uses a Rover 3.5-litre EFi engine combined with a Renault 30 transaxle, and performs exceedingly well on it too. The majority of Ford GT40 replicas (there are others on the market) use Ford small-block cast iron V8 engines, which, it has to be said, are more authentic to the original and less costly than tuning a Rover V8 to produce comparable power output. But it has also been said by more than one owner that the lighter Rover V8,

at around 170 kilos compared with the Ford V8's 225 kilos, produces a lighter, more agile road car; also, of course, with much larger capacity Rover V8 engines available, there is considerably greater power potential, and with Real Steel's adapter kit the Rover can be fitted with small-block Ford engine valve covers. Classic British alternatives to the Anglo-American Cobra genre are the big, bad and brutal Austin Healey 100/4 and 3000 models, which thankfully can be recreated thanks to the vision of the kit car industry. *Pilgrim Cars* of Henfield, Sussex, have their Haldane HD100/300, based on a sound backbone chassis with additional space-frame structures to bolster key areas. The running gear is mainly Ford (Sierra/Cortina), and the Rover V8 can be used to add Healey-style grunt. Then there is the *Sebring Motor Company* with their Sebring SX and Sebring MX. Both utilise a rigid backbone chassis, with fully adjustable suspension and, of course, the Rover V8 engine option, but while the SX retains the classic style of the big Healey, the MX has taken a lower, more aggressive stance with bulging wheel arch extensions.

Any kit car fitted with a Rover V8 engine will be endowed with punchy, flexible performance, but one kit car uses the engine to devastating effect, and that is the legendary Westfield SEight, which in '330' form stands amongst the world's best sports cars. For sheer missile-like acceleration you will need to look to the likes of a McLaren F1 or Bugatti EB110 Super Sport to beat it! *Westfield Sports Cars* of Kingswinford are respected in the industry for building good-quality performance sports cars in the tradition of the Lotus 7 – compact, spartan, but superb in handling and cornering ability, giving true driver satisfaction. Putting a Rover V8 engine in the Westfield was inspired. The car can be supplied fully built with a TVR Power-built 4.3-litre engine, resulting in a car fully capable of harnessing the power and able to accelerate from 0-60 mph in 3.4 seconds and 0-100 mph in 7.9 seconds . The SEight can also be supplied with Rover V8s of lesser capacity and tune, or ready to accept the new owner's engine and gearbox, but the potential of the combination is still apparent.

There are one or two pretenders to the Westfield crown, producing a similar Lotus 7-esque sports car that can be fitted with a Rover V8 engine. Mention has already been made of the Dax Rush. Originally developed in Germany by one Jurgen Mohr and developed for UK road use by Dax, it uses Ford Granada Scorpio running gear to handle Rover V8 power. The Robin Hood uses a stainless steel monocoque chassis and, because the body is slightly wider than its contemporaries, not only can the Rover V8 engine be mounted further back in the chassis, but also a Rover SD1 rear axle can be fitted, with its inherent advantages. The Robin Hood is also extremely competitively priced. Another car of this style worth looking at is the Tiger Super 6, by *Tiger Cars* of Plumstead, London SE18.

The 4x4 market has not been neglected by the kit car industry either, and the construction of the Range Rover, with its extremely robust, separate chassis, not to mention the ready availability of older examples at realistic prices, makes it a convenient basis for a fresh creation. Watchers of the TV programme *Challenge Anneka* cannot fail to have noticed the bright blue and yellow open off-road vehicle she uses on occasions, nor its familiar V8 rumble. The vehicle is in fact a Dakar 4x4 produced by *Dakar Cars Ltd* of Wilmington, a kit car that uses a Range Rover chassis and running gear as a basis. Basically, a suitable donor Range Rover (any year) is stripped of its body and the glassfibre Dakar 4x4 bodywork is substituted. The advantages over building the usual form of kit car are that the Range Rover has a proven chassis and that the complete running gear is left *in situ* together with much of the electrics during the conversion, although much can be done to renovate worn assemblies at the same time. Most of the Range Rover body is stripped from the chassis, leaving the front bulkhead/firewall and much of the floorpan. After the fuel tank is removed the chassis (not the wheelbase) is then shortened at the rear by cutting it off just aft of the rear crossmember, which does not compromise the chassis's strength; in fact the shortened rear overhang enhances the Dakar's off-road ability. Any necessary repairs can then be made to the remaining floor section, particularly the footwells, which have a tendency to rust. The roll cage is then fitted, the floor panels extended slightly, a few brackets welded on, fitment of a Cavalier Mk1 fuel tank, and the new body is bolted and riveted in place. The Range Rover dashboard is retained and, after fitting out with windscreen, seats, lights, etc, the Dakar 4x4 is ready for the (off) road! For half the price of a modest Cobra replica you have a solid, extremely capable recreational vehicle, which out-performs the donor vehicle by virtue of its considerably reduced weight.

Another 4x4 contender in the kit car market is the Eagle RV by *Eagle Cars* of Arundel, Sussex. The appearance is very similar to the later renditions of the ubiquitous Jeep and can be adapted for a number of applications, including the Range Rover chassis.

The Morgan Plus 8 is a very desirable automobile with the classic lines of a traditional British sports car combined with the brutal power of the Rover V8, but anyone who has the means to indulge themselves by buying one of these superb cars will know that the waiting list is very, very long. Enter the Hawke by *G. C. S. Cars* of Orpington, Kent, a roadster from the same classic era and one that can also accept the Rover V8 engine. The Hawke utilises Ford running gear, and a conventional ladder design chassis constructed mainly from 3 inch x 2 inch box section steel. The body is moulded

Reg Woodcock's superbly engineered Rover V8-powered Westfield 11 kit car. The car's injection set-up is unique, designed and built by brother Ray.

ROVER V8

glassfibre with a louvred aluminium bonnet, and was designed from the start to accept the Rover V8 engine, which has resulted in excellent engine accessibility. The oil filter location is often a problem when fitting the Rover V8 into a special application, but this can usually be solved by fitting a remote oil filter as used on the MGB GTV8. The Hawke offers a unique solution to this problem by using an angled plate that can be welded to the oil pump base, lifting it up and away from the chassis member. The threaded tube to which the filter canister is screwed is tapped and an angled extension screwed into it. The result is a very neat installation. *Autotune (Rishton)* of Blackburn, Lancashire, have two very interesting offerings, one of which coincidentally has an ancestry traceable back to the original Buick/Oldsmobile version of the Rover V8 engine. The Autotune Can-Am M1 is a replica of the McLaren M1 open Can-Am race car, intended for use in historic replica circuit racing, which can be, and has been, fitted with a mid-mounted Rover V8. This company also offer the dainty Gemini, which is a replica of the Elva sports car from the 'fifties. Fit a Buick/Rover V8 and you have a replica of the Elva Buick, a very quick, sure handling sports car for road and racing.

Even the magnificent Ford GT40 has not been overlooked by the kit car industry, and here again provision has been made to incorporate the Rover V8 engine as a powerplant worthy of the original car's pedigree. Mention has already been made of the superb DAX 40, the company's bright yellow demonstrator being fitted with a 3.5-litre fuel injected Rover V8, producing a modest 165 bhp, which endowed the beauty with truly exhilarating performance. Other Ford GT40 replicas are the high quality GTS40 by *GT Developments* of Poole, and the Tornado TS40 by *Tornado Cars* of Kidderminster. All these replicas are spaceframe chassis clothed in glassfibre bodywork, and the Rover V8 requires either a Renault transaxle or a Hewland, if you are rich.

Those looking for more modern exotica can choose from a number of Countach replicas, and although by all accounts the kits replicating this Italian exotic may be a lot cheaper than the real thing, they are certainly not in the modest budget category. To replicate the devastating performance of the real Countach a Rover V8 should be considered the minimum requirement! Kits worth investigating are the Mirage by *Mirage Replicas* of Wellingbor-

ough, the Masterco Countach by *Masterco* of Bolton, the Prova Countach by *Prova Designs* of Darwen, Lancashire, who interestingly also offer a Lamborghini Muira replica, and the Sienna Countach by *Sienna Cars* of Warminster, Wiltshire.

Many of these kit cars have racing potential, none more so than the Ultima Sports and Spyder by *Ultima Sports* of Hinckley, Leicestershire, truly a Group C race car for the home builder with a race bred spaceframe, and suspension with racing aerodynamics. Definitely a project for those with serious competition ambitions.

'Thirties style sports cars have a lot of appeal, perpetuated by the desirability of the Morgan Plus 8, and here again the kit car industry caters more than adequately for any demand.

The *NG* range of cars have almost become classics in their own right, having been conceived 15 years ago and still going strong. Various, but closely related, body styles distinguish the NG TC, TD and TF, which use mainly MGB mechanicals (or Marina/Ital as an alternative), and they can all accommodate a Rover V8 to add punch if required. Other kits falling into the ''thirties period' category are the Moss Roadster (or four seater Malvern), by *Moss Cars* of Bath, with Ford or Triumph running gear, the very pretty Marlin Cabrio, by *Marlin Engineering* of Crediton, Devon, which uses Ford Sierra running gear, and, for those who like a more American flavour, how about a 1932 Ford Roadster from *The Chassis Works* in Beaconsfield, or the Ford Model A in a variety of body styles (Roadster, 5-Window Coupé, Tudor Sedan, Sedan Delivery and Closed Cab) from *Scorhill Motor Company* at Walton on Thames in Surrey.

Finally there is the Darrian, by *Team Duffee Engineering* of Lampeter, Dyfed, a car that has been around in one form or another for many years. They are essentially specialist tarmac stage rally cars, and very successful ones too, with a distinguished list of competition titles, including some GT racing success. A glassfibre body, with Kevlar and carbon fibre enhancement of original styling, wraps a spaceframe chassis able to accept a variety of engines, all mid-mounted, and the Rover V8 makes for a very interesting projectile that can handle corners with equally devastating form.

Thus the kit car industry has taken the Rover V8 to its heart and dreamed up any number of interesting and desirable machines capable of exploiting the engine's qualities.

British Airways added their support to the Works Triumph TR7 V8 rally programme by sponsoring the team in both the 1978 and 1979 RAC Rallies

ROVER V8

TVR 350i – Rover
Vitesse 3.5-litre fuel-
injected engine and
arresting looks.
(Patrick Collection)

The NG 'TCR' – a Rover V8 powered sports car along classic lines.

The latest development of the Rover V8 is the 3.9-litre EFi version for North American specification Range Rovers.

ROVER V8

Nic Mann's Morris Minor is a firm favourite with hill climbing spectators all over the U.K. – its performance is stunning

Announced in September 1994, the all-new Range Rover is available with a 4.0-litre or 4.6-litre Rover V8 engine.

MGB GT V8 – a superb combination of character and power. C-7 (Patrick Collection)

An animal – the MG Metro FG8R4. Group B Supercar technology matched with solid Rover V8 power and torque into an awesome combination.

While the new Range Rover may have scaled new heights of sophistication, this has not detracted in the slightest from its off-road capability.

Rover V8 as single seater sprint power-plant. Dave Tilley's March 722 with 'full-race' engine.

Triumph TR8 converted from 4-cylinder TR7 to a very high standard. Better than the genuine article.

The stunning TVR Griffith 500 may go down in the history books as the pinnacle of Rover V8-engined performance motoring – 0-60mph in 4.1 seconds and 0-100 mph in 10.5 seconds!

Chapter Six

Rover V8 Competition Engine

The Rover V8 engine has powered an incredible array of racing machinery in a multitude of different vehicle racing 'classes'. As early as 1970 there had been, an albeit shortlived Rover saloon car racing project using the V8, although by this time Rover was part of British Leyland and the project was therefore managed by the BL Competitions Department. Rover at Solihull had, in pre-Leyland days, pursued their own modest motorsport programme; rallying the P5 Rover, then later the Rover 2000, employing the talents of Roger Clark and appearing at Le Mans with the Rover-BRM gas turbine prototype in the hands of Graham Hill.

The 1970 Rover V8 saloon racer was a ferocious beast whose preparation and racing had been contracted out by BL's Competitions Department at Abingdon. It was the responsibility of Bill Shaw and Roy Pierpoint (who also drove it) to campaign the car which had originally been turned into a rallycross car from a 1966 V8 development hack by Rover. Development of this first car (JXC 808D) was entrusted to *JoMoCo Racing* of Brookwood, Surrey which had been recently formed by two ex-Alan Mann Racing men, Jimmy Morgan and Jimmy Rose. The engine was officially Traco-Rover but was in fact Traco-Oldsmobile, prepared by *Mathwall Engineering* of Cobham, Surrey. Bore was 3.563 ins. with special pistons and Chevrolet con-rods combined with a Traco long stroke (3.5 in) crankshaft to give a capacity of 4.3 litres. Although retaining wet sump lubrication, the considerably modified engine, with hydraulic camshaft followers, four downdraught Weber carbs on Traco inlet manifolds and reworked cylinder heads, produced some 360 bhp at 6800 rpm. The car retained basic Rover suspension but the front had fabricated lower wishbones with higher pickup points and at the rear the De Dion layout was extensively modified. The brakes were massive 12 inch ventilated discs with Lockheed callipers at the front and similar 10 inch diameter discs at the rear.

The bodywork made the staid Rover look pretty sensational with all four doors, sills, bonnet, bootlid and roof in aluminium. Bulging fibreglass wheel arches covered massive 15 inch diameter, 10 inch wide Minilite wheels and Dunlop racing tyres. This first car was used extensively for 'one-off' national saloon car races since a considerable production run would have been required to homologate the car for Group 2 competition.

As it transpired only one other car was built by Shaw and Pierpoint (JXC 806D), essentially the same but built to Group 6 prototype regulations. BL Competitions Department became more involved with this car and it competed in the 1971 Nürburgring 86 hour Marathon de la Route which it led convincingly for 16 hours before retiring. The project died along with the BL Competitions Department which closed shortly after. JXC 806D went to Australia where it continued racing and, after a brief career as an exhibition vehi-

Immaculate red and white aluminium and glassfibre bodywork of the BL – Bill Shaw Racing Rover 3500. *(Bill Price)*

The 4.3-litre Traco/Oldsmobile/Rover racing engine produced 365 bhp. Prepared by Mathwall Engineering. *(Bill Price)*

cle was restored and is now in the hands of a private collector.

It would now be some years before the Rover V8 would receive the full benefit of 'Works' development, although one or two experimental projects were undertaken including the Rover V8-engined Marina coupés built by Leyland Special Tuning in the early 1970s. In South Africa in 1974 a Marina 4-door saloon was built by Geoff Mortimer for Leyland S.A. to contest the National Rally Championship. It entered more than 20 events over a 2 year period, competing against Ford Escort

Roy Pierpoint powers the big Rover around Mallory Park in 1970. *(Chris Harvey)*.

Surprisingly standard-looking interior. Only the racing steering wheel, bucket seats and absence of carpeting give the game away. *(Bill Price)*

ROVER V8

BDAs, Datsun 1800 Twin Cams and Toyota Corollas, managing to finish in the top three on many occasions.

The Marina was fitted with a 3.5-litre Rover V8 which had been tuned by the addition of a locally developed solid lifter camshaft, standard compression ratio, a single 48mm sidedraught Weber on a locally modified inlet manifold, coupled to an MGB 4-speed close ratio gearbox. The engine produced 185 bhp and extremely healthy mid-range torque. The car's suspension used heavy duty Australian components; locally made heavy duty torsion bars, twin shock absorbers each side, special ratio steering rack and 10″ ventilated disc brakes with 4 piston callipers at the front. At the rear there was an Alfa Romeo rear axle using a ZF limited slip differential with uprated leaf springs, twin gas

1970 again and Roy Pierpoint leads Dave Brodie's Escort BDA around Silverstone. *(Chris Harvey)*

Is nothing sacred? A few Marina coupés were built for special rallying events in the early 1970s using MGB GT V8 units. *(Austin Rover)*

The sole Leyland SA/Geoff Mortimer-built Marina V8 saloon on the rough. *(Geoff Mortimer)*

shock absorbers each side, and 9" solid discs. The car sat on 6 x 13 inch Minilite wheels.

This car was driven in the 1975 Total International Rally by Simo Lampinen, but unfortunately failed to finish. It is still running today in club rallies.

TRIUMPH TR7 V8 RALLYING

International rallying has seen a massive increase in public interest through the 1970s and 1980s, fuelled in part by the charisma of a handful of truly exciting cars which have caught the imagination of the 'casual' spectator and the attention of the media.

It perhaps began with the debut of the Lancia Stratos in the winter of 1973 – 74, was closely followed by the Triumph

TR7 V8 and the Audi Quattro, culminating finally with the Group B 'supercars'. The Ford Escort and now the Lancia Delta HF Integral may have proved devastatingly effective, and all credit to them for that, but only a select few have had their name spread through the waiting crowds at the first sound of their approach. The TR7 V8 did just that; the unmistakable sound of its V8 engine blasting a path through the trees, a flash of red, white and blue as it powered sideways through a '90° Right ', the gruff angry growl of 300 bhp and it was gone, leaving behind a stunned silence.

The Triumph TR7 had already been the star of a new era of British Leyland involvement in motorsport following Leyland Cars' announcement in October 1975 that John Davenport would head their official return to the arena. Of the three car team aiming an assault on the 1976 RAC Rally, two would be TR7s, chosen because the production model range lacked a suitable saloon and because it was known then that the TR7 was destined to have V8 power. Development of that power was entrusted to David Wood at BL Motorsport. He had been a development engineer with Ford at Boreham before leaving to set up his own business dealing, naturally, with Ford engines but had been teaching motor technology at Bury St. Edmunds when recruited by John Davenport.

Wood become part of the Abingdon team in August 1977 principally to strengthen BL Motorsport's engineering

production engines were found to be too varied for competition purposes, where equal compression throughout all eight cylinders is of paramount importance, so both block and heads had to be machined to arrive at equal piston heights. Of course, on any V8 engine this can cause manifold alignment problems, not to be taken lightly in the early pre-quadruple Weber days. The blocks were taken from Rover with only the basic machining done because with solid lifters being used the oil drillings to supply the hydraulic tappets were not required. Their omission gave more strength to the block and better oil feed

Preserved for posterity by the Austin Rover Heritage Trust – the formidable Triumph TR7 V8 rally car.

The initial Works Triumph TR7 V8 engine with twin Webers mounted on an Offenhauser manifold via a Repco adaptor.

capability. In the early days of V8 development a lot of engines had been built by Don Moore's *RS Race Engineering* of Cambridge, who had previously been involved in building Dolomite Sprint engines for BL Motorsport. Don Moore (he retired in 1980) acted as an outside engine builder, supplying racing engines to BL which not only kept BL's in-house engine builders on their toes, thus accelerating the development process, but assured them of engine supplies in case of industrial disputes. Like the engineers at Vandervell who had tuned the engine for GKN 47D (see Chapter 8), building Rover V8 engines to produce more power and stay in one piece was a matter of applying sound race engine building principles. There was no pool of tried and tested knowledge to draw on. For instance, crankshaft tolerances on

The first Group 1 Rover V8 racing engine, built by Don Moore's R.S. Engineering of Cambridge.

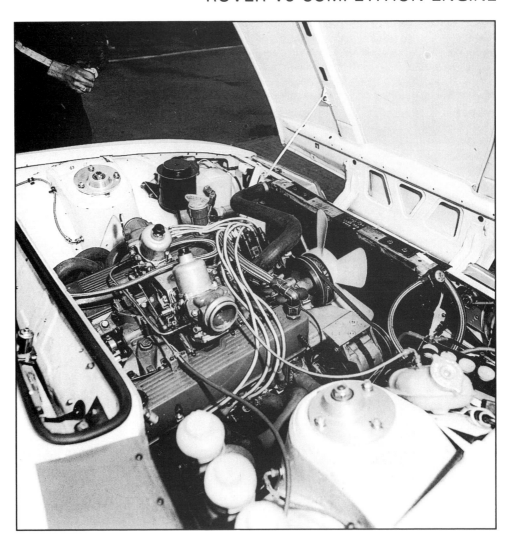

The Pierburg fuel-injection system developed for the Triumph TR7 V8s in 1979-80. This particular version on Reg Woodcock's racing Westfield 11 has been extensively modified.

to the places that really needed it. Line boring was done with everything bolted down to distort the block, which in the beginning had 2-bolt main bearing caps but as engine development progressed BL Motorsport produced their own 4-bolt main bearing blocks which involved asking Rover to cast in extra material to act as a buttress for the special mains caps. Interestingly, when Rover themselves began work on the Iceberg diesel engine project they obtained a few of these competition 4-bolt blocks for assessment.

Development of the engine to produce more horsepower really began with a collection of all the American performance parts then available for the Buick/Oldsmobile engine through such companies as *John Woolfe Racing* in Bedford, who already had a reputation for supplying tuning parts for the Rover V8. Such 'aftermarket' parts as Crane camshafts and Holley carburettors were assessed as a starting point but some were quickly replaced. Holley 4-barrel carburettors, a firm favourite with many looking for more power from a variety of V8 engines were found to be adequate on full throttle operation but lacking in mid-range. The TR7 V8 rally car appeared initially with twin 40 DCOE 13 Webers mounted on a special cast Repco adapter which bolted directly to the carburettor mounting flange of an Offenhauser manifold in place of the usual Holley.

Dry-sumping the engine was deemed essential from the beginning, bearing in mind the inherent tendency of any V8 engine to pump a large proportion of its oil capacity into the upper part of the crankcase, leaving precious little to lubricate the vital power end. It also allows better oil control during the rigours of rallying, a cast sump to strengthen the bottom of the block and more room for the installation of an optimum exhaust system design. With the high rpm the engine was being built to sustain, dry sumping was essential to preserve the distributor drive gear and of course it liberated more engine power (some 20 bhp) to the rear wheels. But as it transpired, the dry-sump system did not solve all the engine's lubrication problems. BL Motorsport started out using heat treated standard Rover pistons with a rev limit of 7200 rpm but later, with Mahle pistons and standard Rover pattern con-rods cast in stronger EN24 material the engine could withstand 8000 rpm or even 8500 rpm! The standard crank was always retained although tuftrided and with oil

drillings repositioned. Some steel cranks were made but were not found to be necessary. The standard ignition system was retained throughout the rally programme. As well as extensive work on camshaft design, the valve gear also received a lot of attention. Solid lifters, adjustable pushrods, steel rockers, bigger diameter rocker shafts, and Schmitthelm valve springs were all added to enhance the engine's ability to operate at high rpm and the valve head diameter eventually

Terry Kaby successfully rallied his TR7 V8 in 1979 – winning the Halewood Stages event, a third in the Russek Manuals and 4th in the Manx International Trophy.

reached 1.65 inches (42 mm) inlet and 1.45 inches (36.8 mm) exhaust. The compression ratio remained more or less standardised at 10.7:1.

The TR8 was homologated for Group 4 (equivalent to Group 2 saloons but with 2 instead of 4 seats) in 1978 and the rallying version of Triumph TR7 V8 was an instant hit with public and press. From its first official public appearance, driven by Tony Pond, in the spectacular Texaco TV Rally Sprint from Esgair Dafydd in Wales, it con-

firmed its claim to be one of the most exciting rally cars in the history of the sport. With the engine (limited to 6500 rpm) and the chassis still in the early stages of development, Pond had his hands full but managed a creditable 2nd against well proved competition. Its first rally was the Granite City Rally out of Aberdeen, crewed by Tony Pond and Fred Gallagher, in twin side draught Weber specification. They won by 12 seconds.

The car retired from the 'Welsh' and

ROVER V8

after rolling in the 'Scottish' retired there too but the highlight of that first year was the domination of the Ypres 24-hour Rally in Belgium, winning by over three minutes against some of the best European teams. The Border Counties Rally had a single car entered so that Pond could do some forest tyre evaluation and it was tyre problems that limited him to a 4th place. American John Buffum came over for a taste of TR7 rallying, V8 style in the Burmah Rally while Pond handled a second entry. He retired with axle trouble but Buffum, also having more than his fair share of problems, finished 8th.

in the dry-sump lubrication system. The Tour de Corse has become known as the 'sabotage' event. It would appear that the TR7 V8s had acquired such a reputation that someone felt it necessary to loosen the gearbox drain plugs on the two cars entered while they were in the security of the *parc fermé*., needless to say, neither car got very far before they came to a grinding halt. A full three car team was entered in the 1978 RAC Rally, with British Airways sponsorship, and Pond/Gallagher finished 4th after being badly delayed in Trentham Gardens with a jammed handbrake calliper as well as a

The Triumph TR7 V8 had many successes. This is Graham Elsmore on his way to winning the 1979 Russek Manuals Rally.

Derek Boyd, partnered with Fred Gallagher was entrusted with a car for the tarmac Ulster Rally and was in a commanding position when a rocker shaft broke, allowing a cam follower to pop out and drop the oil pressure to zero. The Manx International had two cars entered, Pond/Gallagher who won and Boyd/Kernaghan, Boyd going out early with engine trouble. In the Lindisfarne Rally the single car entered for Pond retired with problems

leaking head gasket later in the rally. John Haugland/Ian Grindrod came in 12th and Simo Lampinen/Mike Broad retired. The cars were by now producing 285 bhp at 7500 rpm with peak torque being 246 lb/ft at 5500 rpm, creditable figures, but the power band was relatively narrow.

1979 saw Tony Pond leave the car he seemed so suited to and move to Talbot. The team was restructured around Per Eklund, partnered with Mike Broad, who

American John Buffum's Works prepared Triumph TR7 V8 – HRW 251V – with which he contested many National events.

soldiered on through a fairly inconclusive year. Eklund did however manage to come 2nd in his first TR7 V8 event, the Mintex, and he won the BP Rallysprint. Graham Elsmore, who had come 2nd in the previous year's Wyedean rally driving a 'borrowed' car was now contesting the Sedan Open Championship just as Roger Clark would do in the following year. During 1979 fuel injection was being developed very seriously and tried for the first time in a World Championship event, the 1000 Lakes in Finland. Two cars were entered, one with fuel injection for Eklund who finished 8th and another for Simo Lampinen who retired. The fuel-injection system centred around a Dave Wood-designed crossover inlet manifold, made at Rover and using an advanced Pierburg electronic injection system made in Germany.

Using a special camshaft, the systems metering was controlled via the ignition system and involved a lot of advanced electronics. However, in the confines of the TR7's under-bonnet area it suffered from fuel-lock vaporisation which eventually necessitated a return to Webers. In fact the Pierburg manifold was modified to take 4 side-draught Webers on cast alloy adaptors and this induction setup was tested with a flat plane crankshaft engine for possible use in the Paris-Peking rally Rover 3500s (SD1). The event was cancelled. In the

1979 RAC Rally (again with British Airways as main sponsors) four cars were entered with a fifth loan car for American John Buffum producing over 320 bhp and masses of torque with the fuel injection system. He crashed. Three of them did finish, in 13th, 16th and 17th place, hardly the kind of result worthy of a major Works team.

The TR7 V8 programme did have its problems and in an effort to bring the car to its full potential, development work was proceeding at a rapid pace. The car was not an inherently good handler; it had a short wheelbase, wide track, limited suspension travel and poor driver visibility. Although fast and powerful, it was not an easy car to drive and it took someone of Tony Pond's driving ability, not to mention his enthusiasm and belief in the car, to get the best out of it. When Pond rejoined the team in 1980, along with another star of the sport, Roger Clark, there was a lot of work to be done. The fuel injection system, although providing good power, was proving troublesome when applied to this car under rallying conditions and there were serious problems with the specially built dry-sump lubrication system. The engine was proving capable of 'loosing' a tremendous quantity of oil, holding it where it was not particularly needed and starving the vital reciprocating parts (Per Eklund

The ultimate TR7 V8 rally engine with 4 side-draught Webers. Note they are set back slightly on the engine.

retired from the 1979 San Remo Rally in Italy with just such a problem) and that oil which was finding its way back into the sump was not being scavenged fast enough under certain conditions.

Cliff Humphries at BL Motorsport, with a very limited budget, was doing a lot of testing with quadruple Weber carburation. He had tried four 48 IDF Webers and found fuel surge a problem so he switched to the more suitable 48 DCOEs but finding room for them under the bonnet of a TR7 V8 was not easy. The simple answer was to fix the carbs on to the engine rocker covers with plasticine and close the bonnet, then finding sufficient clearance he had some 'U' shaped manifolds made in steel by Janspeed and began testing. Roger Clark tried them out on his first outing with what was supposedly his private 'Sparkrite' sponsored car, not an official Works entry, and proving quite a handful compared to his more usual mount, the Ford Escort (1979 was the last year of the Works Escorts). By mid-1980, the injection system had been dropped altogether in favour of the four big side-draught Webers, which with new exhaust manifolds produced around 300 bhp at 7000 rpm and peak torque of 268 lb/ft at 5000 rpm.

The oil problems were eventually solved by the use of a bigger twin scavenge oil pump and a 'windage tray', which is a curved metal baffle, more or less the same length as the crankshaft, mounted between the crank and the sump. American racers had pioneered its use in high performance V8 engines, once they had begun to understand the problems caused by the spinning mass of the crankshaft within the confines of the crankcase and how it interfered with oil trying to return by gravity to the sump. With the lubrication problems sorted the engines were now both powerful and reliable.

Richard Hurdwell was bought in from MIRA to apply his considerable skills to the chassis of the TR7 V8 and throughout the year the car began to evolve towards its full potential, helped along the way by the adoption of Michelin radial tyres which were found, almost by accident, to complement the TR7 V8 under many conditions, proving even better once the chassis and suspension had been tuned to suit them.

Eklund came 2nd in the Daily Mirror TV Rallysprint and Pond won the Rothmans Manx Stages Rally using the extremely effective Michelin radial racing tyres they had been forced to try on the Criterium Alpin earlier in the year. The Ypres 24-hour Rally had been missed in 1979 but Tony Pond outdrove the formidable opposition, once again using Michelins. The 1000 Lakes Rally in Finland had a two car entry for Per Eklund and Timo Makinen. While Makinen ran out of fuel, Eklund finished a creditable 3rd. Tony Pond really stamped his authority on the Manx International Trophy, winning by 4 minutes. The Tour of Cumbria was entered as a pre-RAC warm up/evaluation and finished a very encouraging 2nd. For the Eaton Yale TV Rallysprint, Pond shared a car with Formula 1 star Alan Jones and won the event. The 1980 RAC Rally was to be the last factory entry for this magnificent rally car. It was not to be a glorious finale however; Pond lost 3 minutes when he crashed into a stoutly built feeding trough on the first stage at Longleat and lost more time at Calderdale but managed to climb up to a 7th place finish while Per Eklund, John Buffum and Roger Clark all retired.

At the end of 1980 it was announced that the Triumph TR7 V8 rallying programme was over. At the time, the decision was greeted with shocked disbelief by all those who had real faith in the car, but one must bear in mind that in 1979 four-wheel drive became permissible in International rallying and at the Geneva Motor Show in March 1980 Audi unveiled their brand new Audi Quattro. The rally car's success had done a tremendous job in boosting the image and credibility of the production TR7 sports car, as well as highlighting the fact that the TR8 was not available in the UK. Little did anyone know that it would cease production altogether within a year.

In the USA, where the TR8 *was* available to the buying public it was being raced with considerable success by Bob Tullius and in rallying by the previously mentioned John Buffum, although ironically both were competing with Rover V8-engined TR7s before the TR8 appeared in American showrooms. Bob Tullius and his Group 44 operation are probably better known for their exploits with Jaguars but had also achieved considerable success racing Leyland's smaller capacity sports car such as the MGB, Spitfire and TR6. After doing sterling work campaigning Jaguar E Types and XJS in the SCCA Trans-Am series, the fortunes of the Jaguar company declined and for 1979 and 1980 Tullius switched to the TR8, competing eventually

ROVER V8

in the IMSA GTO series which had taken over from Trans-Am as the major championship.

The Tullius-built TR8 racing car was very competitive and was extensively altered for racing in almost every detail. The engine was taken to the limit of the displacement class (4.0 litre,) which with a bore of 89.9 mm and stroke of 78.7 mm was 3989 cc. The engine produced 360 bhp at 8000 rpm and 310 lb/ft of torque at 5500 rpm, had a compression ratio of 12.5:1 and used (successfully) the same BL Motorsport/Pierburg fuel injection system designed by BL Motorsport but applied unsuccessfully to the TR7 V8 rally cars.

John Buffum's rallying TR8 was prepared along the same lines as its European counterparts (he did rally extensively in the UK) for competing in the SCCA Pro-Rally championship, which he won in 1979, but the 3.5-litre engines were prepared by *Huffaker Engineering,* makers of a rather special competition inlet manifold used successfully on the Rover V8 engine by enthusiasts in the UK. His rally engines not only used this manifold but also the Holley carburettor, which along with other special US parts such as Venolia pistons (10.5:1 comp. ratio) and Carillo con-rods, gave 280 bhp at 7000 rpm with 245 lb/ft of torque at 5000 rpm.

All the BL Motorsport Works-prepared cars were snapped up at bargain prices by eager collectors or private rally competitors

John Davenport – Director of BL Motorsport and later Austin Rover Motorsport throughout the TR7 V8 and Rover SD1/Vitesse rallying and racing programmes.

and although the TR7 V8 never became as popular as the Ford Escort in club rallying it is still hard to beat in the amount of driving exhilaration per £ spent category.

THE BIG ROVER – RACING THE 3500 (SD1)

Shortly after the TR7 V8 rally programme got under way John Davenport, Director of BL Motorsport, approached *David Price*

Jeff Allum testing the very first racing Rover SD1 at a wet Silverstone early in 1980.

Group 1 Rover SD1 racing engine in final single Weber form, and good for 260 bhp. *(Patrick Motor Collection).*

1980 and BL Motorsport prepare to campaign two John Price Racing- built Rover SD1s. Jeff Allum (right) and Rex Greenslade were the drivers.

Racing in Gosport, who up until that point had been responsible for the 1978 – 1979 Unipart Formula 3 team which used Triumph Dolomite engines, and asked if they could develop the Rover 3500 for saloon car racing.

They received their first 'in white' bodyshell in the spring of 1979 and built a car to the then Group 1 regulations using engines supplied by BL. These engines, built by *RS Engineering* in Cambridge initially used twin 1 $\frac{7}{8}$" SU carburettors, produced about 260 bhp and proved very unreliable, mainly because of lubrication problems (the regulations prohibited dry-sump conversion) and of course the distributor drive gear proved a weakness at racing revs, which in the early days were

limited to 6500 rpm. Remember, at this time Rover V8 engine development for racing was totally new territory. Gradually engine development, within the limits of Group 1 regulations, progressed. The SU carbs were replaced by a pair of side-draught Webers, mounted on a Repco-type adapter (as used on the early works TR7 V8 rally cars) which was then bolted to a machined Rover manifold, but this did not satisfy the scrutineers for long before RS Engineering were forced to move on to a single downdraught 48 IDA Weber. Alternatives were always being tried, even a 350 cfm 2-barrel Holley (regulations specified the same number of chokes or throttle venturi as standard ie. two) was mounted on an Offenhauser or Huffaker manifold. In 1981 the Group 1 Patrick Motor Sport Rover of Frank Muir managed to get away with using a 'prototype' fuel injection system for a while. Exhaust manifolding was free. The original Group 1 engines used hydraulic camshaft followers and Crane cams but the followers were soon doctored to make them solid (as done later in Group A engines) and sets of pushrods were kept, all of slightly varying lengths, to set the tappet clearance because adjustable pushrods or rockers were not allowed. The first 'Works' Group 1 camshaft was the WL-3, W for Chris Walters their designer and L for Leyland and they progressed in Group 1 to WL-11. Power rose too, reaching 280–290 bhp by the time Group A regulations were announced which radically changed the face of saloon/touring car racing. There were also difficulties at first in stiffening the bodyshell sufficiently for racing, there were no aerodynamic aids homologated for the car and suitable tyres had not yet been developed. With BL Motorsport supplying all the hardware, David Price racing were able to turn this big saloon into a race car weighing just 1050 kilos, which was lighter than the later Group A cars. Testing began at Gaydon in October 1979 using close ratio gear sets in the standard Austin Rover 77mm 5-speed gearbox (the '77mm' refers to the distance between shaft centres).

The Triplex/Esso/Motor-sponsored Rovers of Jeff Allum and Rex Greenslade entered the fray in 1980 contesting the prestigious Tricentrol British Saloon Car Championship (the year that the capacity limit was upped from 3 to 3.5 litres) at a time when the Ford Capri 3 litre had the level of dominance currently enjoyed by the Sierra Cosworth. Rover's first win was

at the British GP support event with Jeff Allum at the wheel and after secret testing at Donington they won the Motor Show 200 race there with a fine first and second placing. The winning car was driven by Alan Jones in his F1 World Championship year.

A Rover had won the Tourist Trophy in 1907 and for the 1980 event, which was a round of the European Touring Car Championship a one-off Rover built to Group 2 regulations was entered for Jeff Allum and Tiff Needell. Against tough

Steve Cole's very successful racing Morgan and had things not been different we might have seen a whole new area of Rover V8 development, with the possibility of a company experienced in Cosworth V8 building applying themselves to the Rover V8'.

In the meantime *Tom Walkinshaw Racing* had been called in to undertake some consultancy work on the Rover's suspension early in the 1980 season, which they did very successfully, and they too put forward a complete proposal for the car's

Rex Greenslade leads Round 4 of the Tricentrol RAC British Saloon Car Championship at Silverstone, 1980. He finished second.

Interior of Patrick Motor Group Racing Group 1 Rover SD1, still surprisingly standard-looking with full dashboard and door trim. *(Patrick Motor Collection)*

Group 2 BMW opposition the Unipart-sponsored car gave a good account of itself but failed to finish. The Rover 3500 was to continue contesting British Saloon and European Touring Car Championships for the next eight years! After this first exploratory season David Price Racing had determined which parts would have to be homologated for the car in order to make it a future success. They had also commissioned *Hesketh Racing* in Towcester, who had previously been involved in preparing Cosworth DFVs for David Price's Aurora series team, to build them a number of Rover V8 engines. Hesketh Racing later evolved into *JGF Engineering* and its head Jonathan Fisher says 'we took the whole project very seriously' but it faded when TWR came into the picture. At the time, Hesketh also built a Rover V8 engine for

future development. It was TWR who were entrusted with the task of taking the car into the British and ultimately into the European Touring Car Championship, but there was a lot of work still to be done.

For the 1981 British Saloon Car Championship there were regularly four cars entered, two by BL Motorsport, (Daily Express/Esso sponsored cars prepared by Tom Walkinshaw Racing) and two *SRG Racing*-prepared machines (with BL assistance) from Patrick Motor Sport who had run a single 'private' Rover 3500 in the

latter half of 1980. The early part of the 1981 season saw the Works cars struggling once again with reliability problems, making little impression on the long standing dominance of the Ford Capri 3.0-litre and the agility of the TWR/Mazda RX-7 of Win Percy. But things eventually came right, the TWR/Rovers winning first at Silverstone (Round 6) and getting their first 1-2 win again at Silverstone in Round 7. Rovers scored another first at Silverstone in Round 11 when they finished 1-2-3, so six out of the 11 championship rounds

1982 and the last year of the Group 1 Works/TWR Rovers, now with Sanyo/Esso sponsorship. *(John Colley)*

Two of these Daily Express/Esso sponsored Group 1 Rovers contested the 1981 British Saloon Car Championship: the first year they were prepared by Tom Walkinshaw Racing.

were won by the Works cars, four of them with 1-2 victories. Peter Lovett and Jeff Allum came first and second in their class, while the Patrick Motor Sport pair driven by Brian Muir and Rex Greenslade provided a strong supporting cast.

1982 continued the close fought battles between the BL Motorsport/TWR Rovers now with Sanyo sponsorship and the Ford Capris which were nearing the end of their BSCC domination and indeed their racing development. Patrick Motor Sport too had a two car team, this time for Frank Muir and Rad Dougall although 2nd placings were the best they could manage. The Capris were to prove very tough opposition with Rovers taking six very closely fought round wins and the Capri five (two of them 1-2-3s), giving Jeff Allum the class win for cars from 2501 cc

to 3500 cc. 1982 also saw Tom Walkinshaw get behind the wheel of a Rover during practice at Thruxton, an event that was to provide its significance later on. This was also the last year that the Championship was open to cars built to Group 1 regulations.

In France René Metge won the French Production Saloon Car Championship in his Marlborough-sponsored Rover 3500. The French regulations were less restrictive than those of BTCC Group 1 and René had begun racing the Rover 3500 in 1980 with a self-prepared car which was very reliable. He finished 18th in the Championship that year and 8th in 1981.

In 1983 René Metge contested the French Championship again, joined by the second Rover of Jean-Pierre Beltoise driving René's 1982 car. In Belgium Eddy Joosen contested their modest saloon championship with a Rover Vitesse and won four rounds. Group 1 was replaced by FISA's new Group A regulations in 1983, bringing the cars into line with those competing in the European Touring Car

1983 and a switch to Group A regulations. The fuel-injected Rover Vitesse appears on the race track for the first time. *(John Colley)*

Championship. This meant a greater restriction on engine modifications but more freedom in the areas of transmission and brakes although bodyshells could not be altered and everything, including the wheels and tyres must fit within those limitations. The maximum tyre width was also dictated by the engine capacity.

With the new Rover Vitesse now in production it was this model that was used as a basis for the TWR/Austin Rover Motorsport team cars, of which there were now three; Jeff Allum and Peter Lovett with their Sanyo-sponsored cars and Steve Soper in a Hepolite Glacier car. These new fuel injected cars produced (to begin with) 290 bhp, which was about the same as the Group 1 carburetted cars but the power characteristics were much improved and the Group A regulations now allowed a Getrag 5-speed gearbox (as used on the racing BMWs).

These new 1180 kilo cars were used to good effect in the 1983 British Saloon Car Championship where they dominated the season. To begin with, only Jeff Allum had a full Group A specification car, because of a shortage of parts but they still managed to qualify 1-2-3 and win 1-2-3 in the first two rounds. In rounds three and four, Rovers qualified 1-2-3-4 on the grid and won convincingly. Round 6 saw Rovers qualify 1-2-4-5-6 fastest with the two Works cars gaining a 1-2 victory. By mid season the cars were being protested in respect of their engines and inner wheel arches, something which was to have serious repercussions later.

Round 7 was another Rover victory and Round 8 at Silverstone saw Works and private Rovers fill the front two rows of the grid and win 1-2-3. The next round was an upset, when Frank Sytner won in his BMW, but the last two rounds were a continuation of the Rover massacre.

The Works Rovers also made their first exploratory entries into the European Touring Car Championship too, entering rounds at Donington (where the TWR XJSs first appeared on home soil), Nürburgring, Spa, the Silverstone TT, Zolder and a single car entry in the Belgian GP support event. They did not fare well, being off the pace and lacking reliability for these longer events. Surprisingly Spa was the best showing. The cars were carrying extra weight because of long range fuel tanks and an air-jack system in this punishing 24 hour classic event. The car of Allum/Soper/Lovett came home 3rd in front of a delighted crowd which included Mark Snowden, Austin Rover's MD who was playing host to a number of Belgian AR dealers as well as assessing the possibility of a full European Touring Car programme for 1984.

1984 was a major year for the Rover Vitesse. The arguments over the legality of the works TWR cars were yet to be settled. Andy Rouse, winner of the British Saloon Car Championship in 1975, had contested the 1983 championship at the wheel of an Alfa Romeo GTV6 sponsored and owned by Industrial Control Services. With an eye to the 1984 championship

Steve Soper joins the team in 1983 and adds a third Hepolite Glacier-sponsored car. Rovers dominate the season

Jeff Allum and Steve Soper – 1st and 2nd at Silverstone 11th Round of BSCC in October 1983.

Andy had sat down with ICS boss Phil Hall and decided that the Rover Vitesse was the car to use. They approached John Davenport of AR Motorsport, who wholeheartedly supported their decision and made certain items of essential hardware availa-

existed, but he was, to all intents and purposes, an independent operation. A Rover Vitesse engine built to Group A rules is a sophisticated racing unit producing 300 + bhp and capable of withstanding 7200 rpm (maximum 7500 rpm) through-

Jeff Allum and Steve Soper – 1st and 2nd at Silverstone 11th Round of BSCC in October 1983.

TWR took the Works Rover team into Europe for their first full season in 1984 with Austin Rover Fleet sponsorship. It was a tough learning year. (John Colley)

Tom Walkinshaw himself defended his 1984 ETCC title at the wheel of a Rover Vitesse in 1985. Here he is at Monza. (John Colley)

Group A fuel-injected Rover V8 as developed by Tom Walkinshaw Racing for the Works Vitesses. (John Colley)

ble to them. Interestingly, Andy Rouse built his own car and engines at his base in Coventry in accordance with his own ideas on how the job should be done. Of course he acquired certain homologated engine and chassis components and drew to a certain extent on the pool of knowledge on racing the Rover Vitesse which already

out a race. The engines built for Group A by Andy Rouse Engineering were fairly typical although camshaft design, cylinder head, injection systems and so on varied as development continued and there were many rather 'exotic' parts specially made which some teams preferred not to shout about too loudly. Legality within the regu-

Andy Rouse wins the 1984 Trimoco RAC British Saloon Car Championship in a Rover Vitesse. Here he holds off Win Percy's Toyota Supra at Castle Donington. *(John Colley)*

lations was often limited by what you could get away with! The cylinder blocks for Group A were what is referred to as 'selected' but were in fact Vitesse 'stiff blocks', introduced in late 1982/early 1983, which have more material on the main bearing webs. The crankshaft with its Freudenberg damper was standard spheroidal graphite cast iron which was ionised for greater strength and crossdrilled for better lubrication of the main bearings. Connecting rods were Group A, that is standard in all but material which was EN24. Pistons as per the regulations were 'free' and Andy Rouse used Mahle forged type, with a raised crown and valve cutouts to give a compression ratio of 11:1. The cylinder heads were polished and ported with phosphor bronze valve seats and guides. Standard Vitesse-size valves were required by the regulations but whereas a production valve has a fuse welded two piece head and stem, Group A valves were one piece and shaped differently behind the head and used Schmitthelm dual, interference fit valve springs. The valve gear was all Group A. The camshaft, rotated by a Reynolds duplex timing gear set, was an AR Motorsport WL15, with hydraulic cam followers which had altered internal valving to make them act as if solid. (In Group A the camshaft is 'free' but maximum valve lift must not exceed that of the production engine). The pushrods then led to adjustable rockers, mounted on a larger diameter shaft, located by steel pillars.

The standard Vitesse cast iron exhaust manifolds had hours of work devoted to them as they were ground out inside to smooth and increase the gas flow. A lot of development work also went into fine-tuning the exhaust system after the manifolds, unrestricted by regulations. On the induction system there were strict limits to the amount of permitted modification but some work was done on the steel trumpets inside the plenum chamber, larger injectors were used and electronic engine management was by a specially developed 'Zytek' unit which optimised the engine's capabilities. Ignition was more or less standard Vitesse although Andy Rouse Engineering had to manufacture their own special hardened gear sets to combat excessive wear at high revs. Because dry-sump lubrication was prohibited a special Group A wet sump was homologated. This was a very carefully and intricately designed unit involving extra capacity, baffling and hinged trap doors to control oil surge during the high G-forces of cornering, acceleration and braking. The standard oil pump, with oil cooler of course, had its relief valve changed to operate at 60 psi and the block was prepared as per normal racing practise with enlarged drain-back areas and a pair of external oil drain pipes running from the back of the cylinder heads to the sump. The alternator and water pump pulleys, using a poly-V belt instead of a standard fan belt, were geared down to reduce rotating speed at racing rpm.

The bhp thus produced rotated an AR Motorsport flywheel and paddle clutch into a Getrag 5-speed gearbox. The car was fully race-prepared to the highest standards with an aluminium roll-cage. The regulations allowed the Rover Vitesse to run on 11" wide rims and racing tyres: Dunlop to begin with, then a switch to Goodyears and finally back to Dunlops, mounted on

Scott, a New Zealander. At the opening round at Donington Park, Andy Rouse's Rover qualified second fastest behind Tony Pond's Rover and won the race, having led from early on. Round 2 at Silverstone saw Andy qualify fastest but he was eliminated at the beginning of the race by a crash that was not of his making. Tony Pond in his TWR-prepared Rover won. In retrospect, Andy feels that the shunt did him a favour because he was able to rebuild the car to incorporate some new tweaks. Oulton Park (Round 3) was something of a problem for everyone and therefore unrepresentative but Andy managed to finish in second place. On to Thruxton and Andy qualified fastest and won in convincing style. Round 4 was back to Thruxton one month later and Andy again qualified fastest but the race was a battle royal between him and the four TWR Works Rovers. Steve Soper won. Andy

The total professionalism of TWR meant the team maintained the cars to the highest standards even at the race track. *(John Colley)*

Ronal centre locking wheels. Stopping was by 12" discs, with four-pot callipers, gas filled Bilstein shock absorbers at the front and Koni oil filled at the rear. The specification was completed by an adjustable front anti-roll bar and either 3.71:1 or 4.1:1 rear axle ratio in a Salisbury limited slip differential.

The immaculate blue ICS Rover Vitesse dominated the 1984 Trimoco RAC British Saloon Car Championship from its début, despite the presence in strength of the TWR works Vitesses whose engines were prepared 'in house' by their own Allan

Rouse came second and Rovers took the first four places! Back to Silverstone where Andy qualified fastest and won. Making his début in an Andy Rouse Engineering prepared (but not built) privately entered Vitesse was Neil McGrath.

The Shawcross Tribunal of Enquiry eventually ruled that the TWR Rovers contesting the 1983 BSCC were illegal in respect of engine rocker assembly and bodywork. Austin Rover disassociated itself from the findings of the tribunal, stating that the cars contesting the 1983 championship were identical to those which had been judged eligible for and had contested selected rounds of the European Touring Car Championship in the same year. They subsequently renounced their claim to the 1983 title and the TWR Rovers were withdrawn in the middle of the 1984 championship. Pressure was put on Andy Rouse (now confirmed as 1983 champion) and ICS to withdraw their Rover Vitesse too but they refused, having invested far too much in their challenge, and the battle for the 1984 title continued.

Round 7 at Snetterton saw Andy qualify on pole and win convincingly against the BMW 635 CSi of Frank Sytner, with Neil McGrath's Vitesse finishing in 5th place. Brands Hatch for Round 8 and Andy had some new opposition in the shape of Win Percy's brand new Toyota Supra. Also another Andy Rouse Engineering-prepared (but not built) Vitesse appeared, entered by Andy's old 1981 Capri racing partner

fastest but this time it was the Colt Starion of David Brodie which upstaged both Rouse and Percy, relegating them to second and third respectively as Brodie successfully fought off Rouse throughout the race.

Andy Rouse had won the Trimoco RAC British Saloon Car Championship for the third time. He was the first driver since Frank Gardner with the SCA Freight Camaro, to win the title outright in a big-class car and it was the first time ever that a British big-class car had won the Series, which had begun in 1958. He had run the entire season on just one Rover V8 engine which had been rebuilt only once. A spare engine had been prepared but never put in the car.

Surprisingly, Andy Rouse switched allegiance to Ford in 1985 having been approached by them and asked to begin race-development of the Ford Merkur (read

The starkly functional cockpit of 1985 Group A TWR/Bastos Rover Vitesse. Note the full door trim. *(John Colley)*.

Charles Sawyer-Hoare. Andy won after a close opening fight with Win Percy who stopped with a puncture after an 'incident'. Win Percy got his revenge a month later when they returned to Brands for Round 9 but Andy was second. Back to Donington for Round 10 and Win Percy again threatened by qualifying fastest but Andy won after one of the finest race-long, wheel-to-wheel battles the Series had seen for years. He had now all but clinched his third BSCC title. The 1984 championship finished at Silverstone (Round 11) and Andy regained his poise by qualifying

Sierra) Turbo on their behalf. ICS boss Pete Hall continued to race their Rover Vitesse in the BSCC during 1985 and development continued. After all, Andy acknowledges that at the time the car was far from over the hill and still reckons it to be one of the best-handling cars in its class even by today's standards.

1984 was also the year that Austin Rover contested, with the Group A Rover Vitesse, the European Touring Car Championship which by this time had become arguably the most prestigious series after Formula 1. Tom Walkinshaw Racing was

ROVER V8

not only contesting the championship with a team of three Jaguar XJ-S HEs but his organisation was also preparing and campaigning a pair of Rover Vitesses (with a third added at major rounds) on behalf of Austin Rover with sponsorship by Austin Rover Fleet, who admitted that 1984 was a learning year, but they were surprised to find just how hard some of these lessons turned out to be.

The Austin Rover/TWR team, under the management of TWR's Eddie Hinckley had a strong international line-up of experienced drivers; Jeff Allum, Steve Soper, Marc Duez, Tony Pond (when rallying commitments permitted), Armin Hahne, Eddie Joosen, Jean-Louis Schlesser, Peter Lovett, and Jean-Pierre Jabouille. Competition in the European Series came from the TWR Jaguars, a host of BMW 635CSis which had long been a dominant force in Europe, and the Volvo 240 Turbo, a most unlikely looking race car campaigned by more than one private team getting Works support. They were fast but they had the aerodynamics of a brick and their handling sometimes bordered on the perilous!

As the 1984 ETCC got under way the Rovers always managed to play second fiddle to the mighty Jaguars in qualifying but had problems in lasting the full race distance. Remember the British Series involved short 'sprint' races of between 40 and 60 miles. In Europe it was 500 km or in the case of Spa, a full 24 hour race so in tuning the Rover V8 engine for this type of event it had to produce plenty of power with good economy because fuel consumption played a vital role of being competitive. They managed to give a good account of themselves, despite mounting pressure from the Volvo camp and having to learn from scratch how to set up the Rover for many of the circuits, but only occasionally managed to get a car amongst the top ten finishers. A third Gitanes-sponsored car was permanently added to the team at the Österreichring event (Round 6). At Spa, supported by a fourth German car Rovers led the race 1-2-3 at one point, Pond taking full credit for getting the Rover he shared with Joosen/Jabouille into the lead, but could only manage a best 8th placing at the finish.

1985 saw the demise of the BMW works team and the sad news that Jaguar would no longer be competing either, preferring instead to concentrate on Group C, again with TWR. Tom Walkinshaw

'Project Scorch' was an attempt in 1985 by David Le Grys on the World Cycling Speed Record. He failed because the wind deflector mounted on the TWR/Bastos Rover Vitesse slowed the car too much. *(John Colley)*

1986 was the only year the TWR/Bastos Works Rover Vitesses raced with these twin throttle plenum injection systems. *(John Colley)*

The Spa 24 Hours is always a tough race and 1986 was no exception. One of the TWR/Bastos cars gets a fresh engine during practice. *(John Colley)*

would be defending his 1984 ETC title at the wheel of a Rover Vitesse now with Bastos/Texaco sponsorship and Dunlop Denloc tyres which were ideally suited to the Rover. Tyre development had played a significant part in the Rover Vitesse's ability to remain competitive and the special Dunlop tyres, with their Kevlar construction sat on 17" diameter rims. The team fielded three Rover Vitesses and the driver line-up consisted of Tom Walkinshaw partnered with Win Percy, Jeff Allum, Armin Hahne, Eddy Joosen, Steve Soper, Pierre Thibault, and Jean-Louis Schlesser. The team had one aim this year; never mind team orders and putting one driver into a championship winning position, just go for it and try to win as many races as possible with the Rover!

The 1985 ETCC kicked off at Brno in Czechoslovakia and the real opposition came from the flying Volvo 240 Turbos of Ulf Granberg/Anders Olofsson and Gianfranco Brancatelli/Thomas Lindstrom who won the first round and the series became a running battle between Rover and Volvo with the hardy BMWs always there ready to take advantage. The Rovers scored a magnificent 1-2-3 win at Monza and won again at Vallelunga, finishing 1st, 3rd and 4th. At home to Donington for Round 4 and a magnificent 1-2-3 for the Rovers. Then it was Volvos turn to shine on their home ground at Anderstorp and then Zeltweg. Still in Austria the circus visited the Salzburgring but again Brancatelli/Lindstrom had the win, with the Rovers second, third and fifth. Round 8 at the Nürburgring in West Germany and only the Rover of Soper/Joosen managed to finish, the other two retiring with oil leaks. Then it was time once again for the classic Spa 24 Hour race and Martin Brun-

dle joined the three car TWR/Bastos team. It was a pair of Rover Vitesses on the front row, leading the field to begin this 2000+ mile race but all three retired and a BMW 635CSi won! Home once again for the Silverstone TT and round 10 of the ETCC. Dave Brodie took pole position with his Colt Starion and BSCC champion Andy Rouse was third fastest in his Ford Sierra Turbo, behind the fastest of the three Rovers, the brand new Vitesse (the 17th TWR had built) of Walkinshaw/Percy which had qualified over three seconds faster than the best Rover managed last year at this event.

The race was a fierce fight but the Rovers took first and second places with Volvo third. Nogaro in France saw the TWR team finish 1-2-3 but Zolder was a mess. The Rover of Walkinshaw/Percy, fastest qualifier, spun on the first corner and was hit head on by a BMW. Only one Rover finished, in third place as the other team car retired with axle trouble. On to Estoril in Portugal and the race was a 1-2 for Volvo after chaos in the TWR pits. Volvo now had the ETC crown but there was one final round at Jarama in Spain which the Rover of Walkinshaw/Percy won. Austin Rover/TWR had lost a very close fight for the ETCC title in 1985 and were all the more determined to make 1986 the year of the Rover Vitesse in European touring car racing. The team once again fielded three cars, but they could now use the definitive Vitesse deep front spoiler which had appeared on production Vitesses from November 1984. The engine was different too. In place of the standard Vitesse single throttle plenum chamber was a new, altogether larger version with twin throttle butterflies. The idea had been developed by TWR, a 'cut and shut' prototype had been built by ARG Motorsport and the whole lot handed over to Lotus for manufacture and testing. In fact the two hundred or so 'twin-plenum' engines had been built and dyno tested at Lotus and final product engineering for the road versions had been completed at Austin Rover, Canley, Coupled with the FISA decision over the winter to scrap the restriction on valve lift in Group A, the Rovers now had a healthy increase in horsepower to take them into the new season.

Apart from managing to find the extra 2 seconds per lap Rover needed every year to remain competitive and the Volvos also benefiting from further testing and development it was another Rover versus Volvo year. Volvo gracefully acknowledged

ROVER V8

that the Rovers were the ones to beat, although the Australian manufacturer Holden (General Motors) were getting in on the act with their Commodore with its heavy but potent 4.9-litre V8. The TWR driver lineup held one or two surprises though. The familiar and successful pairing of Walkinshaw/Percy continued, Steve Soper had gone to Ford, and Volvo star Gianfranco Brancatelli joined the TWR team. The familiar names of Jeff Allam, Armin Hahne, and Jean-Louis Schlesser continued to appear on entry lists.

Round 1 at Monza was a 1-2 win for Rover. Then it was the Donington 500 and a win for the Walkinshaw/Percy Rover. Over then to West Germany and the Hockenheim circuit for Round 3 and a poor race

for the last time at Brno because a new track was being built near the city of Kyvalka. Qualifying was a surprise, fastest was Steve Soper in a Ford Sierra XR4Ti entered by Ford Motorsport Eggenberger with their second team car qualifying second. But the race was a Volvo – Rover battle with Volvo taking first and third and Rover taking second, fourth and fifth.

The Österreichring in Austria hosted Round 7, with four Rovers entered but the best Rover place was fourth behind two Volvos (both eventually disqualified) and a Ford Sierra. On they went to another 'Ring', this time the Nürburgring in West Germany where the BMW 635CSi could still prove a force to be reckoned with, and won. Once more it was time for the Spa

The definitive racing saloon. A 1986 Rover Vitesse in action at the Silverstone TT (John Colley)

Jeff Allum waiting to qualify at Monza in 1986. Jeff successfully raced Rovers for the Works team throughout the six year programme. (John Colley)

for the TWR/Rovers, two retiring with engine trouble. Volvo won. Round 4 was at Misano in Italy and two TWR cars were joined by an Australian 'South Pacific Racing'-entered Rover Vitesse driven by none other than ex-Formula I Champion Denny Hulme, partnered for the race by Neville Crichton and Ron Dickson. This eventful race was won by a BMW 635CSi. Over to Sweden and the TWR/Bastos Rovers qualified first and second on Volvo's home ground. Now two South Pacific Racing Rover Vitesses were entered; the car seen at Misano and a brand new car (Chassis 020, the last TWR Rover to be built), but the race was a Volvo benefit, with the best Rover (Hahne/Brancatelli) coming home second. Round 6 was held

Dennis Leech at Donington in 1987, a good year in which he lost the BTCC Class A honours to Tim Harvey's Istel Rover Vitesse by just one point. *(John Colley)*

24 hour event (Round 9) and the best Rover could do was 6th place. Spa was followed by another classic event, the 50th

Tourist Trophy at Silverstone, and TWR entered two Bastos sponsored cars together with an Istel-sponsored car for

The man behind TWR – Tom Walkinshaw (right) enjoying the celebrations after one of many successes for Austin Rover. *(John Colley)*

ROVER V8

Allam/Hulme. In the race Allam's Rover got the lead when Soper's Ford Sierra retired then Denny Hulme took over and treated the spectators to a display of real driving craft as he reeled off the remaining laps to take the chequered flag. His fourth TT victory at the age of 50, having last won it in 1968!

Round 11 was held at Nogaro in France. One of the TWR/Bastos Rovers retired and one finished well down the field. Then Zolder and Rover came in third. Things improved slightly at Jarama when the pole qualifying Rover of Walkinshaw/Percy came second in the race. Happily in the concluding race at Estoril things came right again. The Walkinshaw/Percy car qualified on pole and came second in the race. The rest of the team came in third and fourth. The Sierra of Soper/Neidz-

The Group A racing engine of Dennis Leech's black Rover Vitesse. This has the twin throttle plenum chamber injection system.

The Rover SD1 was also developed as a rally car. This one, now belonging to Mick Moore is believed to have been built originally for the Paris-Peking event. Chassis number is ARMRR 1GP2 .

wiedz achieved their first win of the year – the shape of things to come?

In addition to its long and illustrious racing career in Britain and Europe the Rover SD1 also proved a very capable rally car. In the spring of 1982 BL Motorsport released news of a Group 2 rally car (GJW 584W) which had been built during the winter of 1981/82 to assess the SD1 as a possible competitor in some of the long distance rallying events such as the forthcoming 1983 Paris-Peking Rally (cancelled). Much of the testing of the new car was done by Colin Malkin with early involve-

ment by Michelin after encouraging results with their tyres on the TR7 V8 rally cars. The Rover incorporated many competition developments from the Group 1 circuit race cars but the engine was pure TR7 V8, with four sidedraught Webers, producing over 300 bhp. The Unipart-sponsored car, following in the footsteps of the Triumph TR7 V8, made its public début in the Pace Petroleum Rallysprint at Esgair Dafydd with Tony Pond at the wheel.

That first car went in 1983 to Ken Wood who had won the Scottish Rally Championship in 1982 with a Triumph TR7

V8 (he won the 1983 title with the Rover) and Tom Walkinshaw Racing built two new Rover Vitesse rally cars to Group A specification, with 300 bhp fuel injected engines. Initially the cars weighed in at some 1350 kilos but as development progressed this weight dropped to 1290 kilos. In September that same year Tom Walkinshaw, partnered by John Davenport, entered his first rally, the Bianchi Rally in Belgium, and climbed to 8th place before

sorship and Works assistance. Russell Gooding acquired a Group A Vitesse and in the National Rally Championship Ken Wood and Bob Fowden competed with Group 2 cars while Chris Tilley, David Clibbery and Andy Carve campaigned Group A versions. Tom Walkinshaw, again partnered by John Davenport, finished his first rally, the Russek Manuals event in August and in the same month Tony Pond/Rob Arthur gave the Rover its first Group A vic-

Tom Walkinshaw and John Davenport tried their hand at rallying in this Group A Vitesse in the 1984 Silva Stages rally. It retired.

crashing out of contention. A couple of weeks later the re-shelled car was entered in the Rothmans Manx International Rally, crewed by Tony Pond and Rob Arthur but the car retired on only the second stage with differential trouble. The back axle was proving a weak link of the car and was to receive serious development in 1984.

1984 saw the Rover competing strongly in national rallying events. Bob Fowden, who had earned a considerable reputation at the wheel of a Triumph TR7 V8 throughout 1980, 1982 and 1983, moved to a Rover SD1 with Castrol spon-

tory on the Hunstruck Rally in Germany. Tony Pond was becoming increasingly involved with the Metro 6R4 in national events but still found time to get behind the wheel of a Rover. He dominated the Rothmans Manx International in September and entered the 1984 RAC Rally in a Unipart/Daily Mirror sponsored car, but crashed in Knowsley Safari Park.

Computervision had been major sponsors of the Metro 6R4 rally programme and in 1985, while development of the Group B supercar continued they supported a Rover SD1 (B565 A0X) for Tony

111

Pond/Rob Arthur in the Shell Oils Open Championship, with Mike Stuart driving a second Computervision car in selected events. The Rover was a consistent top Group A finisher in the series, Pond finishing 6th overall in the championship, 2nd in Group A and 1st in Group A cars over 2000 cc. Rover, as a manufacturer finished 4th in the championship. But the main thrust for AR Motorsport in rallying had to be on an international level with the Metro 6R4 and the big rumbling Rovers would, along with a number of TR7 V8s, be left in the hands of private teams to campaign.

So with the TWR/AR Motorsport Rovers gone from the European racing scene it was left for private teams and individuals to use the big cars in national events and where better than the British Saloon Car Championship. With the Works cars pulling out of the championship midway through the 1984 season and Andy Rouse going over to Ford in 1985 it

was left to Pete Hall, in Andy's 1984 ICS Rover Vitesse, Neil McGrath, Mike O'Brian and Dennis Leech to continue representing the marque in 1985 and 1986. With Andy Rouse continuing to dominate there was only the occasional opportunity for Rover to shine. Shine they did too in Round 5 of the 1986 BSCC held at Brands Hatch when because it was a prestigious Grand Prix supporting event, two TWR Rovers made an appearance. Supported by private entrants, the Rover Vitesse, in a week when its replacement the Rover 800 series was announced, took five of the top six places! In the 1987 British *Touring* Car Championship there were four Rover Vitesses doing battle with the new force, the Ford Sierra Cosworth RS500, and they managed to give a very good account of themselves. In the big class the Rover Vitesse of Tim Harvey took three wins, Dennis Leech one, and various Sierras the other five, enabling Tim to take the Class

Tony Pond and Rob Arthur rallied their Computervision Group A Rover Vitesse with great success in 1985. *(John Colley)*

A (2501cc & above) title in his John Maguire Racing prepared, Istel sponsored, car. Dennis Leech with his privately entered car was only one point behind Tim.

It was Dennis Leech who remained the sole Rover Vitesse campaigner in the 1988 British Touring Car Championship amongst a horde of Sierra Cosworths. Dennis had first campaigned an ex-Patrick Motor Sport Rover in the 1982 BSCC having entered the fray with an ex-David Brodie Ford Capri the year before. He had previously com-peted in Formula 5000, raced a Ford Mustang and owned, at one time or another, a couple of Ford GT40s, so he certainly appreciated the virtues of the V8 engine. A privateer, Dennis prepared his own car and built his own engines, but managed to contest the championship with determination for six years. He won only once and get a second place but was always a strong qualifier and always featured in any race his limited budget enabled him to enter. He built a new car

The immaculate Ford 100E-bodied quarter mile race car of Paula and Stan Atkins.

Major motivation in the form of a 4.5-litre Rover V8 producing over 400 bhp on nitrous!

around a new TWR/AR Motorsport shell (with additional work by Andy Rouse) for the 1987 season and later received limited support from Land-Rover for his efforts. But by 1988 the Sierra Cosworth was an overwhelming force in British Touring Car racing. As Dennis said 'by pushing the Group A rules I might be able to squeeze another 50 bhp from the Rover, but I need 150 bhp to be competitive against the Fords'. Two thirds of the way through the 1988 season Dennis gave up the struggle – Ford were back!

The Rover V8 engine has in recent years gained new prominence in drag racing with the Rover V8 Challenge, which

under various guises and sponsors has seen Rover V8-engined, full bodied drag racing machines compete at a high level in two classes, Street Rover and Pro Rover. All vehicles competing in the Challenge must be road legal, with full bodywork, working lights, cooling system and four wheel brakes. Street Rover machines must also use road tyres, be limited to 3.9 litres, and have induction limited to carburettors with four inlet chokes (or factory fuel injection), with more restrictive engine modifications. However, the Pro Rover class cars use racing slicks, have no engine capacity restrictions, free induction, including the use of supercharging

The Rover V8-powered rear wheel drive Pro Rover drag racing car of Kev Jenkins holds the e.t. record of 9.41 seconds!

or turbocharging, and much more potential for creative engine modifications. Cars in Pro Rover are built purely for racing and this is reflected in the quarter mile times and speeds. A top Street Rover challenger is capable of times as low as 11.27 seconds at speeds of 135 mph, while in Pro Rover class leaders are completing the quarter mile in 9.43 seconds with terminal speeds approaching 150 mph!

The telling factor in Rover V8 Challenge drag racing is the use of nitrous oxide by all the competitors, although it is not compulsory, and it is this factor alone that produces these very impressive performance figures within the current regulations. The knowledge and skill of the engine builders, the standard of vehicle preparation and the ability and reaction times of the drivers all contribute enormously to the performance and competitiveness of this very exciting racing; however, the use of nitrous oxide injection systems, varying in sophistication as much as the engines and vehicles themselves, has pushed their quarter mile performances to levels worthy of star billing in the drag racing programme.

The championship is run over six rounds, with varying points awarded for results, plus bonus points for top speed and low elapsed time at each meeting. A typical Street Rover field consists of at least a dozen competitors, racing Rover SD1 saloons, Rover V8-engined Ford Escorts and Morris Minors, and even a kit car or two with elapsed times of between 11 and 12 seconds. The Pro Rover fields are ten cars with elapsed times of between 9 and 11 seconds. The machines in Pro Rover are more sophisticated, with recognisable bodyshells of Rover 200s, Ford Escorts, TR7s, and even 100E Populars, but they generally cloak tubular chassis, with sophisticated multi-link racing suspension, aluminium panelled interiors, racing transmissions and state of the art racing engines. Rover V8 Challenge racing can be accomplished certainly at Street Rover level on a modest budget, and the nitrous systems can endow even a converted road car with competitive performance. What the racing needs is greater involvement in Pro Rover from companies

involved in supplying tuning parts and engine building expertise for the Rover V8, to increase the 'grudge' factor and accelerate engine development.

In the early years of the Rover V8 Challenge it was the Ford Cortina Mk1 of Steve Green that was the car to beat. In 1994 two cars have set the pace in competition and the standard in preparation, the Rover 200 of Kevin Jenkins and the Ford 100E of Paula Atkins. The Rover 200 won the 1994 Pro Rover Championship and holds the e.t. record at 9.41 seconds (at 143 mph). Kevin began racing in the Rover Challenge in 1986 in a Ford 100E that ran a best of 11.25 seconds. He then raced the Bob Nixon Ford Pop with the same engine and held the e.t. record at 9.63 seconds (148 mph) until Ian Hampstead took the record in dominating style with a 9.47 second pass in April 1993. For 1994 the new state of the art Rover 200 (built by Chassis Craft) uses a Real Steel-built and developed 4.3-litre (actually 4384 cc) Rover V8, which has a 77 mm stroke steel TRW crankshaft, Childs & Albert aluminium con-rods, Ross forged pistons, Real Steel camshaft, and a single 650 cfm Holley carburettor on a Huffaker inlet manifold. The nitrous oxide injection is a '175 bhp' system by NOS Systems and, when actuated, the engine produces 425 bhp with 460 lb/ft of torque, or a mere 382 bhp without!

The equally fine Ford 100E of Paula and Stan Atkins also débuted in the 1994 season, although the team already have considerable experience in the Rover V8 Challenge. The car was built by JMW Performance to impeccable standards and has run a best of 9.43 seconds over the quarter mile. The Rover V8 engine was built by J E Engineering in Coventry, the main sponsor. It is a 4.5-litre unit, with a J E cast 80 mm stroke crankshaft (cross-drilled) with a 94 mm bore, Omega forged pistons, Carillo steel rods, Crower camshaft, Group A rocker gear, and quadruple Dellorto 45 DRLA downdraught carburettors mounted on J E Engineering manifolds. The nitrous oxide system was supplied and set up by Hatton Enterprises and, when activated, the engine produces 442 bhp and over 400 lb/ft of torque.

Chapter Seven
Into the Nineties

As the 1980s drew to a close and a new decade began, the future of the Rover V8 engine was certainly assured for many years still to come, but in production terms its application was now restricted to the Range Rover and Land Rover, both engines and vehicles emanating from the same Lode Lane factory. The engine was continuing to be manufactured in large numbers and had more performance orientated applications than ever in the products of Morgan, TVR, Ginetta and Marcos, but the Rover Group itself had moved on in the large luxury saloon market to front wheel drive with the Rover 800 series, where the Rover V8 engine no longer had a place.

But the new decade ahead was being heralded by some exciting new developments that had begun in 1989 with the introduction by Land Rover of a 3.9-litre (3947 cc) version of the engine, which sustained interest in the Range Rover and maintained an acceptable level of performance for the important North American market in the face of ever increasing emission restrictions. The increase in capacity, the first in production terms since the engine was unveiled by General Motors in 1961, was accomplished by increasing the bore to 94 mm. The resulting engine was rated at 185 bhp at 4750 rpm with 235 lb/ft of torque at 2600 rpm, although later versions pushed this figure slightly higher.

In the same year Land Rover launched its first all-new vehicle since the Range

Rover. It was called Discovery, and in the range was a 3.5-litre version, powered of course by the Rover V8 engine.

DISCOVERY

The idea of adding a third product line to the Land Rover range was born in 1985-6. The company already had a long term strategy based on the replacement of the Land Rover 90 and 110 range and a new Range Rover, but acknowledged the need to add a third model between the two. It had been widely recognised that as the Range Rover continued to move 'up market' there was an opportunity to introduce a vehicle in the lower priced personal sector.

The Discovery project got the green light in late 1986, but with a planned introduction for the 1990 model year, the new vehicle had to be ready by late 1989, which meant that a new approach to product development was needed to achieve that objective. Discovery is based on a Range Rover chassis, retaining the Range Rover's engine, gearbox, transfer box and axles, but deleting the self-levelling strut.

Discovery was launched at the Frankfurt Motor Show on September 16th 1989. It is interesting to note that it was available initially as a three door only, with no word on the possible availability of a

The Land Rover Discovery was a very important new addition to the model range, available initially with the 3.5-litre Rover V8, but later acquiring 3.9-litre EFi power.

four door. There was of course a four door version planned from the beginning, but this was a marketing ploy to help differentiate Discovery from the Range Rover, which by this time was selling predominantly as a four door. Likewise Discovery was only available with a 3.5-litre carburetted version of the Rover V8 (there was also a Tdi option), despite the fact that the Range Rover was using the 3.9-litre EFi version of the engine and could be ordered with automatic transmission, which was not available with Discovery. This was all done initially to position Discovery in a wholly separate sector of the market and it worked very well.

Discovery was not launched in the all important North American market until March 1994, by which time worldwide sales had comfortably exceeded the 100,000 mark and the second generation face-lifted models had appeared. In the UK it is the best selling four wheel drive vehicle, but in the USA it faces tough competition from the likes of Jeep (Cherokee) and Ford (Explorer).

With the Range Rover moving steadily and inexorably upwards and becoming ever more expensive, the cost of adapting the vehicle for specialist tasks has risen too. So Discovery has moved naturally into this lucrative territory, and the Police were quick to adapt it as an alternative to the Range Rover. The Discovery 100 inch wheelbase has been extended by Land Rover Special Vehicles division to 116 inches for ambulance conversions, while the three door Discovery has been made available as a commercial, with the rear side windows blanked off, and called appropriately the Discovery Commercial.

Specialist conversions in the luxury and performance market have been slow to adopt the Discovery, although mechanically there is no obstacle to applying to it the same enhancements as have been used on Range Rovers over the years. However, by their nature specialist performance versions of the Discovery V8i will be expensive.

The four door version did come along about a year later, and the carburetted Rover V8 was replaced by a 163 bhp EFi version (designated the V8i), although the turbo-diesel engine was by far the most popular powerplant. Another year elapsed before the Rover V8 version was again upgraded with the introduction of the 3.9-litre EFi catalysed engine from the Range Rover, producing 182 bhp at 4750 rpm and 231 lb/ft of torque at 3100 rpm. Performance of the Discovery V8i obviously benefited, and, with a weight of between 1975 and 2020 kilos depending on specification, the 0-60 mph time is a very respectable 10.8 seconds for the manual version (11.8 for the automatic), with a top speed of 106 mph (105 for the automatic), far in excess of any that the diesel versions could muster.

ROVER V8

Clearly Discovery was being moved up market into territory recently vacated by the Range Rover, which itself was continuing to move inexorably up market. No doubt another product line will be introduced beneath Discovery, although it is doubtful whether such a vehicle will require the power of the Rover V8 engine.

It had taken Land Rover no less than 22 years to exploit the potential of bigger capacity Rover V8 engines when they introduced the 3.9-litre version of the engine in 1989. In September 1992 they took another giant leap forward with an even bigger version of the engine, taking the increased 94 mm bore and adding a 76 mm stroke crankshaft for no less than 4.2 litres! The reason for the bigger engine was the launch of the new Land Rover flagship, the Range Rover LSE.

RANGE ROVER LSE

Early on in the development programme of the LSE, Land Rover had made the decision to incorporate an uprated version of the Rover V8 engine, but, as we shall see, the conclusion to their own engine development programme was being reserved for another project. In searching for more power and performance Land Rover turned to the independent specialists who between them had been building a variety of uprated Rover V8s for the past decade. This assessment work culminated in the purchase by Land Rover of the base specification of a 4.2-litre version from J E Engineering (formerly J E Motors) of Coventry. Alex Stephenson, Managing Director of Land Rover – Power Train Operations, said at the time, 'It's always preferable to design from a known base rather than from a clean sheet of paper, and I was keen to capture some of the wide experience of stretching our engine which exists outside our own organisation. J E Engineering have a record of providing reliable engine conversions to Range Rover, so it was logical to use their specification as a starting point for the new 4.2-litre V8.'

And well it might, because the 3.9-litre version that had first appeared in a Range Rover in 1989 had also been sourced from the same company. The aftermarket industry had developed the engine into areas the factory had been slow to exploit, and now that development work was being taken on board by the factory.

At the time of its launch the Range Rover LSE represented the latest flagship in the Land Rover range, a luxury vehicle reaching new heights of opulence and performance, building still further on the strength of the Range Rover appeal. The LSE was not just a new specification – it represented the most significant development of the original vehicle since it had first appeared in 1970. It had a 108 inch wheelbase (standard Range Rovers and Discoverys are 100 inches), air suspension, traction control and a 200 bhp 4.2-litre Rover V8 engine. The result was a Range Rover that was to set the scene for

Bigger, better, and more sophisticated and expensive, the Range Rover LSE also needed a new 4.2-litre version of the Rover V8 to complete the picture.

the completely new version, due in 1994. It was roomier, quieter, smoother, more powerful, more refined and had more space for rear passengers. But its on-road improvements had not been accomplished at the expense of off-road ability.

The new air suspension system debuted on the LSE, but made available later as an extra on Vogue SEs, is a highly sophisticated version of that used on lorries, with the four coil springs replaced by four variable rate air springs, leaving the axles, radius arms and front and rear anti roll bars unchanged. Each wheel has a ride height sensor that continuously reports to a control unit located under the driver's seat. This control unit sends instructions to a reservoir of compressed air, which charges the springs via a complex series of valves. When the LSE is on the move the system is self levelling regardless of the vehicle load or what is being towed, and offers five different ride height settings with a 5 inch range: high profile (for off-roading), extended profile (for grounding situations off-road), low profile (for added stability at speed), normal (for on-road), and access mode, when the LSE lowers itself for ease of getting in and out.

The Range Rover LSE also lays claim to being the first off-road vehicle to be equipped with traction control, operating on the rear wheels only as an extension of the ABS system, slowing a spinning wheel with the brakes and ensuring that torque goes to the wheel that has the most traction.

As previously stated, the 4.2-litre engine took the 94 mm bore of the 3.9-litre unit and added a 77 mm stroke crankshaft although this has since been revised to a 76.2 mm stroke giving a capacity of 4292 cc. The compression ratio was 9.5:1, although again this has been revised to 9.2:1, and the engine received a revised camshaft profile. Although the Lucas L-Jetronic fuel injection system was essentially unchanged from the 3.9-litre, it was reworked to suit the bigger engine. Power was increased modestly to 200 bhp at 4850 rpm and torque went up to 250 lb/ft at 3250 rpm, but the torque delivery was tailored for improved mid-range response. Although heavier by some 140 kilos, the Range Rover LSE can accelerate from 0 to 60 mph in just 9.9 seconds and go on to a top speed of 112 mph.

So an additional product had been added to the Land Rover range and it had benefited from the developments made to the Rover V8 engine, but Rover Group had not forgotten the performance potential of the engine, nor, it seems, had they forgotten the MGB GTV8 either.

MG RV8

Although the MGB GTV8 ceased production in July 1976, and the MGB itself was terminated in 1980, the MG badge lived on in a variety of sporty saloon variants from the Austin Rover/Rover Group range. In the early 'nineties brand new MGB roadster bodyshells were available from British Motor Heritage, ostensibly for restoration purposes, but this led on to a surprising and exciting development in the form of a limited production Rover sports car code-named Adder – the MG RV8.

Officially launched in October 1992 and celebrating the 30th anniversary of the MGB, the MG RV8 was the result of a confident and successful Rover seeking to reintroduce a line of sports cars bearing the MG name, and the MG RV8 represented its announcement of this intent. Appropriately dubbed a 'retro-look' roadster (the original MGB was never offered as a roadster in V8 form), it uses a bodyshell manufactured by British Motor Heritage at Faringdon in Oxfordshire from a combination of original and new tooling, the unpainted shell being sent to Rover Cowley for assembly.

The new roadster has to be the most desirable MG ever, combining contemporary roadster features, considerable luxury, V8 performance and instant classic status. The MGB roadster form has evolved considerably, with new front and rear wings, moulded sills, fully integrated front and rear bumpers, new styled headlights and tail lamps and a new one piece windscreen frame. The restyled wheel arches accommodate a wider track.

The engine is a 3.9-litre Rover V8 built by Land Rover, with electronic fuel injection and a pair of three way closed loop catalysts. This is backed up by the familiar Rover 77 mm 5-speed manual gearbox, which has complemented the engine for many years and in so many applications. The engine, with its 9.35:1 compression ratio, is rated by Rover as producing 190 bhp at 4750 rpm and 227 lb/ft of torque at 3200 rpm. This endows the MG RV8 with a 0-60 mph time of only 5.4 seconds and a claimed top speed of 140 mph! The suspension is familiar to any MGB owner, but it has received considerable development and refinement. The front double wishbone layout with coil springs and Koni dampers is mounted on a modified version of the original MGB crossmember. The front swivel hub and stub axle assemblies are all new with improved suspension and steering geometry to complement modern tyre technology. The rear suspension has Koni dampers in place of the original MGB level arm units, and the rear axle (3.31 to 1) features a Quaife torque bias differential originally developed for rally cars, which optimises torque transfer under varying road conditions. Front and rear anti-roll bars are fitted.

With the new found power of a fuel injected Rover V8, the MG RV8 needs high performance braking, and the system is all new, developed in conjunction with Automotive Products – Racing Division. There are 270 mm ventilated front discs with four pot callipers and 9 inch rear drums, backed by a dual circuit and servo assistance. Rolling stock is Michelin MXV3 205/65 x 15 tyres on 6J lattice spoke alloy wheels.

Driving the MG RV8 is a joy. It has a real quality feel about it, and is obviously very well made. The ride is smooth and effortless, remaining stable at speed over a variety of road surfaces, although the soft springing does eventually produce body roll. The Rover V8 engine remains quiet, but with a wonderfully muted V8 burble that makes you ever aware of the power within. For those who have experienced

and enjoyed the MGB in their youth and desire a nostalgic indulgence, the MG RV8 will not disappoint; in fact it now has some of that luxury and refinement that one requires as one gets older!

Modern day classic – the charismatic MG RV8 took the MGB legend and elevated it to new heights of luxury and, more importantly, performance.

THE DEFENDER 90

The current Land Rover vehicle range includes the 'Defender' 90, 110 and 130,

3.9 litres of fuel injected, silky smooth power – the iron hand in the velvet glove.

which in all configurations have the Rover V8 3.5-litre option. The engine in this application has twin SU carburettors, an 8.13:1 compression ratio and produces 134 bhp at 5000 rpm with 187 lb/ft of torque at 2500 rpm. The Defender name is used to denote the modern day versions of the original and legendary Land Rover workhorse, much developed and civilised but still instantly recognisable.

Land Rover have successfully sold the Range Rover and Discovery in North America, but buyers in this demanding market get one other option in the range, the Defender 90. Buyers in North America do not like diesel engines, so you would have thought the 135 bhp Rover V8 version would suffice. Not so. Lucky buyers get this sole model, launched in 1994, unique to the Defender range with a 182 bhp, 3.9-litre fuel injected Rover V8, a 5-speed gearbox, four wheel disc brakes and enough off-road extras to make this offering a Land Rover with real 'attitude'. The Defender 90 is the only 'open V8-powered sport utility' available in the USA straight from the showroom, with bright red and yellow paint options, a hefty black roll cage, optional alloy wheels and enough power to take it from 0-60 in just 8.5 seconds – it is *the* vehicle for serious off-road buffs.

THE NEW RANGE ROVER AND THE RV8 ENGINES

It was August 1989 when Land Rover first began work on their most significant development of the Rover V8 engine since its introduction in 1967. The Rover V8 was needed to power the next Range Rover, at that time code-named 'Pegasus' but later designated '38a', and to do so would mean meeting a number of objectives. The engine would need to provide higher performance in its base specification as well as a high performance derivative. Engine refinement would have to be improved to contribute to the increased overall refinement of the vehicle. It would have to present a reduced package size in order to meet the overall packaging targets of the new vehicle. Fuel economy would have to improve (never the engine's strong point), it would have to comply with all emissions legislation in all the vehicles' markets, and there would have to be reduced service time and ownership cost.

The design of the Rover V8 dates back to the mid-1950s, and it is a credit to the original design and the engineering team charged with the task of improving the V8 engine, that the criteria were achieved. What is interesting is the path they followed and the changes made to the design, which have facilitated the application of state of the art automotive technology and addressed weaknesses in the GM design that have frustrated engine tuners for decades.

The original research into a high performance derivative involved supercharging the 3.5-litre Rover V8, but as the power output rose, so the crankshaft manifested its weakness. At this point it has to be stressed that for mass production purposes engines are subjected to very rigorous and severe testing, often exceeding those encountered in racing because the main components are required to have a life expectancy of 150,000 miles or more. Strengthening the crankshaft required bigger bearing diameters. Aside from the lubrication and bearing surface benefits the bigger bearings result in greater overlap, or more material 'joining' the successive journals and counterweights.

Boring the cylinder block to accommodate a larger crankshaft with larger diameter bearings aggravated inherent weaknesses in the block casting, something that those building Rover V8s for racing have known about for many years and which the factory addressed by making available a limited number of cross-bolted blocks for competition purposes. So the first step in the development process was to

Purposeful and rugged with form that follows function, the Rover V8 3.9-litre EFi engine provides torque for plenty of off-road action.

make detailed changes to the block casting, but important details that have enabled substantial progress to be made in terms of rigidity and ultimate strength. All production 3.9, 4.0, 4.2 and 4.6-litre blocks are now the same casting (HRC 2411), which then receives the appropriate machining applicable to the final engine specification.

The cylinder block has been made significantly stronger by the addition of stiffening ribs in key areas (along the block sides near the main bearing webs, for instance) and, more importantly, both 4.0 and 4.6 litre blocks now have cross-bolted main bearing caps. Of course Land Rover have produced cross-bolted blocks before, but they were special items and expensive, one of the reasons being that the main caps had to be individually ground to match the block. The new blocks have this feature productionised, although they are now a press fit in the block. The cap material has also been upgraded from grey to SG iron. The interior profile of the block has been altered to make room for the redesigned crankshaft with its bigger bearings and bigger counterweights. The cylinder liners are 5 mm shorter and the oil pick-up from the sump no longer fits into the block casting, from where the oil made its way to the pump via a drilled gallery; the pick-up on the new engine is direct to the pump, but more on that later.

There are two new crankshafts, one of 71 mm stroke for the 4.0-litre and one of 82 mm for the 4.6-litre version. The main bearing size has gone up from 58.4 mm to 63.5 mm and the counterweights are larger, although of the same number as before. These new crankshafts will not fit into older engines because there is insufficient room for the bigger counterweight to rotate inside the block. The stroke of the 4.0-litre crank is identical to the old 3.9-litre, as is the cylinder bore of 94 mm, so the capacity of these two engines is the same.

The new Range Rover 4.0 V8 – size and status undiminished, new heights of refinement and on-road ride, but off-road ability always unrivalled.

To complement the new Range Rover, the Rover V8 engine has been comprehensively redeveloped for new heights of power and refinement.

The '4.0-litre' tag was used to differentiate between the two engines. The new crankshafts are also longer to drive the new oil pump, which will be discussed later.

A new connecting rod design has been produced for the new 4.0 and 4.6-litre engines. They are made from forged steel and now have balance pads on both the small and big ends; the screw-in bolts retaining the caps are of a more robust design and are manufactured to extremely fine tolerances. The 4.0-litre engine uses a rod 155.2 mm in length, and the 4.6-litre is 149.7 mm with a 55.5 mm big end bearing diameter, the older version having a 50.8 mm big end bearing. The increase in length was done to reduce the angularity of the rods in the engine, thus reducing vibration. The small end size has been increased from 22.2 mm to 24 mm.

The pistons are also new and are a common design between the 4.0 and 4.6-litre engines. The capacity of the bowl in the piston crown varies slightly between the two engines (4.0-litre, 13.23 cc/4.6-litre, 22.29 cc) to determine the compression ratio. To maintain equality of material thickness on the piston crown they are different castings. Having said that, the compression ratios are the same for both engines – 9.35:1 – although lower 8.2:1 compression pistons are available. The original 3.5/3.9-litre engines have pistons 80.9 mm long overall, with a compression height (or crown height) of

Top The all new serpentine belt drive for the engine's ancillaries. *(Stefan Piasecki)*

Middle The new four bolt (cross-bolted) main bearings in the new cylinder block casting. *(Stefan Piasecki)*

Right Cylinder block front detail, showing the main bearing caps, and the longer crankshaft to drive the new oil pump. *(Stefan Piasecki)*

123

49.5 mm, while the longer stroke 4.2-litre engine uses a piston 72.85 mm long with a compression height of 45 mm. The new 4.0 and 4.6-litre engines have a shorter piston of 66.6 mm, with a compression height of only 35.9 mm. As already stated, the gudgeon (or wrist) pin diameter has been increased, but the new engines also have a gudgeon pin offset. The 4.2-litre engine was the first production Rover V8 to use this feature, but on the new 4.0 and 4.6-litre engines it has been increased from the 0.55 mm of the 4.2-litre to 0.60 mm. The reason for this offset is to produce a slight side loading on the piston at TDC, thus eliminating piston slap – all part of the infinite attention to design detail by the Land Rover engineers in their quest for refinement.

Not only are these compact pistons lighter (the crowns are relatively thin), but they are also factory balanced to +/–2 g. The top ring has gone from 1.8 mm wide cast iron to 1.2 mm chrome steel, while the second and third rings remain the same as the old engine.

Great things were expected of the new cylinder heads, and rumours abounded among Rover V8 aficionados of new designs, single overhead camshafts, four valves per cylinder, and other exotic possibilities. The reality may disappoint, but the heads have received sufficient attention to warrant careful examination. To retool completely new castings is a very expensive exercise, so the existing heads have been worked on very comprehensively with dynamometer and flow bench testing, resulting in heads with a claimed flow increase of 5 per cent, enough to meet the performance criteria required. Modifications had to avoid any changes to the water jacketing, which would have

meant expensive retooling, so the inlet and exhaust port have, according to Land Rover engineers, been enlarged to the maximum possible without compromising reliability. In theory this could be bad news for the aftermarket head modifiers, although it will take back-to-back flow bench and dyno tests to prove whether the

The new crankshaft no longer has a distributor drive gear on the end, and the cam is also positively held in the block by a retaining collar. The drive sprocket is also new.
(Stefan Piasecki)

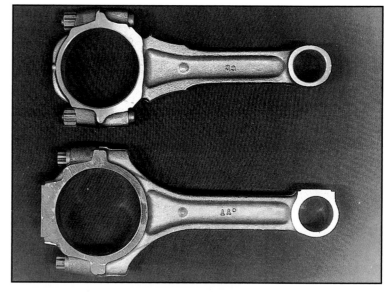

The new connecting rod (top) compares favourably with the older design (bottom). The new 4.0 and 4.6-litre engines use different length rods.
(Stefan Piasecki)

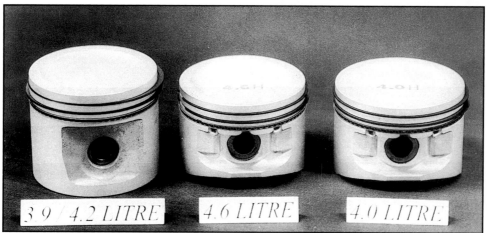

The factory has added two more pistons to the already bewildering choice available to Rover V8 engine builders.
(Stefan Piasecki)

new factory heads have any real performance potential.

The valves are a carry-over from the previous versions developed originally for the legendary Vitesse, both the inlet and exhaust being unchanged in diameter, and the inlet valves having the stems waisted behind the valve head to improve the gas flow. The amount that the valve guides protrude into the ports has also been reduced, and at the other end the guides have a stepped top to incorporate a hi-tech oil seal. The single valve springs remain unchanged and all the remaining valve gear, rockers, rocker pillars, rocker shafts, pushrods and camshaft followers remain unchanged.

The cylinder heads are now retained on the block by only ten bolts, the outer row, the so-called 'outrigger' fixings, beneath the exhaust manifolds having been dispensed with. Cylinder sealing on the 4.6-litre engine was found to be marginal under certain conditions, so the engineers sought more effective sealing. They discovered that tightening the outer row of bolts added no cylinder sealing clamping force, but actually tilted the cylinder head over slightly and aggravated the gasket problem. The steel shim head gasket has gone, being replaced with a new composite material gasket that is thicker, so the thickness of the cylinder head deck has been reduced to maintain the required compression ratio. This has resulted in combustion chamber volumes of between 28 and 31 cc (balanced on individual heads to within 1 cc, of course), as opposed to the 'old' heads, which have chambers in the region of 36 cc. The cylinder head fasteners themselves are now flange bolts of the same diameter, but they are not re-useable and must be replaced every time the head is re-fitted.

Camshafts for the new engines proved a major challenge for the engineering team, since Rover possessed limited experience in camshaft design for pushrod engines. For the past ten years or so all camshaft work has been on single or double overhead designs. Achieving the performance targets on the 4.6-litre required a new design, providing performance with refinement but without reducing valve train durability. As a result the 4.6-litre has an asymmetrical lobe design and a faster opening rate coupled to a slower closing rate, and is considered by Land Rover to be as 'wild as possible' while maintaining the necessary refinement. The 4.0-litre on the other hand has the same profile as the 3.9-litre except that the timing is retarded by 4 degrees – see the Camshaft Chart on page 178 for more details. The camshaft material has also been upgraded to Profall 55. Incidentally, these camshafts will not fit the older engines, having had alterations made at the front to accommodate a new drive sprocket, although the camshaft drive is still by simplex chain.

The front cover has been completely redesigned, improving the packaging of the engine and reducing its overall length by 75 mm. The new cover has no provision for a distributor mounting or drive because the new engines have no distributor, and a completely new design of oil pump is incorporated inside the cover, driven off the front of the crankshaft. This gives greater low rpm pressure and an increase in capability of 25 per cent, partly to cope with the demands of the bigger bearings. The oil pressure relief valve, a sticking point on the old engine is now totally redesigned and is incorporated into the pump, while the oil pick-up from the sump is now direct into the pump and the oil filter head is an integral part of the cover casting. The water pump, mounted high on the Range Rover version of the old front cover, is all new, with an increased capacity of 200-210 litres per minute (up from 160), and using a 60 mm pressed steel impeller instead of the old 100 mm cast version. It also rotates in the opposite direction to the previous engines.

The exhaust manifolds are identical for the 4.0-litre and 4.6-litre and are no longer cast iron, but fabricated from thin wall (1.5 mm) stainless steel of 30 mm diameter and encased in a triple layer heat shield. This may seem a major departure for a

The distributor has now been replaced by this 'coil pack', which is actually four double ended coils controlled by the engine management system.

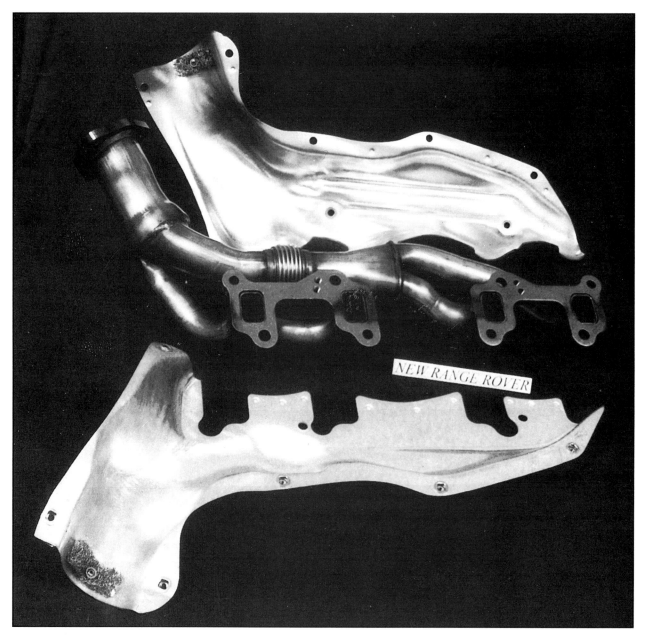

NEW RANGE ROVER

major manufacturer and a performance bonus, as well as having a considerably higher unit price. The reason that they are deemed necessary is emissions. All vehicle emissions are at their worst in the first 2 minutes after start-up, and to reduce this effect the catalytic converters have to reach 350 degrees celsius as quickly as possible. The reduced weight of stainless steel greatly assists this process. New composite manifold gaskets match the new manifolds to the revised exhaust ports.

The induction hardware, ie inlet manifold, plenum base and plenum cover, remain essentially unchanged, although the plenum cover has been redesigned for cosmetic reasons and now has the idle speed control on the side instead of the

back. The inlet manifold also has a repositioned water take-off for packaging reasons.

The engine management system has been substantially upgraded and is known as GEMS (Generic Engine Management System). Designed by Sagem-Lucas, it has been jointly developed by them and Land Rover especially for the Rover V8. It has the familiar hot wire mass flow sequential fuel injection with lambda sensor control for optimum catalyst efficiency. The GEMS system has fully programmed ignition control with knock retard, which continually monitors all cylinders for signs of detonation or pinking, retards the ignition on any cylinder where it is occurring and gradually advances the ignition back to its original

The new exhaust manifolds are made from welded steel tube, encased in a heat shield. They have performance potential, too!
(Stefan Piasecki)

value. The system allows fully optimised fuelling and ignition characteristics across the entire operating range of the engine, improving the part load specific fuel consumption by 5 per cent. The system also enables the new Range Rover to meet Californian OBD2 legislation, which requires the system to interrogate itself continually and indicate to the driver, via a dash warning, if emissions exceed the permitted level by 50 per cent. There are also self diagnostics that are logged for dealer interrogation. As previously stated the distributor has gone, to be replaced by four double ended ignition coils, and the engines use Champion RN11YCC double copper cored spark plugs with a service life of 30,000 miles!

Other detailed design features of the new engines are a completely closed engine breather system, rigid cast alloy mountings for ancillaries, serpentine multi ribbed drive belt with automatic tensioner, and a thermostat now mounted in the bottom hose. This so-called coolant return thermostat, achieves a more even engine warm-up and gives great coolant temperature stability, which is important when using electronically temperature controlled air conditioning. The standard fitment is now a Magnetti Marelli A127i 100 amp alternator (120 amp optional), a ZF power steering pump and a viscous coupled Eaton 425 mm diameter fan. All new components on the engine are metric and therefore use metric fasteners, so the Rover V8 is now a mixture of metric and imperial. As other new components are introduced they too will be metric.

When faced with the considerable power outputs of bigger capacity Rover V8 engines, it is easy to be cynical about the conservative power outputs of factory engines. Land Rover sell vehicles in a fiercely competitive marketplace where discerning buyers demand exceptional standards of refinement and reliability as well as out-and-out performance, so the engineers have to build engines that can meet a tough and often conflicting set of criteria. Much of the development effort devoted to the Rover V8 has been aimed at improving the refinement of the engine while at the same time meeting the on and off road performance requirements of the all new Range Rover. As has been seen, virtually every component of the Rover V8 has been 'massaged' or redesigned. In addition, very thorough attention has been paid to engine balancing, a major contrib-

utor to refinement, so each reciprocating or rotating component is now balanced as it is manufactured. The crankshaft is balanced on a Schenk machine to a tolerance of +/–15 gcm, the connecting rods are balanced end to end to an overall tolerance of +/–2.5 g, so tight that they no longer have to be segregated into sets, and the pistons are balanced to +/–2 g.

But what of the new Range Rover itself, for which the new RV8 4.0-litre and 4.6-litre Rover V8 engines have been so carefully developed? Officially launched on Thursday 29th September 1994, the new Land Rover flagship had been an open secret for some considerable time prior to its unveiling. Originally code-named 'Pegasus', it was the subject of considerable press rumour and speculation, eventually acquiring a new, more anonymous code name of '38a' in the final months prior to launch.

The new five model Range Rover range had been five years in the making, cost £300 million to develop and confirmed Land Rover's position as the manufacturer of the world's most luxurious, technologically advanced four wheel drive vehicle. The new luxury flagship model not only surpasses the off-road ability of the old Range Rover (still in production and known as the Range Rover Classic), but is also now able to compete with the world's best luxury cars in on-road ride and handling.

Successfully restyling the Range Rover was an enormous challenge and one that Land Rover chose to meet by being evolutionary rather than revolutionary. The styling retains many of the key design features as well as retaining the commanding driving position, distinctive front end, large glass area, E pillar, close wheel cuts and split tailgate, although it is on first impressions not as imposing on the road, its size being played down by its styling. Compared with the original Range Rover, the new one retains the wheelbase of the LSE introduced in 1992, but has wider track, wider and longer body, and its shape is softer and more aerodynamic (Cd 0.38).

Land Rover designed a completely new chassis for the new Range Rover, a stronger ladder frame intended to improve handling, ride comfort and stability as well as being able to withstand the rigours of off-road running. The old Range Rover frame is made from 2 mm gauge steel, but the new frame is made from welded box sections of high strength micro-alloy steel

127

varying in gauge from 2.5 mm to 4 mm, with four crossmembers, one of them removable to allow access to the engine bay. A great deal of attention has been paid to the suspension system of the new Range Rover, in keeping with the desire to build a world class vehicle both on and off the road. The familiar beam axles are in fact all new, being both lighter and stronger, and the rear suspension replaces the A-frame concept; two lightweight composite radius arms provide location of the axle and act as an integral roll bar. Lateral location of both front and rear axles is by a panhard rod. Roll stiffness, always a weakness of the original Range Rover, has been increased by 30 per cent, together with improved rate of roll, giving great cornering confidence.

As previously stated, Land Rover were the first to use electronic air suspension on a 4x4 vehicle with the Range Rover LSE, launched in 1992. The system has been further refined and is now standard on the new Range Rover. It retains the five height settings, some revised, but increases the options available to the driver. ABS is standard on all models, with ventilated 297 mm discs on the front and solid 304 mm discs on the rear. The electronic traction control, also introduced on the LSE in 1992, is carried over as standard on the new HSE models.

Steering remains a re-circulating ball power-assisted system, mounted to minimise kick-back when the vehicle is operating off-road. All new cast alloy wheels with five-stud mountings have been designed in three styles for the new Range Rover. There is a 7J x 16 inch three spoke, a 7J x 16 inch 'five-hole' for the SE models, both using 235/70 R16 105H tyres, and a 'prestige' five-spoke 8J x 16 inch for the HSE models using 255/65 R16 109H tyres.

The detailed design and development of the new 4.0-litre and 4.6-litre Rover V8 engines has already been discussed. In the new Range Rover the 4.0-litre engine produces 190 bhp at 4750 rpm with torque of 236 lb/ft at 3000 rpm, while the 4.6-litre produces 225 bhp at 4750 rpm and 277 lb/ft of torque at 3000 rpm. Fuel consumption of the 4.0-litre manual is 27.2 mpg (auto is 26.8 mpg) at a constant 56 mph, or 15.2 mpg (auto is 14.0 mpg) on the urban cycle, while the 4.6-litre achieves a very creditable 24.8 mpg at 56 mph or 12.8 mpg on the urban cycle. The new Range Rover also has a 2.5-litre 6-cylinder diesel option.

Transmission is either a Land Rover R380 5-speed manual, first introduced in March 1994, and either a ZF HP22 4-speed automatic on the 4.0-litre or a ZF HP24 4-speed automatic for the 4.6-litre. Both have four shift programmes: high range/normal for on-road economy, high range/sport for enthusiastic driving, low range/normal for normal off-road and heavy load towing, and low range/manual for severe off-road conditions. All are selectable from a single 'H' gate single lever selector system.

With a vehicle kerb weight of 2090 kilos the 4.0-litre manual, accelerates from 0 to 60 mph in 9.9 seconds and has a top speed of 118 mph, while the slightly heavier (2100 kilos) 4.0-litre automatic goes from 0 to 60 mph in 10.4 seconds and has a slightly lower top speed of 116 mph. The 4.6-litre automatic (no manual available) has a 0-60 mph time of 9.3 seconds and a top speed of 125 mph.

With the new 4.0-litre and 4.6-litre engines in production, what are the prospects for the older design of 3.5, 3.9 and 4.2-litre engines? Well, the good old 3.5-litre carburetted engine is still in production at Land Rover, being used by DAF in their Sherpa V8 commercial, and can still be found in the Land Rover Defender 90, 110 and 130 models, producing 134 bhp at 5000 rpm and 187 lb/ft of torque at 2500 rpm on a lowly 8.13:1 compression ratio and SU carburettors. After October 1994 this particular version of the engine was no longer sold in Europe due to emission legislation, but will soldier on in other "third" world markets in this application.

The 3.9-litre is of course continuing in use with the Discovery V8i and has found a very healthy demand from the specialist manufacturers such as Morgan, Marcos, TVR and Ginetta. Land Rover have now taken steps to standardise the specification of the engine that they supply to these specialists, using the 1994 Discovery specification engine as a basis and making alterations to the alternator bracket, drive belt and the like. Of course these companies are free to make whatever additional modifications they wish, but they are supplied with an emissions legal powerplant, which is their principal concern when sourcing engines in this way. To date the bigger 4.2-litre engine has not found favour in the same way, and its future is less certain with demand for the Range Rover Classic LSE being an unknown quantity now that the new Range Rover has been introduced into the range.

The Janspeed Le Mans
TR7 V8 Turbo – a 1980
British Le Mans challenger
that came to nought, but a
magnificent effort
nonetheless.

The one and only TVR
420 SEAC racer.
Powered by a 4.2-litre
Rover V8 and brutally
powerful with it.

Early days. Racing the Group 1 Rover SD1 in 1981 with a two car Works team.

The Rover Vanden Plas – luxury with effortless grace thanks to Vitesse specification fuel-injected Rover V8. *(Patrick Collection)*

The next generation of Range Rover with the next generation of Rover V8 – still synonymous with each other after all these years.

ROVER V8

The Group A Rover Vitesse entered the racing scene in 1982 and Sanyo sponsored the works team for two years. *(John Colley)*

After Andy Rouse won the 1984 Trimoco RAC British Saloon Car Championship in this Rover Vitesse, ICS boss Phil Hall continued to campaign it when Andy switched to a Ford. *(John Colley)*

The 1984 Spa 24 Hour race and Tony Pond guides one of the works Rovers around the rain soaked circuit.
(John Colley)

The 1986 Silverstone TT and Denny Hulme wins this classic for the fourth time. Both the race and Denny are 50 years old. A victory to savour.
(John Colley)

The essence of European Touring
Car Racing in 1984, 1985 and
1986. The Rovers battling it out
with the Volvos and ever present
hordes of BMWs.
(John Colley)

The Rover Vitesse also raced successfully in individual European saloon car championships. This is the Austin Rover France car of Jean-Louis Schlesser.
(John Colley)

Will we ever see the like
again? The definitive
racing Rover Vitesse.
Austin Rover cancelled
the programme at the end
of the 1986 season.
(John Colley)

V8

Chapter Eight

Taken To The Limit

Remarkable automobiles are the stuff of day-dreams, not only firing the imagination of schoolboys and enthusiasts but often introducing technical innovation or ingenuity which is both fascinating and highly commendable.

The four machines examined here vary widely in their purpose and application but they are all the more outstanding for being powered by the same engine, a fact which represents no compromise in their composition or performance, indeed it is the core of their excellence. They represent in no uncertain terms the versatility and capability of the Rover V8 engine.

GKN 47D

When this car was given its first public showing at the 1969 Racing Car Show at Olympia on the Vandervell Products stand it caused a sensation.

It was the brainchild of Claude Birch, the then chairman of Guest Keen & Nettlefolds (GKN). It was his idea to contract Lotus to build an unique Rover V8-powered car, based on the Lotus Europa, which would act as a mobile test bed and showpiece for the multitude of automotive components then made by various companies within the GKN Group. Although based on and bearing a very strong visual likeness to the Lotus Europa,

GKN 47D incorporated strong elements of the Lotus Type 47 sports racing car which was itself based on the Lotus Europa road sports car. The Type 47 had first appeared at the end of 1966 with a mid-mounted Cosworth-Ford twin-cam engine and Hewland FT200 5-speed gearbox. The Type 47 received intensive development through 1967 and was sold to privateers as well as campaigned by a Works team.

GKN 47D utilized the well known box section backbone chassis of the Europa but whereas the Europa chassis divided at the rear bulkhead into a Y on either side of the engine, on GKN 47D the box section chassis ends at the rear bulkhead. Overall it is 10 inches longer, extending from the front suspension, rearward to the rear bulkhead line. From there the engine is carried as a non-stressed member on a tubular frame extending from the rear of the box section. Front suspension is by unequal length fully adjustable wishbones of welded tube, with Armstrong co-axial coil-over-damper units and cast alloy uprights. At the rear the suspension is by reversed lower wishbone and single-tube top links. Double trailing arms go forward to pick up on the rear of the box section chassis. As on the front, Armstrong coil-over-damper units are used and Girling disc brakes provide retardation for all four wheels. The front and rear brake systems are split both for safety and to allow the use of a racing style balance bar between the two master cylinders. Front and rear anti-roll bars are fitted courtesy of Vander-

GKN 47D as it first appeared at the 1969 Racing Car Show at Olympia. *(Haymarket Publishing).*

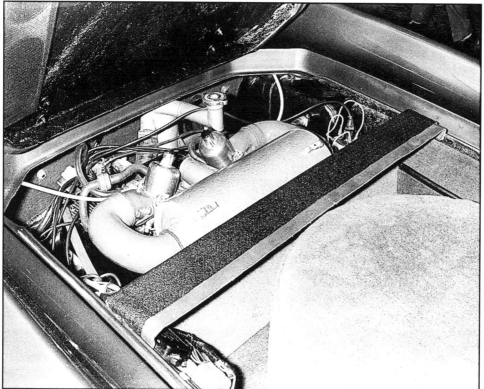

The standard Rover 3.5-litre lurking in the confines of the engine compartment. *(Haymarket Publishing)*

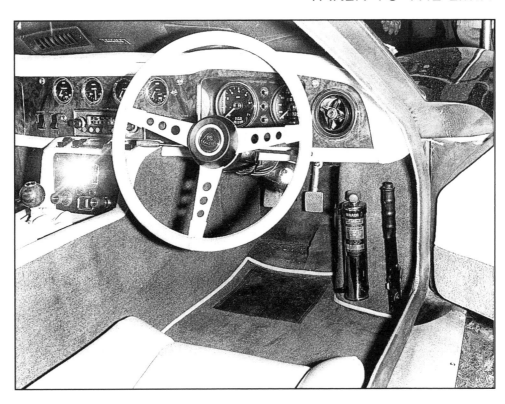

The interior was finished to a very high standard. This was after all a high performance Grand Touring car. *(Haymarket Publishing)*

vell Products (makers of the famous Vanwall racing cars).

Steering is by rack and pinion, mounted on the front of the box section chassis, the column being adjustable and having an energy-absorbing section for safety. The 13 x 7.5 Kent alloy wheels are held on by bronze three eared knock off spinners.

As previously mentioned, the engine is carried on tubular extensions of the box section chassis, these extensions being a pair of triangles ending in a ring frame or bulkhead which acts as a rear engine and gearbox mount and provides attachment points for the rear suspension. Front engine mounts attach to the two triangular chassis extensions.

To the casual eye, the fibreglass bodyshell is that of the Europa, but there are differences. To begin with it is longer, to accommodate the longer chassis and wheelbase; 94 inches instead of the Europa's 91". The overall length of the car was also up from 157.25" to 160.5". The rear deck panel is slightly higher than the Europa and there are two air intakes as found on the Type 47 just below the twin fuel filler caps required because there are two 9 gallon fuel tanks one on each side of the engine where the Europa has a single 7 gallon tank. There are also interior air extractor vents on the extreme rear quarters of the car above the bumper line.

The spare wheel is carried on a light, tubular cradle above the gearbox, releasing the front compartment for luggage.

Particular attention was paid to the cooling system. A pair of front-mounted radiators received ducted air, with assistance when needed from a pair of electric fans operated either by thermostat or manual switch. The radiators are connected in parallel, with engine coolant going to both after first passing through a swirl pot, the purpose of which was to remove steam and aeration. An oil cooler was also included, mounted in the engine compartment and fed via a duct.

The interior is decidedly up-market, in line with Europa S2 specification, retaining the superb Europa fixed, very supportive seats and dash layout (with 180 mph speedometer!). Electric windows and tinted glass add that touch of luxury. When first built the car was powered by a standard Rover 3.5 litre V8 and rightly so. Member companies of the GKN group were suppliers of a good number of standard components for this engine, from the IM 25 alloy used in the block and cylinder head castings, through connecting rods and a host of fasteners and small components, to the bearings which are the product of Vandervell Products of Maidenhead. A 7.25" two plate Borg & Beck clutch transmits power to a ZF 5DS 12-NR2 five speed gearbox, connected to the engine by a

139

specially cast Kent Alloys bellhousing.

The engine as originally fitted was pure P5B/P6B specification but the car's performance was initially disappointing because the engine was not even producing its rated power ie. 140 + bhp (DIN). It did not take long to establish that this low power output was caused by the exhaust system Lotus had been forced to adapt to the confines of the engine compartment.

Having taken delivery of the car and given it an initial assessment it was handed over to GKN's Vandervell Products in Maidenhead for serious development. Their priority was more power from the engine and with the almost complete absence of any detailed tuning knowledge in the UK, the staff there really did start with the basics and follow time honoured principles for extracting more power.

A lash-up exhaust system by Vandervell yielded an easy 30 bhp, bringing the power up to 150 bhp; a lot nearer the standard figure. From this makeshift system, with assistance from Rover, Derringtons made a proper 4-branch, exhaust system starting with four-branch manifolds which paired together cylinders 6 & 8, 4 & 2, 1 & 5, and 3 & 7 in 1.25" OD pipe leading into 1.5" pipe and finally a crossover expansion box at the rear of the car.

All good engine tuning begins with a camshaft change and this programme was no exception. They first tried an Iskenderian 282 HY cam, which came with stronger valve springs, adjustable push-rods and high rev/anti-pump lifters. The bottom end of the engine was balanced, the standard pistons being retained and the conrods polished and lightened to 112 grams each. The cap half of the main bearing had a groove machined in it for improved lubrication at high rpm and a smaller flywheel was also fitted.

Modest work was done on the cylinder heads; the inlet and exhaust ports were reshaped and polished as were the combustion chambers which were then balanced in capacity, resulting in a 10:1 compression ratio. The inlet manifold also received some attention, having the runners polished and matched to the cylinder head ports. The carburettor flanges were bored to take 2 inch SU carburettors. Although the port work was of a very straightforward nature the flows were checked by Weslake and there were marked improvements. With $\frac{7}{16}$" of valve lift the standard inlet valves flowed 79 cfm (cubic feet per minute) but Vandervell's work produced 88 cfm. For exhaust the

flow went up from 69 cfm to 84 cfm. The inlet valves were also machined: the step was removed from the edge of the seat and the radius behind the valve head was reshaped (as per Vitesse valves) for better flow. the valves were also polished. In the course of the engine rebuild Vandervell incorporated other detailed modifications; for instance the valve spring retainers had to be modified to suit the smaller Iskenderian valve springs, the rocker pillars were packed to raise them $\frac{3}{32}$" and they were dowelled in position. The adjustable pushrods also had to be shortened by $\frac{1}{16}$" and of course everything was checked for clearance, such as the piston to to valve etc.

The engine was dyno-tested in this form and produced the following power figures:

RPM	3000	3500	4000	4500	
BHP	119	138	158	176	

RPM	5000	5500	6000	6500	7000
BHP	182	192	196	192	185

This was the final result of engine development in 3.5 litre form and the next, rather ambitious stage was to enlarge the engine to 4.4 litres using a kit supplied by Traco in California, who at the time were really *the* name in race engine tuning this aluminium engine. The parts were actually meant for the *Buick* version but Vandervell could find no one who had applied them to it. Everyone they contacted had been using the parts to enlarge and tune the *Oldsmobile* version of the engine. No one, to their knowledge had yet tackled the Rover V8.

The components supplied by Traco consisted of Buick 300 crankshaft with 0.600" longer stroke (the journals were ground to Rover size), a special crankshaft torsional vibration damper, a set of special 'slipper' type pistons by Alcoa in 0.062" larger diameter, piston rings and gudgeon pins, connecting rods (actually for a Chevrolet small-block engine), an Engle camshaft and a pair of inlet manifolds to mount 48 IDA Weber carburettors. The standard cylinder liners were machined out (in situ) by 0.062" to take the new pistons

GKN 47D on the road. Acceleration of 0-60 mph in 5 seconds was shattering. Top speed over 160 mph. (Quadrant/Autocar)

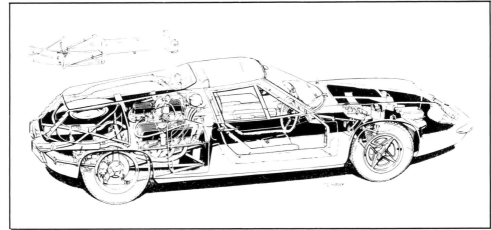

The Holster cutaway, showing the backbone chassis and tubular extensions around the engine. (Haymarket Publishing)

and the new crankshaft was fitted after some machining which included shortening it, together with another new specially made flywheel and made-up front pulleys to match the Traco damper. The block also had to be relieved to clear the crank webs. The whole process of careful assembly and balancing was done again and further work was done on the cylinder heads to match the new inlet manifolds. The combustion chambers also received further attention resulting in 11.4:1 compression ratio. The inlet manifolds themselves had to be modified to take 45 IDA Webers and not the 48 IDAs they had been designed for. Although the Engle camshaft was fitted, the rest of the Iskenderian valve gear parts were left in place. There then began a period of engine trials and parts assessment.

The first weakness to make itself apparent during early dyno testing when Vandervell were subjecting the engine to sustained 6000 + rpm was the ignition system. A new Lucas transistorised ignition system was fitted (with no vacuum advance) and the timing was set at 4° BTDC. Further testing resulted in a broken rocker arm on No 1 exhaust valve which bent the push rod, these being standard Rover aluminium rockers. In this form the engine was producing 288 bhp at 5500 rpm with a peak of 296 bhp at 6500 rpm.

Concerned with what seemed to be excessive valve gear loads they then switched back to the milder Iskenderian camshaft used in the 3.5-litre build which resulted in power peaking at 5500 rpm with 278 bhp, although interestingly they got their best 3500 rpm power reading with 197 bhp. Next on the agenda was a switch to 'street' 2 inch SU carburettors with UVP needles and blue springs, a good combination, but ultimately less powerful, bearing in mind that absolute maximum horsepower is not always conducive to good driveability.

After consultation with Rover they decided to take a Buick manifold, originally intended for a Rochester carburettor and modify it to take the pair of SUs. They did not consider the Rochester carb to be worth testing. Power was still poor by comparison and it was at this stage that excessive wear in the distributor drive gear was noticed.

With Rover supplying stronger experimental rockers and the latest production nickel plated rocker shafts (introduced to combat excessive wear) Vandervell felt

confident enough in the valve gear to try the Engle camshaft again. The SUs were finally discarded in favour of the four downdraught Webers, restoring the peak power to 296 bhp at 6500 rpm, but the distributor drive gears were still causing concern. Vandervell, having established that the wear was occurring between 5500 rpm and the test limit of 7000 rpm did what they could to improve lubrication to the distributor drive gears, suspecting torsional crankshaft vibration. The Traco damper was discarded and the front pulley arrangement modified to accept the Rover damper. After rebalancing and a complete rebuild, an airbox/filter was designed, made and fitted, the carburettors re-jetted to suit and the engine finally deemed ready for active service.

The car was driven by many people, at the invitation of the GKN Group, proving an exhilarating drive for those who cared to extend its performance capabilities to the limit. 0-60 mph time was 5 seconds, 0-100 mph in just over 11 seconds and 0-130 mph in just over 19 seconds. Covering the quarter mile from a standing start took just 13.1 seconds, with a terminal speed of 108 mph. Maximum speed was 163 mph. It was at one time considered for racing but was a little too heavy at about 18 cwt and finding suitable VR rated tyres for the 13 inch

The well engineered installation of the 4.4-litre Rover V8 engine with ZF transaxle. Spare wheel mounted in the foreground. *(Quadrant/Autocar).*

wheels, even for the road, was a problem. Graham Hill tested it at Thruxton once, but did not like the ZF 5-speed gearbox, which he had endured in his F1 Lotus, but he arranged for his friend HRH Prince Charles, with bodyguard as passenger, to take the car for a blast around the circuit.

The car was stored at Vandervell for some considerable time, then after a thorough rebuild was sold in 1984 and is now cosseted by its new owner in the USA.

the highest accolade and to win is the pinnacle of motoring achievement.

In 1980 a Triumph TR7 V8 Turbo was entered for the Le Mans 24 Hours, the marque not having raced there for 19 years and its appearance was accompanied by a display of patriotic fervour which would, at the end of the day, turn sadly into something more closely akin to the Dunkirk spirit.

In 1977 Janspeed Engineering in Salisbury had a redundant TR7 in their work-

The Janspeed Le Mans TR7 V8 Turbo. Has been timed at 201 mph on the Mulsanne straight at Le Mans.

JANSPEED LE MANS TR7 V8 TURBO

Les Vingt-Quatre Heures du Mans has become, since its inception in 1923, one of a select number of great annual motor sport events: held in such high esteem as the Indianapolis 500, the Monte Carlo Rally, the Paris-Dakar Raid and more recently the Tooheys 1000 (formerly the James Hardie 1000). Le Mans is regarded as the ultimate test for sports racing cars, a venture of such excellence and prestige that to simply compete is the life-long ambition of many; to finish is deserving of

shops which had been used to facilitate development work for BL Motorsport in Abingdon, who were at this time gearing up for the Triumph TR7 V8 rally programme. Janspeed decided to use the car as a basis for a Modsports racer but were thwarted by a change in the Modsport rules.

Without any specific aim in mind the project began to escalate and Neville Trickett was called in to style the racing body panels which would greatly improve the aerodynamics and cover the enormous racing tyres the car now had. 1977 was also the year that Janspeed became involved in turbocharging the Rover V8 engine and at the 1978 Performance Car Show the red, white and blue Janspeed TR7 V8 Le Mans Turbo was revealed to an appreciative public. The Le Mans tag had been added because by now Jan Odor of Janspeed favoured the idea of entering the car for the race in the Group 5 Silhouette class, at that time dominated by the Porsche 935. He may have wanted to take the car to Le Mans but various business commitments meant that the project was not that high on his list of priorities and in 1979 it was handed over to ADA Engineering. This fortuitous turn of events had come about when endurance racer John Sheldon had seen the car at the Alexandra Palace show and was impressed by the idea of racing an all-British sports car at Le Mans. He then involved ADA (Anglo-Dutch-American) Engineering, a company bought in 1977 by Ian Harrower and Chris Crawford, who had experience in successfully competing at Le Mans and whose company specialised in race car preparation. Together they approached Jan Odor who agreed to loan them the car but they were then left to develop it and provide the finance, which at the time did not seem a problem. They were confident that by having the car there, a physical reality rather than just an idea, they could obtain sufficient sponsorship.

In April 1979 Janspeed began preparing a very special Rover V8 engine for the project. The basis was a standard 2-bolt mains aluminium block strengthened by a massive cast alloy dry sump/girdle. Four were cast specifically for this project. One went on to the Le Mans car, one went on to a similar twin turbocharged engine built for a rallycross Triumph TR7 V8 but using blow-through sidedraught carbs; one to TVR and one remains, unmachined, at Janspeed. As well as acting as the dry sump it incorporates, in one solid casting, the main bearing caps and when bolted down it ties together the whole bottom end of the block and adds immense strength.

Not content with this radical piece of engineering Janspeed then went on to modify the cylinder heads and block so that they were held down by 5 bolts around each cylinder. This was not done by using Oldsmobile heads either, they drilled the standard Rover heads and welded threaded tabs on to the block on the inlet port side. Head gaskets are not used, instead the cylinder heads were machined to take 'O' rings and the combustion chamber volume was equalised at

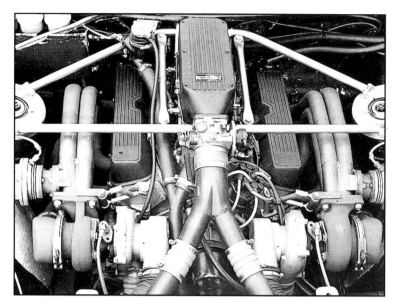

36.4 cc, with compression ratio 8.96:1. The cylinder heads themselves were fully polished and ported with 44mm inlet (concave face) and 35mm exhaust (flat face) valves. The cylinder bore is 90mm and originally the stroke was the standard 71.1mm but later developments altered the capacity slightly, although the standard crankshaft was always retained. The connecting rods are Chevrolet small block 5.7″ (they have the same 2.0″ journal size) originally fitted with Cosworth pistons. The engine was first built with a WL-9 camshaft but this was changed for a special Piper camshaft which uses solid Crane cam followers and Crane adjustable pushrods. In fact, once ADA Engineering began testing the car one of the problems they encountered was very erratic valve

The specially-built twin turbocharged 3.5-litre Rover V8 is capable of producing in excess of 500 bhp.

The block 'girdle' designed by Janspeed for the Le Mans engine to add rigidity to the cylinder block. This one is unmachined.

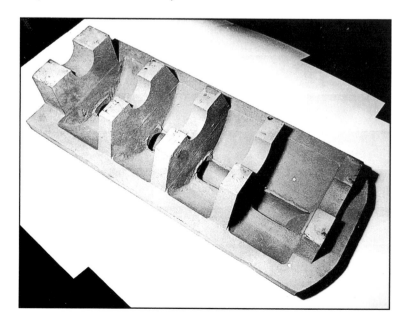

The cockpit bears little resemblance to a production TR7 but still has wind up windows!

timing due to the severe flexing of the valve gear and this was beefed up at an early stage. They fitted what amounts to a Group A racing setup of the time ie. steel rocker pillars, large diameter rocker shaft and Bahco 1.4:1 ratio adjustable rockers. Lubrication is by a dry-sump system built entirely by Janspeed specifically for this demanding application, which included the necessary lubrication to the twin turbochargers. Those turbochargers are S4-104192 Turbosonics, by Rotomaster and the total system into which they were originally installed makes an interesting comparison with modern systems. Basically the turbochargers sucked through a pair of 2″ SU carburettors, so from the outset a volatile fuel/air mixture was in the system, which after being pressurized by the turbocharger went through two stage intercooling before being fed into the engine. This intercooling consisted of an air-to-air primary system and then a Freon cooled secondary system which had its origins in an air-conditioning unit. Even those involved with the project look back on such an innovation with amazement but at the time it was a logical means of achieving the kind of performance required within the limits of their budget and the technology then available. The one big disadvantage of this particular turbocharging arrangement; having the fuel introduced upstream of the turbos, with such a highly tuned engine was that any backfire or similar detonation could have explosive consequences. One of the intercoolers looked as if it had taken a load of buckshot after one such incident!

The car meanwhile was made ready for Le Mans and ADA Engineering applied their considerable skills to making sure the car was up to the task. They double skinned the humble TR's monocoque in all critical areas, adding strength to the roof and scuttle. The unique body panels were also strengthened with Kevlar, very little of the actual steel exterior body panels being left apart from the roof and the drastically narrowed boot lid. Even the doors were reproduced in glassfibre, retaining their winding windows and all the front panels could be removed via Dzus fasteners. The suspension was by Triumph-based McPherson struts with Bilstein inserts at the front and at the rear the 'live' BL axle was replaced, in accordance with the Group 5 rules, with an equally 'live' Jaguar axle with a 2.77:1 ratio. As a temporary measure an American made Muncie T10 4-speed gearbox was fitted and still remains on the car today. Brakes were 12″ ventilated discs with four-pot callipers and the 15″ diameter Compomotive wheels were 10″ wide at the front and 14″ wide at the back.

The financial aspect of the Le Mans campaign was a constant, uphill struggle

Sculptured for velocity – front wing detail. One of a number of specially designed body panels on this car.

and despite determined efforts by everyone involved the project was grossly underfunded. These were times of recession, companies tightening purse strings and fighting for survival. Marketing and publicity budgets were being restricted and sponsorship money was in very short supply which not only made it difficult for individual teams but the sport in general. With the Triumph TR7/TR8 about to go out of production there was only passing interest from BL for such a patriotic and determined effort. No doubt they would have been eager to cash in on any success!

The car, now ready to take to the track, received very little testing and a planned sortie to the Silverstone 6 Hour race had to be cancelled to conserve funds. So with virtually no testing miles under its wheels the car was proudly taken to the 1980 Le Mans 24 Hour race, accompanied by members of the TR Register who had shown their loyalty and interest by putting money into the project. It had by now attracted some interest from the press but a big sponsor was still not forthcoming and money that had come in amounted to little more than donations from well wishers.

After successfully passing scrutineering

The 'TRS' road-going replica of the Janspeed Le Mans TR7 V8 Turbo, built by Dave Bennett and Del Lines in Weston-super-Mare.

the 1068 kilo car, resprayed in British Racing Green specially for this outing, failed to qualify. It was to have been driven by John Brindley, Ian Harrower and John Sheldon who incidentally did the fastest lap in the car at 4 minutes 37.1 seconds and it was timed at 201 mph on the Mulsanne straight. Everything was being put to the test at the same time as trying to qualify the car. There were all sorts of irritating problems, such as a whole batch of wheels with balance problems which would probably not even have been noticed at road speeds but at racing speed perfect balance was crucial and only four were found to be usable. There was also propshaft vibration at high speed, steering and gearbox problems as well as numerous small faults present in any new project. The engine was totally new territory and would rarely fire on all eight cylinder. Mind you, when it did it produced an enormous amount of power.

So the car came back an honourable failure, but undeterred and convinced of the car's potential it was re-entered for the 1981 Le Mans. It was tested by Derek Bell at Silverstone and went, in May 1981 to the Silverstone 6 Hours where Ian Harrower qualified with a 1 minute 44.7 second lap which was easily a match for

ROVER V8

Front airdam of the 'TRS' differs from the Janspeed car. Bodywork finish is superb. Car now proudly owned by Andrew Massey.

the Porsche 935s. But it halted practice after crashing heavily at Becketts while being driven by John Brindley and becoming a non-starter. It was not able to make it to Le Mans, either . . . The car's final race was in the Flying Tigers Brands Hatch 1000 Kms on September 27th that year. On this occasion driven by Bill Wykeham and Ian Harrower, it qualified 30th fastest after fuel surge problems and a broken rocker shaft. During the race, after a very early pit stop, Bill Wykeham spun the car at Stirling's Bend and it stalled. He could not get it restarted.

One final entry in the 1982 Le Mans 24 Hours by ADA Engineering (who by now owned the car), to be driven by Ian Harrower and Bill Wykeham was the last hope, but lack of funds saw that foray cancelled. They had finally concluded that developing a car like this, without adequate backing, was not going to work. It was the end of its competition career.

After a short spell in a motor museum the car was sold in 1983 to the British Sports Car Centre for a knockdown price and after a few 'test runs', was parked in a corner where it gradually disappeared from view beneath various spare wheels and body panels. There it languished, gathering dust. It was eventually brought to the notice of Peter Nott, a sports car racer, who had always retained an interest in the car and he was astonished to learn that this brave little legend was in need of

a benefactor. He raised the money to rescue it and on 17th September 1985 proudly trailered the Janspeed TR7 V8 Turbo home where he set about restoring it to its former glory.

The engine was not capable of running but initial investigations pointed to something like a broken camshaft as the possible culprit so in October '85 the car was taken back to its birthplace – Janspeed. Everyone there was astonished to see their prodigy return and in their hands the engine received a long and careful rebuild. On 7th October 1985 the engine was lifted out and the car remained there

The engine of the 'TRS' is less dramatic, but still packs a punch. Engine number is EXP 251

The Janspeed-built, twin turbocharged engine of John Buckham's car. Dual sidedraught Dellortos and no intercooler.

John Buckham's Sussex Transmission Engineers rallycross TR7 V8. (Bill Mantovani)

until 19th March 1987, partly because the engine damage was far more extensive than was first thought and partly because Peter Nott had to pour considerable quantities of hard earned money into having the work done properly.

The engine had at some stage been run without the intercoolers, resulting in a dropped inlet valve on cylinder number 7. This had sent shrapnel into cylinders 1 and 6, thankfully without damaging the bores but the pistons and heads had suffered. It was no use simply putting the engine back together in its 1980 form; the technology of turbocharging having

advanced considerably in the intervening years and it was now possible to assemble a system of much greater sophistication. But first the engine had to be rebuilt. The Cosworth pistons were replaced with a set by Omega on the same Chevrolet conrods. The crankshaft, block and dry sump system were all deemed sound. The WL9 camshaft which had once been tried was now installed, with an Auto Power Services/Duplex timing chain set. The compression ratio was lowered still further to 8.05:1 in anticipation of higher turbo boost, by the Janspeed method of boring into the cylinder head slightly with a cutter the same diameter as the cylinder bore.

The turbochargers were mounted on stainless steel exhaust manifolds with additional support from a pair of beautifully fabricated and fully rose jointed (to allow for expansion) triangular brackets. They sucked through a giant pair of special air cleaners, then the heated air was blown through the new intercoolers before entering the single Janspeed plenum chamber. This was in fact fabricated from sheet alloy, although in its crackle black finish it looks cast and machined, sitting as it does on top of an almost standard Rover Vitesse inlet manifold. The whole system is finally controlled by a specially programmed Micro Dynamics ECU which represented the single most complex aspect of the whole installation.

The car was put on the dynamome-

ter at Janspeed, while they were working to set up the engine's electronics but it easily exceeded the dynamometer's maximum capacity of 250 bhp at mid-range rpm. The true potential of the engine, running on the kind of boost it is quite capable of sustaining, may never be known. The engine has cost far too much for its new owner to ever put it at risk but most people agree that in its original form

500-550 bhp was a realistic figure.

Peter Nott trailered the car back to Le Mans in 1987 for the Historic Cavalcade and its appearance amongst the Ford GT40s and the Bentleys met with more than a little curiosity and amazement. But a Mulsanne Straight timing ticket reading 193.5 mph needs no comment. The passenger was speechless too!

The car spawned two interesting spin-

Nic Mann's incredible Morris Minor working hard at Gurston Down in 1987. The car is the current class record holder at this hill climb course. P8-17

off projects which deserve a mention. The specially designed bodypanels made for the Le Mans car inspired a road going replica with Dave Bennett of Bodylines in Weston-Super-Mare undertaking the considerable amount of bodywork involved and Del Lines also of Weston taking care of the mechanical side, which included the installation of a tuned Rover V8 3.5-litre engine. The result, dubbed the TRS, is a stunning creation which transformed the TR7 bodyshell into something altogether more aggressive and purposeful.

The second spin-off concerns the one other twin-turbocharged engine built to a similarly high competition specification which went into John Buckham's Sussex Transmission Engineers rallycross Triumph TR7 V8. John had been successful in rallycross, driving a BDA-engined Escort but was looking for a new project for the future, possibly a TR7 V8. At the time there were other successful Triumph TR7 V8s in the sport (Richard Painton's for example) and the idea took a leap forward when a customer brought his Rover SD1 into John's transmission business because it needed a beefed up automatic transmission to handle the power from a new Janspeed twin turbocharged engine. John was impressed by the installation and after discussions Janspeed prepared a competition unit. It was built along the same lines as the Le Mans car, with a cast alloy crankcase girdle, 'O' ringed cylinder heads with five bolts around each cylinder and full dry sump system. The turbocharger installation was simpler than the Le Mans car though, being a blow-through system, without intercooling, using a pair of Dellorto sidedraught carburettors mounted on a fabricated adaptor which was in turn bolted to a Huffaker inlet manifold, but the horsepower was there in considerable degree.

The engine went into a brand new Triumph TR7 bodyshell built to rally specification, with lots of BL Motorsport bits. Originally the car ran with an automatic gearbox, which enabled the car to be held at the startline on the brakes while the engine was brought on to boost, then on the green light the brakes were released and POW! But the automatic gearbox gave poor engine braking on deceleration so after two meetings a ZF gearbox from an Aston Martin was substituted. Sorting the engine was a long process, mainly because there was a fault with the fuel return to the tank. On a blow-through turbocharged system the fuel pressure must always exceed boost pressure otherwise the carburettor becomes pressurised. Because of this high fuel pressure, there has to be a system to provide constant return of fuel to the fuel tank which on this engine was not working properly. They assumed the engine was over-choked, so reduced the carburettor size, which made it run leaner, which in turn led to overheating. When a twin turbocharger installation like this overheats, it melts things! The problem was eventually sorted but about the same time John found business demanding more of his time, leaving little for sport so the car was pushed into the garage and left. It is still there.

MORRIS MINOR V8 TURBO

The Morris Minor has many attributes which have enabled it to enjoy popularity long after it ceased volume production. It is roomy, frugal on fuel, cheap to insure and cheap to run but with a 0-60 mph time perhaps unkindly described as 'occasionally' it is certainly not a performance car. It requires a tremendous amount of work and effort, not to mention a rather wicked sense of humour, to turn the definitive, mundane motor car into one of the quickest road driven cars in the world.

Nic Mann's 1960 Morris Minor has almost achieved the status of legend in its eight year gestation period from extremely rapid turbocharged Rover V8 engined special to phenomenally quick road driven hillclimbing and sprint competition car. But the story goes back a good deal further than that.

This immaculate machine has been owned by Nic for some 20 years. He originally bought the Minor for £60 as a replacement for his mother's Austin A40 which he had put into a ditch. Nic began competing with it in sprints using a MGB engine which he later turbocharged but in 1979 decided to make some radical alterations by fitting a Rover V8 engine. The engine, actually a pre-SD1 unit, came from a local scrapyard and fitting it required the removal of all the Minor's body/chassis structure forward of the front bulkhead. A tubular structure was then fabricated to carry the engine and front suspension, which consists of fabricated unequal length, coil sprung wishbones with Vauxhall Ventora front uprights and an adjustable anti-roll bar. A one-piece, front-hinged glassfibre moulding replaces the steel bonnet and wings. The rear axle initially was from a Mk2 Cortina with LSD, located by four equal length links and a Panhard rod. It proved strong enough at this stage of development, although Nic occasionally replaced half-shafts as a precaution. The engine was checked over thoroughly and rebuilt, retaining the stock block, crankshaft (tuftrided) and connecting rods but fitted with Ford cast pistons giving a compression ratio of 6.5:1. A Crane solid lifter camshaft was fitted, with of course solid lifters and adjustable pushrods, retaining the standard Rover timing gear set. The cylinder heads were untouched, apart from stronger valve springs and thorough reconditioning as were the standard Rover P6B exhaust manifolds which were and still are the only ones that will fit in the space available. A standard wet sump (baffled to counter surge) and oil pump were also retained although the oil pump was later fitted with a high-volume kit simply as a way of uprating the pre-SD1 pump which was slightly inferior to the later SD1 type.

It is in the single turbocharger installation that the ingenuity involved becomes apparent and although Nic has been developing and refining the car over a period of years the engine was enormously powerful from the beginning. The first set-up used a Tecalemit mechanical fuel injection system. Switzer turbo supplied by BTN Turbochargers, (commercial vehicle turbocharger reconditioners), and no intercoolers. The Tecalemit fuel injection system relied purely on throttle position and

engine rpm for fuel metering so Nic added an enrichment device to increase fuel flow during turbo boost. This throttle butterfly was located downstream of the turbocharger on the inlet manifold plenum, with injectors mounted very close to the inlet ports. For road driving the wastegate was set at 15 psi but for hill-climbing the air cleaner was removed because of its restriction on airflow and the wastegate was reset to give 22 psi. The engine was mated to a Rover SD1 5-speed gearbox, with either a standard or a close ratio set of gears which has a locking mechanism to prevent the weaker fifth gear from engaging, unless speeds in excess of 130 mph are needed during competition.

In this 'Phase One' form the engine was capable of propelling the car to 0-60mph times of 4.4 seconds and 0-100 in 9.5 seconds. These are staggering figures, but the system could suffer from vapour lock problems, and although it worked well on full-throttle applications, still needed refinement in normal driving and the fuel consumption was very poor. The car has never been trailered to a meeting and with only a 6 gallon fuel tank, consumption was important.

So the following year Nic applied his considerable engineering talents to adapting the standard Rover inlet manifold and its pair of SU carburettors. The new system he devised has the turbocharger blowing through the SUs with parts from the Tecalemit fuel injection system providing fuel enrichment under boost. It was during

The car has always been immaculately presented and has been tested more than once to establish its phenomenal performance.

this stage in the engine's development that Nic, in collaboration with Aldon Automotive and David Vizard, also began experimenting, somewhat tentatively at first, with nitrous oxide injection. The intention was to use the nitrous oxide (N_2O) as a turbo-lag eliminator, providing the necessary additional horsepower until the turbo boost came on, after which it was cut off by a pressure switch. The turbocharger too had been changed to a larger capacity Garrett AiResearch T04B and a huge intercooler now sat in front of the engine, where the radiator had been. There were now two throttling points, one being the normal throttles of the SU carburettors which mainly controlled the engine during low throttle openings and the other just upstream of the turbo which took over once the flow rates increased. By carefully balancing the two, Nic was able to maintain a reserve of air in the long inlet tract for better low rpm response while at the same time protecting the turbo from surge and the consequent loss of boost at gearchanges. In this form the engine was producing around 400 bhp (500 bhp with nitrous oxide)and the car as tested by *Autocar* could accelerate from 0-60 mph in 3.4 seconds (using second gear only), 0-100 mph in 7.9 seconds and to 130 mph in only 13.7 seconds.

The engine was not the only area of the car to receive further development. The greater power and the need to transmit that power effectively to the road meant that the Cortina axle had to be replaced, this time by an independent Jaguar-based system with twin inboard discs, acquired once again from a scrapyard. Its massive 3.3:1 ratio Salisbury differential housing is very solidly located, via a fabricated sub-frame to the rear of the car, and the bottom 'wishbones' triangulated with rose-jointed links. All the rubber compliance was removed. The front mounted MGB radiator had to go to make way for the intercooler and engine cooling is now taken care of by a Range Rover radiator, with twin electric fans, mounted in the boot directly over the rear axle line. The rear wheel arches were redesigned to scoop in much needed cold air and the resultant warm air exits the boot area through a line of holes just behind the rear window. The steel wheels by this time were replaced by Compomotive alloy wheels. For road use they are 6.5 x 13 " with 205/60 Pirelli P6 tyres on the front and 8.0 x 14 " with 225/60 Pirellis on the rear. For competition use Nic fits 10 x 15 "

Compomotive wheels on the front and 12.5 x 15 on the rear, mounting Avon racing tyres, although Dunlop and M & H tyres have been used in the past. These racing wheels and tyres are carried to meetings on a roof rack and when fitted need polished alloy spats to be covered, quickly and easily attached by small nuts and bolts.

In its Phase Two form, with twin SU carburettors, the engine was a big improvement but it was still not possible to get the fuel metering exactly right over the whole rpm range. Carburettors are not sensitive to air density and over a couple of years Nic began to formulate plans for a more refined fuel injection system. Fuel metering on a turbocharged engine must take into account all normal factors such as engine rpm, throttle angle, etc., but also boost and charge air temperature, at which point the 'science' begins to get very complicated. Air flow metering simplifies all this – only the *amount* of air being consumed by the engine needs to be known in order to add the correct quantity of fuel.

Nic decided that what he needed as a base system was Bosch K-Jetronic fuel injection which coincidentally is used in V8 form on the Porsche 928. Sounds expensive and so it is, but Nic was able, through the co-operation of Josh Sadler of Porsche dealers 'Autofarm' to obtain a secondhand system from a scrapyard in Belgium. Josh was a fellow hillclimb competitor who campaigned various 'hairy' Porsche 911s. His performances in road driven cars were for many years Nic's inspiration and set the target for his performances at various venues. Eventually though, Nic could regularly get the better of him!

The advantage of the Bosch system is that although it is a sophisticated piece of precision equipment it is mechanical, so relatively easy to work on. It deduces airflow from a sensor (a large 'flapper' valve) and tends to lag slightly behind the engine's fuel needs. Thus the system possesses *relatively* poor throttle response – this is inherent in its design – but Nic knew that this could be overcome to a large extent. The flapper valve was installed ahead of the turbocharger and Nic spent many hours studying the system, understanding exactly how it operated, before altering its fuel flow capabilities. A Rover production fuel injection manifold was acquired to mount the injectors. This is not a Vitesse-type manifold but an old North American specification type which has a much simpler layout in the central plenum chamber base area. This was machined to take the Bosch injection nozzles in the usual place, in the manifold runners near the ports and a new plenum chamber cover fabricated to take the pipe from the turbocharger. The intercooler was doubled in size and the boost was now capable of being raised even higher to 25 psi.

Once this Phase Three turbocharging system was installed and working Nic turned his attention to the nitrous oxide injection system. He was finding that the nitrous oxide could be used with boost for big gains in mid-range horsepower, not just as a compensator for turbo lag (which was still a problem) and began using it in ever increasing amounts. But the state-of-the-art 8-port systems that were so popular at the time, with an individual N_2O/fuel nozzle into each port, proved unsatisfactory. Controllability was poor and response unpredictable which was a problem in hillclimbing where accurate control was paramount. He found that above a certain temperature, regardless of pressure, the nitrous oxide held in the pipes and nozzles would vaporise and when the system was actuated all the engine would get for the initial burst would be vapour, which was less effective than the liquid form. The pipes and nozzles needed to be kept cool, so that the nitrous oxide remained liquid right up until it was needed which meant moving the system away from the engine. The result eventually was a totally progressive nitrous oxide injection system, controlled by the throttle position via a needle valve and injected immediately after the intercooler. The extra fuel required with the nitrous oxide was injected into the plenum chamber for good distribution, which meant also that it reached the engine slightly before the N_2O. The purpose of the system was to remove turbo lag by running at low boost (9 psi) over three quarters of the accelerator travel, which gives progressive and virtually instant throttle reaction principally due to the N_2O. At about three quarter throttle boost is raised to 15 psi with virtually instant effect, which provides enough performance for the majority of hillclimbing situations. If however, still more is needed the last bit of the throttle travel operates a spring loaded switch which slams the wastegate (which under these circumstances would be passing a lot of exhaust gas) shut and the engine receives 25 psi boost – instantly. The result is massive quantities of horsepower and devastating acceleration. One further refinement; a

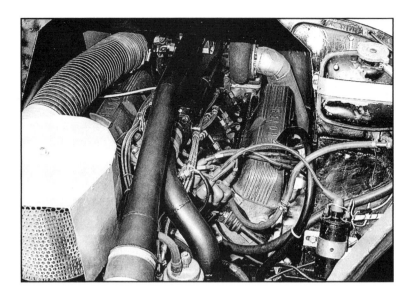

later development, was water injection which permits the safe use of about 27 psi boost, but only for specific events such as the Brighton Speed Trials (half-mile straight).

Throughout the car's long competition life it has never suffered any kind of terminal engine component failure. In over a decade of competition the car has only once failed to get home after an event under its own steam and that was after a major 'off' at Loton Park during the car's MGB-powered days. It is built from fairly mundane components even by 'fast road' standards, firstly because it 'delivers the goods' without having to rev beyond 6500 rpm and secondly because Nic simply does not have the budget to invest in hi-tech racing parts. Were this car trailered to meetings and its engine only capable of delivering such awesome power for a minute or so during a hill-climb, sprint or

Hidden away, almost in the middle of the car. The turbocharged Rover V8 engine capable of producing over 500 bhp.

The Garrett AiResearch TO4B turbocharger, with wastegate in the right foreground, sits at the rear of the engine.

drag race, needing afterwards a thorough and careful overhaul before another attempt, it would still be remarkable. The fact that the Minor V8 Turbo has been regularly loaded up with four racing wheels on a roof rack, tools and hydraulic jack, and an overnight bag, started up on a cold morning, reversed out of its modest garage and driven quietly out of its village home en route to a meeting somewhere in the UK makes this a truly incredible car.

There have been a few minor problems which have needed remedial work as well as incidental developments along the way. The original Ford cast pistons were prone to blowing the ring lands and eventually Nic had a set of 6.5:1 compression ratio pistons specially made to his design by Jahn's of Los Angeles. It was fortuitous that he ordered nine because one lost a gudgeon pin circlip, and ruined a bore. He returned to press fitting gudgeon pins after that experience. Nic has also had a camshaft made to his own specification by Crane although apart from a duration of over 300° and a valve lift of 'about' 0.50" he insists it is unremarkable. The high cylinder pressures too have caused one or two problems, like *bending* a con-rod (in compression) and after removing the cylinder heads during one routine overhaul Nic found that some of the thick metal washers under the head bolts had broken. This had been caused by the heads actually lifting off the block, a fact confirmed by carbon rings around the head gaskets. The block decks were bored

to take larger diameter head bolts with heli-coils and despite retaining the standard Rover metal gaskets the problem has not returned. The standard Rover rocker shafts and aluminium rockers have also been retained without problems, although a rocker shaft has broken occasionally, a fact Nic puts down to the later shafts being of inferior quality. The cylinder heads too have come in for some attention by Oselli Engineering in Oxford, who collaborated with Nic on the modifications. The requirement was mainly for greater exhaust flow for which, in addition to conventional polishing and porting, larger Mercedes sodium filled exhaust valves were fitted. The sodium melts at operating temperature and flows up and down inside the hollow valve stem as the valve opens and closes. When it is at the bottom of the stem, near the valve head it absorbs heat and when at the top of the valve stem it dissipates that heat, via the valve gear into the engine oil thus helping to lower combustion chamber temperatures in a critical area and preventing 'knocking' at high boost.

Nic has competed very successfully in hill climbing and sprinting events all over the UK, including the odd foray to the Channel Islands and the Isle of Man. His car is a firm favourite with spectators, although Nic competes mainly as a means of measuring the performance of the car as he has developed it and putting his engineering theories to the test against the clock. In 1982 he tried his hand at drag

The interior showing the offset driving position and the extent to which the engine intrudes into the passenger compartment.

ROVER V8

racing, competing in the Streetracer Championships, an annual event which required cars to be driven to meetings and raced on road legal tyres, which ruled out slicks or racing compounds. He was racing against many seasoned competitors in some mighty machines; for instance a 327 cu. in. Chevrolet V8 with N_2O injection, a Lotus 1600 Twin Cam with N_2O injection, a 440 cu. in. Mopar V8 with N_2O injection and a Ford 390 cu. in. V8. All these potent engines powered machines capable of putting up very impressive $\frac{1}{4}$ mile performances but Nic won the first prize of £500, recording a fastest elapsed time of 11.80 seconds over the course. In 1983 he took the money again with slightly slower 11.96 seconds and in 1984 pocketed another £500 with a winning 11.76 seconds and a terminal speed of 128 mph – his best terminal speed of the day 130 mph. Compare that with a Dutton Phaeton which competed in the same event with 3.9-litre Rover V8 power, which managed a 13.4 second elapsed time and a terminal speed of 104 mph. At Blackbushe that same year he recorded his quickest ever quarter mile of 11.1 secs/130 mph but that was on hillclimbing slicks. In 1985 Nic qualified with an 11.46 secs/133 mph but was eliminated by a staging rule on the start line but he was back the following year and took his revenge. Racing this time for £700 he raised his fastest terminal speed to 135 mph and recorded a fastest e.t. of the day of 11.68 seconds. The final was against the 429 cu. in. Ford V8 engined Ford 105E of Rob Houlston. Nic won with 11.82 secs/129 mph.

But drag racing was really just for fun, the more serious competition was done at hillclimbing and sprint events all over the country where the car competed in the Special Saloon class, over 1300 cc capacity. In its class Nic's Morris Minor is the current record holder at Gurston Down, Shelsley Walsh, Wiscombe, Prescott and Bouley Bay (Channel Islands). At sprint events he holds the record at Colerne, Weston and the classic Brighton event where he has beaten John Welch's sophisticated X-TRAC 4WD Rallycross Escort and the Morris Minor has run the $\frac{1}{2}$ mile in 17.7 seconds at 159 mph! It was most recently tested by *Autocar & Motor* magazine on racing tyres and on paper was able to out perform three of the world's true Supercars – the Ferrari F40, Porsche 959 and Lamborghini Countach. The Morris Minor recorded a 0-60 mph time of 3.1 seconds (against a Porsche

959's 3.6 seconds), a 0-100 mph of only 6.9 seconds (none of the supercars have been tested at less than 8 seconds) and 0-150 mph in 17.2 seconds (the Ferrari F40 is capable of doing it in 18.5 seconds). Remarkable is a wholly inadequate word under the circumstances.

So next time you are sitting at the traffic lights in your brand new Ferrari F40 and a small, white saloon pulls alongside you, be careful, you may be about to experience the most embarrassing moment of your life. Being left for dead by a Morris Minor!

There is no space up front for the radiator so it sits in the boot, over the rear axle. Nitrous oxide bottle is on the right, battery on the left.

METRO 8R4

A ride around a rally stage in the passenger seat of this MG Metro '8R4' is an unforgettable experience. Here the power of a highly tuned Rover V8 engine is harnessed to the ultimate transmission system, capable of putting all its considerable horsepower on to the road surface, regardless of whether that surface be smooth tarmac or gravel-strewn mud. Its traction is equalled by enormous braking power and if the acceleration is akin to stepping out into an empty lift shaft, then the brakes can be compared with hitting the bottom. From the word 'go' the loud angry bellow of over 300 bhp shoves you irresistibly forward, no discernable sensation of building up speed, just a sudden maniacal rush. Then the noise drops as the brakes interrupt your rocket sled ride and despite the security of the seat harness, your legs push solidly against the floor, seemingly trying to stop you pitching nose first into the windscreen. But you slow smoothly, the car's speed wiped off without drama, then it is flung into the first corner with an easy measure of opposite lock and once facing in the right direction, another unbelievably noisy onslaught. After the initial shock you try to take in the surroundings, but features either side blur as you stare fixedly at the next corner which your reason tells you has no hope of being negotiated. But suddenly the speed has gone, the stones clatter against the underside as the car slips easily sideways, the engine a flat growl, still at seemingly impossibly speeds, then down a gear and away you go once again. So it goes

The Metro 'FG8R4' built by FG Rallying of Bromyard.

The highly tuned 3.9-litre Rover V8 engine sits easily in the engine bay meant for a V6.

157

A 'standard' MG Metro 6R4 fitted with V64V engine looks no less bulky than the Rover V8.

on, an experience which leaves you dazed, the straights reduced to short sharp blasts of acceleration, the corners opened out before you by the phenomenal grip of the car. Coming back into the parking area you sit in mild state of shock – with a grin across the full width of your face!

When Austin Rover Motorsport took the decision to compete on equal terms with the world's best in the Group B supercar category, they entered into this technological warfare with a weapon that could not be compromised by any other considerations. It had to be capable of taking on, and beating the most advanced rally cars ever built, cars which had pushed forward the boundaries of rally car performance to a point we shall not see again for many years to come.

The development of the MG Metro 6R4 began soon after the brutally powerful Triumph TR7 V8 rally programme had been dropped and thoughts were turned away from the traditional concept of taking a production road car and adapting it to the special needs of world class rallying. The fact that this new mechanical package was wrapped in the bodywork of Austin Rover's Supermini, with sporty MG identity, coincided purely with the need to keep the overall size compact.

The layout, design and engineering was undertaken with a great deal of input from Williams Grand Prix Engineering. Four wheel drive was a must – Ford had abandoned their Escort 1700T because its rear wheel drive layout was obsolete before the car was even finished – but in one area Austin Rover Motorsport made a significant departure. The currently 'fashionable' turbocharger was passed over in favour of a larger capacity, normally aspirated engine with its instant throttle response, good engine braking and with no turbocharger(s) there would be no excessive underbonnet temperatures to worry about. Honda were going to supply a competition engine based on the V6 used in the current Rover 800 series, but in order to get the new machine rolling and capable of putting in some test and development mileage a Rover V8 was cut up to produce a 2495 cc V6, fitted with a pair of triple-choke downdraught Weber carburettors. In this form the car was entered in several national stage rallies where homologation was not required.

Once the car had shown its potential the decision was taken to go ahead and build the 200 examples needed for homologation into Group B and the car that was finally unveiled to the public in 1985 differed considerably from the earlier prototypes. The wheelbase was longer, the track increased and larger 16 inch diameter wheels fitted. The bodywork too was even more radical, leaving only the roof and windscreen of the Metro production car. It was a squat, purposeful and supremely functional machine that was now ready to

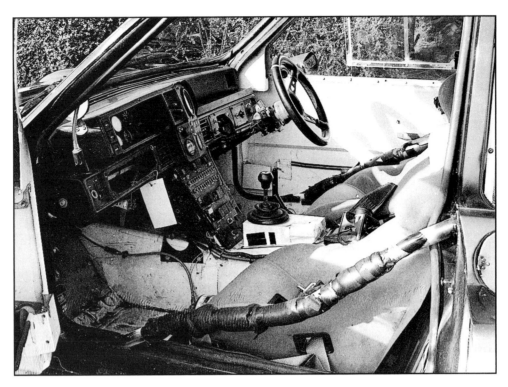

Interior of the 'FG8R4' is certainly functional. Has been converted from left to right hand drive.

enter the fray. For the engine compartment Austin Rover Motorsport engineer David Wood had designed a brand new four-valves per cylinder, all alloy V6 (the Honda engine would not be coming) producing 250 bhp in 'Clubman' form, but for the 20 evolutionary examples eligible for International events the power would be up to 380 – 400 bhp.

The new MG Metro 6R4's first competitive event was a real baptism of fire – the 1985 Lombard RAC rally – where the spotlight of the world's media would be upon it. The car of Tony Pond (the other dropped out) gave an excellent account of itself and proved the car's ability to compete. But all through 1986, when the car contested the World Championship, the spectacular little machines proved fragile, the engines having problems, particularly with cam timing belts and the transmission needed frequent attention. But the car had its successes and when Group B cars were suddenly outlawed it found and still finds continued success in National events and rallycross. It is already being sought by collectors.

When the Group B supercars were outlawed, following the tragic accident in Corsica which killed Lancia star Henri Toivonen and his co-driver, the MG Metro 6R4 in Clubman form at least was available at something of a bargain price. Mike Gibbon of FG Rallying approached Austin Rover Motorsport about buying one of these Clubman specification cars as a rolling chassis. A price was agreed, but it appeared that someone within the organisation learned of the intended use of the car and vetoed the sale unless the car was bought complete with engine. Mike however was not interested in spending money on the V64V engine because he had other plans – the car was going to be Rover V8 powered! The search for a suitable car continued and eventually Mike secured the purchase of a full Works specification rolling shell from RED the rallying preparation specialists. This was no Longbridge-built 'Clubman' version, this was an Abingdon-built car, driven by David Llewellyn in the 1986 RAC Rally. Mike's acquisition boasted Kevlar, not glassfibre bodypanels, alloy not steel roof, fully adjustable suspension, and a host of other refinements which made the car considerably superior.

It is quite probable, although by no means certain, that this was the first MG Metro 6R4 to be fitted with a Rover V8 engine, which made it an ambitious, innovative and indeed brave project. Such a bold step also illustrates just how certain Mike was that a Rover V8 engine in the MG Metro 6R4 was the right combination.

Whether the Rover V8 should have been used originally in the embryonic MG Metro 6R4 is academic, since the whole thrust of Group B development was stopped in its tracks. Whether the engine

was even considered as an option in the early stages no one will admit to and had Group B continued, the Rover V8 would have had to be considerably developed to keep pace with the need for more power which the turbocharged cars were always managing to find. Claims that the Rover V8 was too bulky for this application have been firmly dismissed now, though. The engine is 4″ longer than the V64V engine and fills the engine bay a little more but it fits, the car works with it in and accessibility to the engine is first class.

Mike and his team at FG Rallying wasted no time in getting on with the job, once the car had been thoroughly checked

over. The Rover engine went in with few problems although it was obviously not a straight swap. The bellhousing had to be specially adapted and the block required some machining. The special cast alloy sump had to be sectioned and a new piece welded in to fit the longer Rover cylinder block. The exhaust manifolds had to be specially made to mate with silencer boxes which sit across the back of the car.

One of the biggest problems was plumbing in the dry-sump lubrication system. The mounting of the oil pump was accomplished without too much difficulty but no existing pipe fittings were compact enough to provide the tight bends needed

The 'FG8R4' blasts off around a special stage with a video camera on the roof to record the action.

The block originates from an engine built for American John Buffum who came to Europe to rally during the TR7 V8 programme. It has a steel crankshaft, Group A conrods and Omega 10.4:1 compression ratio pistons. The cylinder heads are FG Rallying's own, fully reworked with larger inlet and exhaust valves with their own dual valve springs. The camshaft is a Group A Works rallying specification, similar to a Crane F256, with solid lifters and adjustable pushrods. The rest of the valve gear is more or less to Group A specification, with large diameter rocker shafts and steel rockers etc. Power output is estimated to be over 300 bhp with masses of mid range torque.

The rest of the car is Austin Rover Motorsport MG Metro 6R4 – the engine sits between the rear wheels, slightly to the left, with the flywheel facing the front of the car, fairly high up in the tubular and sheet steel chassis. Engine power is transmitted forwards into the five speed, close ratio gearbox which sits between and below the seats, then forward again into a transfer box, which moves the propshaft line to the right of the engine/gearbox. In this transfer casing is the FF-type differential with a viscous coupling splitting the torque (35% front/65% rear) to front and rear differentials. Drive to the rear wheels goes through a quill shaft, running alongside the engine, to the mechanical rear differential which is housed in a casting incorporating the dry-sump. A short cross shaft goes through the sump to take drive to the left driveshaft. Drive to the front wheels goes forward via a propshaft to the front solid-mounted differential and from there to the two driveshafts. The fully independent suspension uses Bilstein struts with twin, dual-rated springs. At the front the struts work with wide based bottom wishbones and an adjustable roll bar while at the rear the struts fit to reverse wishbones with adjustable front links and a blade type anti-roll bar. The brakes on all four wheels are massive ventilated discs with four piston callipers and the rack and pinion steering has variable power assistance.

The car, with Rover V8 engine installed and plumbed in, worked instantly. There were some gear selection problems to be sorted out before it could be thoroughly tested but these had nothing to do with the V8 installation. The result is a truly fantastic car. It has proved to be *much* quicker than an MG Metro 6R4 in 'Clubman' form which is how the car is

in such a small space. The problem really did have everyone scratching their head until a company specialising in hydraulics for fork lift trucks came to the rescue. The whole lot was sorted out in no time.

The engine itself came from FG Rallying's previous 'company car', a full Works Triumph TR7 V8 which had needed a massive bonnet bulge to clear the four Dellorto downdraught carburettors which replaced the works sidedraught Weber setup. For the Metro 6R4 – now dubbed the '8R4' the 45 Dellortos were replaced by 48 DRLA Dellortos and later, engine capacity was increased to 3.9-litres. It also packs a host of other top quality rallying components.

now rallied, in fact one suspects that it could even give a full International specification 6R4 a run for its money especially when reliability is essential.

Apart from sprints, hillcimbing and appearances as a rally course car, it has seen no serious competition, but this does not detract from the concept, which seeks to offer a realistic alternative to the expensive and delicate V64V Austin Rover Motorsport engine. For those in a position to compete in national rallies with an MG Metro 6R4, which is still a very exciting and competitive car today, the installation of a Rover V8 engine, in an advanced state of tune has obvious advantages. The FG Rallying MG Metro 8R4 is a promotional tool for the company's business, a demonstration of their abilities and commitment to the sport. Others, such as Bristol's Dave Appleby have built these hybrid machines and compete regularly with considerable success, as do the European-based machines with which J E Motors of Coventry have been involved.

This concept received another boost, not to mention a considerable step forward in development when the Toleman Group unveiled their challenger for the 1988 Paris-Dakar Rally 'Raid'. The car was the TG88 Metro Raider, which had begun

life as an MG Metro 6R4 but was then lengthened 9.5 inches and widened by 2 inches. The balance of the car was changed by increasing the wheelbase, which meant moving the rear wheels further back in relation to the rest of the car and moving the 3.9-litre fuel injected Rover V8 engine forward, so that it did not sit between the rear wheels to the extent that it does on the normal 6R4. The radiator was now in the rear. The front suspension layout was retained but at the rear the struts were replaced by double wishbones and dual coil over water and air cooled shock absorbers. The steering was also redesigned to withstand severe shock loads. The transmission too had received a lot of work; the front and rear differentials were now by Quaife who had also modified the central differential so that it locked up if required. All three differentials and the gearbox incorporated a cooling system.

Unfortunately the car did not fare too well on its début outing. In the first stage it became stuck in soft sand and after a long struggle to free the car it ran out of fuel. The full potential of this new design has yet to be realised and the team have ambitious plans for future events.

Chapter Nine

Getting Technical

The standard Rover Vitesse is a big car. It weighs 1424 kilos and the fuel injected V8 engine produces 190 bhp at 5280 rpm with 220 lb/ft of torque at 4000 rpm. It can accelerate from 0–60 mph in 7.1 seconds, goes on to 100 mph in 20.4 seconds and reaches a maximum of 130 mph. By any standards this is a performance car.

When discussing 'street' performance it is important to maintain a sense of perspective between what is realistically achievable within a given budget, what is sufficient to meet performance requirements and most importantly – the vehicle's intended 'driveability'. A good road engine need not have maximum horsepower or enormous torque, but it does need to be docile at tick-over and low rpm, have good pick-up and smooth power delivery, a usable spread of power and torque over the rev range encountered in normal driving. It must start easily, not overheat in traffic and have reasonable fuel consumption. For the average driver the Rover V8 can be modified to produce far more power and torque than in standard production form (without the expense of fuel injection), yet fulfil all the above criteria and remain reliable.

It must be emphasised that to go for ultimate power output, often available in rpm ranges that can seldom be used on the road, has trade-offs in other areas of driveability that can lead to a fussy, lumpy and temperamental engine which is a pain to drive everyday in traffic. The very virtues of a big capacity V8 – its even torque delivery, lazy revving and power with reliability can be destroyed by trying to tune the engine too highly. Greater power also involves more and more uprating of the vehicle's running gear. Its suspension, brakes, wheels, tyres and in some cases even its body/chassis structure will have to be capable of handling that power in safety.

All the options will be explored here, from choosing parts to build a good strong road engine, from modifications that can be done in the driveway with the engine in the car, right up to the more specialised sphere of building no-compromise competition engines which may involve selecting all the right parts for the job.

REBUILDING TECHNIQUES

Stripping and rebuilding the Rover V8 engine, be it for a specific repair or for restoration, is very similar to working on any normal overhead valve 4, 6 or 8-cylinder engine and certainly a lot simpler than many overhead camshaft types. You have a lot more cylinders obviously, and so more pistons, valves and pushrods etc., which means greater component costs, even for something as straightforward as a rebore.

Because V8 engines tend to go on for ever without complaint, always starting

A nicely prepared Rover V8 with Holley 4-barrel. Chrome rockers are by Roverpart.

easily and running smoothly, they are often neglected and many secondhand engines will show signs of infrequent oil changes and resultant excessive wear in certain areas, usually obscured by a heavy build-up of thick black sludge inside the engine.

It is not within the scope of this book to give step by step instructions on the stripping and rebuilding of the Rover V8 engine. A good Owners Workshop Manual will cover the subject in detail and general rules on engine dismantling, inspection, measurement of wear, rectification, essential machining, and scrupulous cleanliness during rebuilding apply to this engine as to any other. Likewise it is not possible within the limits of this book to describe in detail the techniques used in building a high performance Rover V8 engine. Firstly, this would need a whole book of its own and secondly, the techniques of machining and assembly involved in building any performance engine are well documented elsewhere although any specific deviations from normal practice when applied to the Rover V8 will be covered.

Firstly, examine the engine externally for oil or coolant leaks and when the oil is drained from the sump check for any gritty or metallic particles, then make a note to investigate possible causes during dismantling. Once the coolant has been drained, remove the water pump and

check for signs of corrosion in the water passages. Aluminium engines need the correct antifreeze in the cooling system all the year round as a corrosion inhibitor and some owners are not as careful as others. Remove the intake manifold and the metal gasket beneath to reveal the lifter gallery and check the condition of the valve gear and the presence of oil sludge. A relatively clean gallery will indicate an engine that has had regular oil changes. The engine can be dismantled very easily, without special tools, with the possible exception of the front pulley which may need a puller

Scrupulously clean. A standard 2-bolt main bearing Rover V8 being built at J E Motors.

if firm leverage proves insufficient. All moving parts should be carefully checked for wear, particularly the camshaft and valve gear, bearings and valve guides. If the engine is to be completely stripped it is most important that *all* the oil ways, particularly in the cylinder block and crankshaft, should be thoroughly cleaned and blown out with compressed air. If the original pistons are to be retained (but probably fitted with new rings) carefully clean out the ring grooves using a broken piece of piston ring as a scraper. The cylinder bores should be cross hatched honed, before refitting the piston/connecting rod assembly.

The camshaft must be removed with extreme care to avoid damage to the bearings and if the camshaft bearings show signs of wear or damage they will have to be replaced. Replacement sets are available from a Rover V8 specialist such as John Woolfe Racing or Auto Power Services and will have to be fitted by an engine specialist. Be sure to inspect the timing chain and gears as well as the distributor drive gear, both on the distributor and on the end of the camshaft for excessive wear too. Never fit a new camshaft without fitting new hydraulic tappets (or followers).

There is nothing unusual about the cylinder heads either. Care has to be taken when de-carbonising the combustion chambers because you are dealing with soft aluminium, not cast iron, and check all machined faces for flatness after they have been thoroughly cleaned. Check all the valves for straightness and the valve guides for excessive play, check pushrods for straightness by rolling them one at a time on a sheet of glass, and replace the rocker shaft if it shows signs of wear. Be sure to clean out all bolt threads but try to avoid using taps to clean threads in aluminium because they are delicate and helicoil sets are expensive. For the same reason *always* use a torque wrench (you will probable need more than one)) when tightening fasteners, particularly into aluminium, and lightly lubricate the threads with a 50–50 engine oil/paraffin mix. The oil pump, once inspected for scoring or gear wear and reassembled, must be packed with petroleum jelly to assist priming on initial engine start-up. A priming tool is available.

When building an engine from scratch, keep all assembly areas scrupulously clean. Always inspect new parts very carefully to ensure they are both correct and in perfect condition. There is nothing more frustrating than trying to fit a new component that is not correct (possibly damaging something) or finishing an assembly job only to discover that the wrong part has been supplied and having to begin all over again. However, that is not to say that one should assume that because engine parts are new or re-machined they should or will simply bolt together without any attention to final adjustment. Many people try to save money by buying parts they need to rebuild or tune a Rover V8 and cannot grasp the fact that although they may have paid a lot of money for such specialised components they cannot simply bolt them together and turn the ignition key. The main reason that engine building is so expensive is because an enormous amount of time, skill and care goes into building *any* engine, especially one that is being put together from a collection of parts from a variety of different sources. A built engine, either supplied ready to fit, or installed in a car which has been delivered to the engine specialist, has probably been slowly and carefully assembled, the rotating and reciprocating parts checked for binding or fouling at every stage and when everything has been trial built, with grinding, polishing and relieving where necessary, the whole engine is dismantled, re-checked and then finally re-assembled. It is possible to build a good engine at home in the garage, but only with the careful choice of parts, specialist help in machining and balancing, a sensible, methodical approach and a lot of care. *Never assume anything* – check and check again.

Of course, there are many areas of engine work that can be tackled in the garage or on the driveway with a good set of tools. For instance it is well within the bounds of any competent DIY mechanic to fit a new camshaft, provided that the fitting instructions are followed correctly and the camshaft specification requires no machining to other engine parts. It is possible also to fit perhaps a new inlet manifold and carburettor or new exhaust manifolds and system, without getting involved in a major undertaking. But, buy a block, crankshaft, connecting rods and pistons to build a big capacity engine, or fit a high lift camshaft with solid lifters and you are going to have to put some work into it if a smooth reliable engine is to be the end result. This applies to building or modifying any performance engine. You have been warned!

165

ROVER V8

CYLINDER BLOCKS

There are four different cylinder blocks made for the Rover V8 engine. The first was obviously the original and referred to as the pre-1981 block. The point that has to be considered with these blocks is that prior to 1973 they had rope rear crankshaft oil seals instead of rubber lip type. These seals were not particularly efficient and difficult to install correctly. The older blocks can be converted to lip type rubber seals by boring the seal housing in the block $3\frac{7}{8}''$ diameter by $\frac{7}{16}''$ deep. For the front crankshaft seal either an SD1 front cover can be fitted (they are expensive) or the original cover can be converted. Oselli Engineering for instance will carry out front and rear seal conversions for a modest sum. The front crank seal was changed to a lip type with the introduction of the SD1 engine in 1976. From 1981 onwards the block received extra webbing on the front, behind the timing gear and across the lifter gallery, beneath the inlet manifold. Next came the Vitesse 'stiff blocks', introduced late 1982/early 1983 which have additional internal material around the main bearing webs and these are now the standard production block. There is absolutely nothing wrong with the standard block when used in normal road and semi-competition states of tune.

The ultimate for competition is the cross-bolt block, also known as the X-block or 4-bolt mains block which has not been used in production at all but can be obtained from certain specialists which are produced from time to time by the Factory for 'competition purposes'. They have special main bearing caps which are not only located by the usual pair of bolts going vertically into the block but are also held in place by a bolt coming through the block wall, near the sump line, into the main bearing cap from either side. This adds to the block's rigidity as well as firmly locating the main bearing caps. Cross-bolt blocks were originally made by BL Motorsport for the Triumph TR7 V8 rallying programme, adopted by Land-Rover for the 'Iceberg' diesel engine project and subsequently produced more recently by Land-Rover for the Paris-Dakar engines. For racing it is undoubtedly the best block to use, although perfectly good racing engines have been built without them and they are not readily available. Some engine builders resort to using a block strengthening plate or 'girdle'. These may be cast or machined from alloy and incorporate

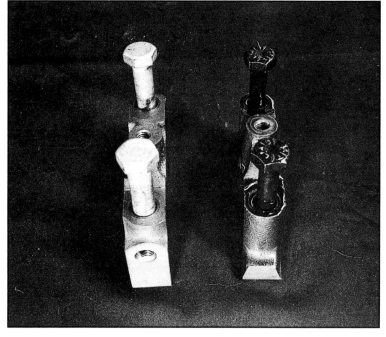

A rare 4-bolt main bearing block, also referred to as an X-bolt or cross bolt block. The ultimate for racing.

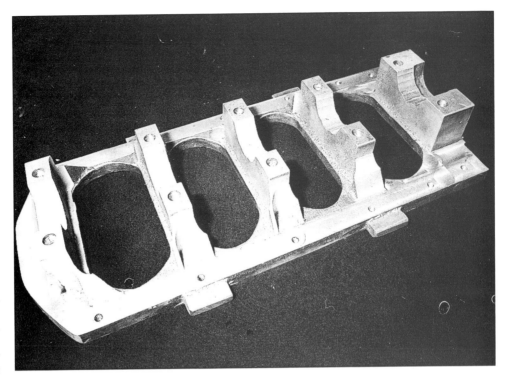

A prototype cylinder block 'girdle' designed by J E Motors, incorporating main bearing caps. (Not fully machined)

Main bearing caps. On the right a standard 2-bolt cap. On the left a 4-bolt cap with threads for bolts coming into the cap through the side of the block.

the main bearing caps, requiring the block to be line bored after fitting. Others are cut from steel plate and bolted to the block at the sump line. The object in both cases is to add rigidity in this critical area.

Some blocks (both 2-and 4-bolt) produced by BL Motorsport cannot be used with hydraulic camshafts and lifters because the appropriate oil passages have not been machined into them. It is also possible to 'stud' the deck surfaces of the Rover V8 block although the machining involved is expensive. This not only provides excellent cylinder head location but it can also save a valuable, modified block from the scrap heap if the head bolt threads become damaged or worn excessively through repeated rebuilding.

The bearing caps on a Rover V8 are cast iron and if the engine has been subjected to excessively high rpm they fret against the block, a phenomenon which can be easily recognised when the bearing caps are removed. Block alignment can be checked simply by inserting a known straight crankshaft, tightening down the caps and noting whether the crank rotates freely. It is also worth checking that both deck heights are equal by measuring them from the axis of the crankshaft, but remember that no more than 0.030″ can be removed from the face of the block or cylinder heads before inlet manifold alignment becomes a problem. Bore finish on the standard engine is straightforward

honing to a cross hatch pattern but bore finish is very important to good oil consumption and plateau honing is highly recommended. With aluminium block and cast liners it is not necessary to use deck plates when machining.

There are one or two procedures that should be followed when preparing a block for engine assembly which will assist engine lubrication. Most important is the careful enlargement of all oil drain-back holes in the cylinder heads and lifter gallery area. A couple of hours working with a grinder to remove all traces of casting flash – which will also prevent the slight risk of any of it breaking off and falling into the engine – and polishing all the rough or sharp edges from the block internals will assist the drain-back of oil to the sump. Another trick is to radius the inside of the angle where two drilled oil passages meet with a small grinding wheel, in particular the two oil holes visible in the front of the block when the front cover is removed. Also drill a couple of holes through the front lifter gallery bridge into the timing gear area, this not only helps return oil to the sump but adds lubrication to the timing gears. If the block has been rebored or relined for larger capacity check the lower edge of the liners and deburr if necessary. Remember to thoroughly wash the cylinder block after any machining work and replace any core plugs and oil gallery plugs including the Welch plugs.

167

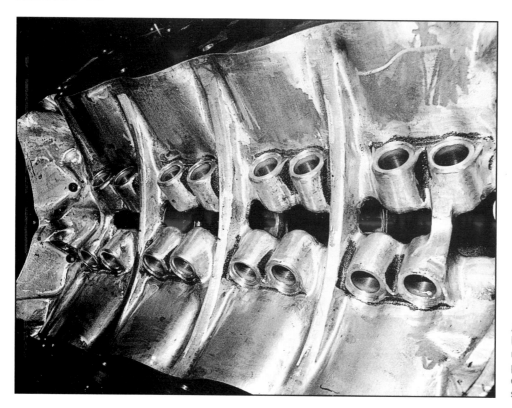

A fully race prepared lifter gallery with all the upper surfaces polished to aid rapid oil drainback to the sump.

The compression ratio of the engine is stamped by the factory on the block. On early engines the stamp can be found on the rear of the block above the bellhousing flange and on later engines it is on the left-hand deck surface, visible between the middle two cylinders when looking down through the exhaust manifold on that side. However, the compression ratio is not dependent on the block or cylinder heads but on the pistons.

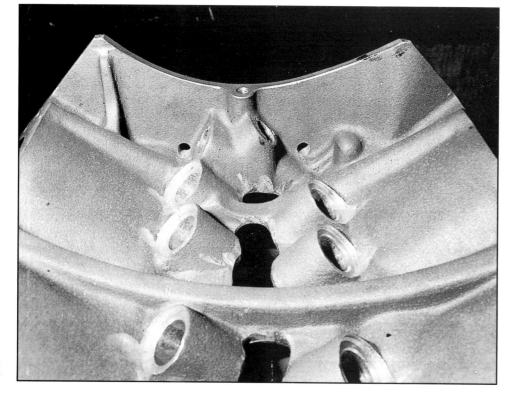

The lifter gallery, looking towards the front of the block. Note the two small holes drilled to aid oil drainback and timing chain lubrication.

A 'stroker' crankshaft. These cranks, originally designed for a diesel version of the Rover V8 can be machined for 77mm or 80mm stroke.

Carillo steel connecting rods for the Rover are probably the best money can buy, but the best does not come cheaply.

CRANKSHAFT

There is really only one sensible choice here and that is the standard item. This cast spheroidal graphite iron, five bearing crankshaft has proved capable of putting up with virtually anything the engine builders and tuners can dream up, once checked, polished and tuftrided. However, one cannot stress too strongly the importance of having the crank, along with the conrods, pistons, flywheel and front pulley properly balanced if you intend to rev the engine beyond 6000 rpm for anything other than occasional bursts. Because the Rover V8 in production form is not a high revving engine the factory balancing has only ever been sufficient to meet production requirements. Group A racing partic-

ularly in the European Touring Car Championship 'endurance' races was probably the severest test for the standard crank, but anything other than the standard crank is illegal in Group A regulations, so they were fillet rolled on all the journals and then ionized and apart from isolated cases, crankshaft failure was never a weakness of the engine. In racing and rallying, the standard crankshaft, properly prepared, has regularly withstood 8000 rpm. For racing, the oil supply is improved to the main bearing by cross-drilling, ie. the existing oil journal holes are drilled completely through, resulting in an additional opening located 180 degrees opposite the original. Also, instead of one half only of the main bearing having an oil groove in it, the other half is also grooved, achieving 360-degree oiling of the bearings. This practice is not of course unique to the Rover V8. Vandervell can supply heavy duty bearings for the Rover V8.

Steel crankshafts were made (forged, not machined from billet) but they were never legally homologated for any racing class and are now very rare. Even rarer are the small number of flat plane crankshafts (machined from solid) that were made for experimental purposes by Austin Rover Motorsport. There are still a number in existence but they really rank amongst the 'exotica'.

CONNECTING RODS

The standard Rover V8 connecting rod is an alloy steel forging with a press fit gudgeon (or wrist) pin. In keeping with the engine's reputation for possessing a strong bottom end, the connecting rods are very good for most performance applications and are safe to 7000 rpm if tuftrided, carefully checked and prepared. Group A rods are exactly the same in appearance, and are forged from the same pattern, but in stronger EN24 material, weighing 540 – 546 gms as opposed to the standard rod's 501 – 509 gms. There are also Cosworth forged steel rods (actually Chevrolet Vega forgings), slightly longer than the standard item which can be an advantage with a higher revving engine.

Another alternative is the Chevrolet small block connecting rod from the 1964–67 327 cu. in. engine, which has an identical 2.0 inch journal size but must

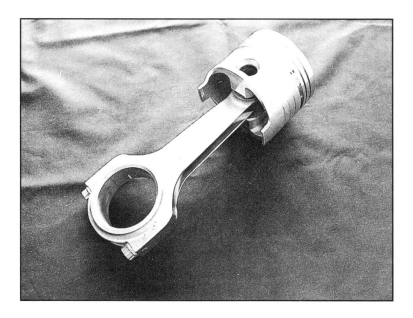

have about 0.100″ removed from the offset sides to fit correctly. The centre-to-centre length is only slightly longer at 5.7″ on the Chevy compared with 5.660″ on the Rover, which might involve removing some material from the top of the piston to maintain a given compression ratio, depending on the piston used. This also opens up all sorts of expensive possibilities for using Chevrolet-sized Carillo steel rods which are probably the best available (at a price) and even aluminium rods although they have restricted fatigue resistance which makes them only suitable for sprint type competition events.

PISTONS

The pistons used on a Rover V8 engine determine the compression ratio so it is not necessary to machine either the block deck faces or cylinder heads. On any V8 engine such machining will effect manifold alignment, although if the engine is fitted with quadruple downdraught or sidedraught carburettors with their independent manifolds, this is not critical. Everyone agrees that the closer the pistons go to the cylinder heads at the top of the stroke the better for power, but as a general rule the compression ratio should be kept below 10:1 for road use.

Having said that, one of the most often used methods of boosting performance on an SD1 engine is to install a set of 10.5:1 cast pistons from a pre-1973 engine which give a compression ratio of 10.25:1 on the SD1 engine because of the slightly greater combustion chamber volume. Any of the standard cast Rover pistons can be used and over the years engines have been built with a variety of compression ratios so there is a wide choice. Being cast they have their limitations but certainly a set of cast pistons are well up to the task on a tuned engine provided it is not going to be revved beyond 6000 rpm, except for the occasional burst. The main problem with standard cast pistons is that relatively little material joins the piston crown to the skirt and they can separate under stress. There are other cast pistons available, from Omega for instance, which are of stronger design and available with valve cutouts in the crown for use with high lift camshafts. Forged pistons are more expensive and have to run greater skirt-to-bore clearance

which can mean a slightly noisier engine.

There are a wide variety of cast and forged pistons available, both with flat tops and raised crowns, with and without valve cut-outs from manufacturers such as Omega, Cosworth, Mahle and Venolia. Choice really depends on the desired compression ratio (Group A race engines ran 11:1 +), intended engine operating rpm, camshaft used and the budget involved.

CYLINDER HEADS

There are only two different cylinder head castings for the Rover V8. One casting was used up to the introduction of the new

Standard Rover V8 piston is adequate up to 6000 rpm, above that there is a risk of them cracking.

A stronger 'performance' Rover cast piston with valve cutouts for valve clearance when high lift camshaft is used.

Rover 3500 (SD1) in 1976, using 12.7 mm reach spark plugs and known as 'pre-SD1' heads. The other was first used on the new Rover 3500, uses 19 mm reach plugs and is known as the SD1 head. The Vitesse cylinder head is identical to the SD1 head except for the valves which are uniquely Vitesse and some very slight differences in the port area although the casting is the same. The principal difference between all three heads – pre-SD1, SD1 and Vitesse is the valves. The pre-SD1 head had 38 mm inlet valves and 33 mm exhaust valves while the SD1 head has 40 mm inlet and 34 mm exhaust. The Vitesse valves are the same diameter as those on the SD1 head but are waisted behind the head of the valve ie. more material is removed from the tapered area behind the head of the

A Rover V8 piston selection. Left, 4.2-litre standard, centre, 4.4-litre flat, right, 4.2-litre competition forged piston.

A fully modified and polished big valve combustion chamber.

Group A piston with raised crown for high compression and valve cutouts for valve clearance.

valve and a short way up the valve stem. In addition the throat area behind the valve is slightly larger (about 0.040") and the valve is recessed slightly further into the cylinder head (about 0.120"). However, Vitesse valves are weaker than standard SD1, causing problems in early Group A racing engines, although this should never cause a problem on a road engine. The factory have now abandoned Vitesse valves on the fuel injected engine (or EFi) used on the Range Rover. The actual port shape on both head castings is virtually the same and was only altered on the SD1 head to achieve smooth flow behind the slightly larger valves.

For performance the Vitesse cylinder head is the best, although in fairness the pre-SD1 heads are not that bad and the

Inlet Ports – those on the right are standard. Those on the left have been enlarged and polished to the limits of the casting.

Exhaust Ports – standard at the bottom of the picture, fully ported, and polished at the top.

SD1 are only marginally better and may be fitted with the Vitesse valves. Likewise, SD1 valves can be fitted to pre-SD1 heads, but they are not a straight swap; there is machining involved. If one intends to modify a pair of cylinder heads then it is best to start with a pair of the SD1 type but there are no hard and fast rules on port and combustion chamber modifications.

There is certainly not an abundance of surplus material separating the ports from the coolant passages, so creative port shapes and profiles are not really possible, although here again the SD1 type head casting is slightly superior. Modified heads are available from several Rover V8 specialists and the extent to which they are modified largely depends on how much you are prepared to spend. Some are

Crane camshafts for the Rover V8. Crane produce eleven different profiles for the engine and are very popular.

simply gas flowed with standard sized valves; others have enlarged ports (they cannot be enlarged that much), polished combustion chambers, bulleted and shortened valve guides, altered valve seats and larger valves. The largest appear to be 43 mm inlet and 37 mm exhaust as fitted to a pair of J E Motors 'Big Valve' heads. To fit them, valve guides of larger than standard o.d. are fitted in holes drilled with a greater centre-to-centre distance between inlet and exhaust. New valve seats also have to be fitted. This offsets the new valves away from each other thus allowing the larger head diameters to fit. However, such big valves are more effective with enlarged bore sizes as this reduces the shrouding effect of the cylinder walls.

It should also be stressed that extensively reworked heads are not only very expensive but ultimate engine breathing only becomes critical at high rpm and 'competition' heads are not suitable or practical for road use. Modified cylinder heads will not, in isolation, yield that much more power. Like any area of engine tuning, they must be part of a unified tuning plan but they do enable the engine to exploit the full benefit of better camshafts and induction and exhaust systems.

There is another area open to exploration in the search for better engine breathing and that is adoption of the aluminium cylinder head used on the 1964 Buick 300 engine. Although the Buick 300 engine had a cast iron block the 1964 version had aluminium heads with a combustion chamber volume of 54 cc, larger ports and valves which can be bolted to the Rover block using 4 bolts around each cylinder and the Buick 300 head gasket. Apparently it is also possible to fit 45.7 m (TRW/Volvo) inlet valves on these heads too but finding a pair of them might be another matter!

Valves – left to right: A Vitesse exhaust valve, J E Engineering large inlet and exhaust valve, Group A inlet and exhaust valve.

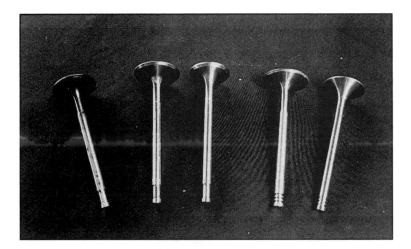

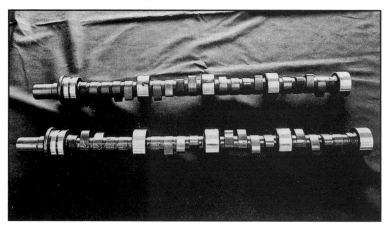

CAMSHAFT & VALVE GEAR

Unfortunately, there are no hard and fast rules or standardized combinations in engine tuning and this applies more readily to the subject of camshafts than any other. There is a huge range of camshafts available for the Rover V8, from uprated road, through fast road, semi or club competition, specialist competition, to ultimate full race. In practice this means that depending on the camshaft selected and assuming that the rest of the engine has been built to be compatible with that camshaft one can go from a moderately powerful engine with an even tick-over and smooth, tractable power delivery over a wide power band that is a positive delight to drive on the road, to an engine that will barely tick-over at all, coughs, splutters and stumbles at low rpm, making it virtually undriveable in traffic, hardly produces any power unless the rpm are well up but pulls like a train when revving at 5000 rpm, requiring frequent gearchanges and a clear road ahead!

Of course all engine tuning is a compromise and a camshaft must be selected to suit the specific application of the engine and the vehicle it is to power. There is a tremendous variety of camshafts currently available for the Rover V8 and there appears to be considerably more development mileage left in this area too. The Camshaft Chart in this Chapter details a wide range of those available from leading suppliers but it is by no means comprehensive. If one is rebuilding a high mileage engine the camshaft will almost certainly be worn and in need of replacement anyway and a camshaft change is probably the single biggest improving factor when tuning an engine so it pays to give plenty of thought to the subject before making a final choice. If the camshaft is for a regularly used road car and its use will not involve any other engine modifications, the choice will be limited to fairly mild camshaft designs. At the other extreme, if it is intended that the engine is to be supercharged then a high-lift, short duration camshaft, such as a '½-race' type, is recommended by some tuners as ideal.

Manufacturers sometimes make claims for specific gains in horsepower if a particular camshaft is used, but these figures will vary according to the engine in which the camshaft is fitted and what other modifications have been made to that engine. There are no hard and fast rules.

When Vandervell did their comprehensive development work on the GKN 47D special the camshaft they used was an Iskenderian 282HY which had valve timing of 36/76/76/36, valve lift of 0.440″ and duration of 282°. This was an hydraulic lifter cam and was supplied to Vandervell with anti-pump up lifters but adjustable pushrods. With some minor cylinder head work and a free flow exhaust on the engine, in initial 3.5-litre form it was good for nearly 200 bhp. Interestingly, this camshaft remained in production for something like 15 years, which means either Iskenderian did not update their designs very much or more likely, once they hit on a good one they stuck to it! From the sixties onwards there have been a number of American camshafts from Iskenderian, Crower, Engle, Racer Brown and the current market leader Crane but most of their grinds were based on developments for other engines such as the bigger Buick 300 or even the Chevrolet small-block. One camshaft that was developed specifically and very successfully for the Rover V8, especially in fuel injected form, was the BL Motorsport WL-9. This has valve timing of 19/57/57/19, valve lift of 0.435/0.430″ and duration of 256°. This camshaft is still available through specialists. One of the most popular camshafts for road engines was the Crane H214, now superseded by the H216, and also popular is the Piper HR270 (or its Mk11 version the HR270/2). Both these camshafts can be fitted to the engine without other modifications, a weekend swap on the driveway, and with BAF needles in the SUs will produce instant additional power and even improve fuel consumption.

The standard Rover V8 camshaft has not changed throughout the engine's life and has a lift of 0.390″. The pre-SD1

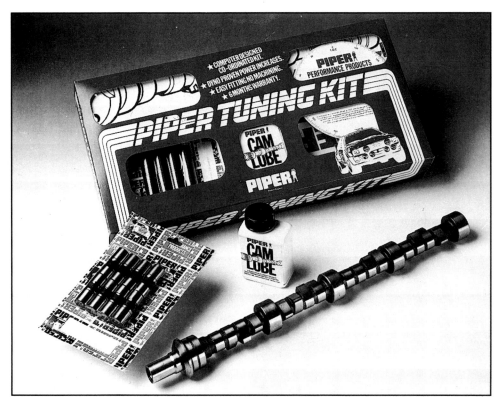

A Piper camshaft kit – Piper produce five different camshaft designs for the Rover V8.

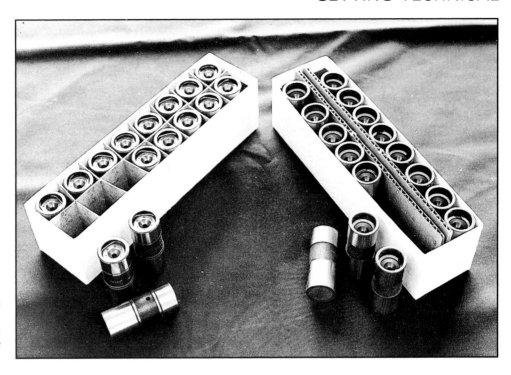

Crane camshaft followers (or lifters). Hydraulic 'Hi-Rev' on the left, solid on the right.

Crane roller rockers for the Rover V8. The roller acting on the tip of the valve reduces friction and wear.

engines used double (interference fit) valve springs but the SD1 engine went over to single valve springs. They are perfectly satisfactory in the production application, and for one to break does not necessarily mean a dropped valve, but if an aftermarket camshaft is to be fitted with anything exceeding that 0.390″ lift they have to be changed. In fact if the engine is intended for anything other than normal road use they really should be changed. Many of the Rover V8 specialists have their own double valve springs, interference fit, with an opposite wound inner spring, often referred to as 'heavy duty'. The ultimate valve springs for the Rover V8 are Schmitthelm, as used on the Group A racing engines, but these are 'exotic' and for normal performance applications a good quality set of heavy duty double valve springs with matching caps and collets are sufficient. When installing new valve springs it is important to ensure that they are right for the camshaft. If too weak, the cam followers will have difficulty following the profile of the camshaft lobe, too strong and they will sap engine power and cause rapid camshaft and lifter wear. Refer closely to the valve spring requirements of the camshaft selected and the valve spring installed height.

The camshaft manufacturer will know whether machining or other alterations are required to an engine in order to be able to operate with certain camshafts. High lift (or 'wild') camshafts bring with them problems. For instance if a camshaft with a valve lift of say 0.460″ is used on an unmodified cylinder head almost certainly the valve spring will be compressed to such an extent that it will become coil bound ie. the spring coils will be crushed against one another resulting in breakages or the valve collet will hit the top of the valve guide with equally expensive results. In addition, the higher lift will push the valve further down into the cylinder to the extent that it may strike the top of the piston (which will be on its way up). It does not take a degree in physics to realise that two engine components trying to occupy the same space at the same time will often as not end up lying side by side in the

175

sump! There are also problems of possible rocker arm interference on full lift and the need to maintain correct valve gear geometry which has to be taken into consideration.

So over a certain valve lift the valve spring seat in the cylinder head may have to be recessed, to give the spring more room and the valve guide may have to be reduced in height. The 'installed height' of the valve spring must be set exactly as per the camshaft specification (shimmed if necessary) and lastly, pistons with valve reliefs must be installed or appropriate reliefs machined into the existing pistons.

Cam followers, tappets or 'lifters' as they are referred to in the States are another area for careful consideration. One often repeated piece of advice, but equally often ignored, is *never* change a camshaft without fitting a new set of followers or in no time at all you will have to replace both – again. The standard SD1-type Rover hydraulic items are perfectly adequate up to 6200 rpm and are always worth using on a road car because they require no

maintenance, are quiet in operation and will act as a rev limiter. After about 5500 rpm they tend to pump up, eventually holding the valves open slightly. The next stage is hi-rev lifters which resist this pumping up until higher rpm (eg 6800 rpm) are reached. They are made by Crane but also available as 'heavy duty' lifters from Auto Power Services, Oselli and others. Always soak new hydraulic lifters

This is the 4.2-litre engine in the TVR 420 SEAC racing sports car. The valve gear has large diameter rocker shaft, steel Volvo adjustable rockers and steel rocker shaft pillars.

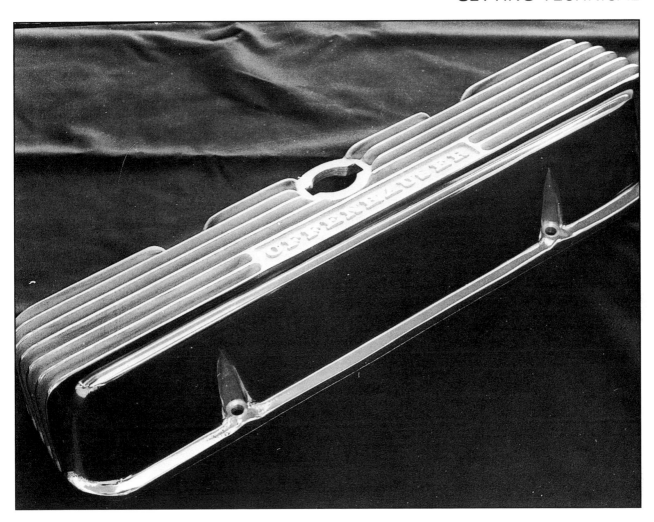

The finishing touch. Polished alloy Offenhauser rocker covers, originally cast for the Buick engine but available for the Rover V8.

Cloyes 'True-Roller' matching timing set. Crank sprocket has three keyways for precise valve timing.

in engine oil for as long as is practical before fitting – days if possible. For engines operating at higher rpm solid lifters must be used, again available from Crane and with them comes the necessity of being able to adjust the tappet clearance. This is usually accomplished by using Crane adjustable pushrods but systems have been devised to use rockers with adjusters. For instance both Crane and Titan make adjustable rockers (the Crane is a cast alloy, anodized roller rocker) but neither work quite correctly, being something of a compromise and need very careful assembly with possible grinding in places to achieve satisfactory clearance and action. The Group A system is good, it uses bigger diameter shafts, steel pillars and a cast steel rocker with normal type adjustment, in fact a Bahco type Volvo 144 rocker was originally adapted but such setups are no longer widely available. The standard rocker arms are alloy and satisfactory but steel ones are available if heavier duty use is envisaged and the standard alloy rocker shaft pillars are more than ade-

quate for hydraulic cams. Here again, steel pillars are available, BL Motorsport used fabricated ones, but they are expensive. The rocker shaft can be replaced with a tuftrided item at little extra cost over the standard items. The standard Rover pushrods are okay for any road engine, in fact they have even been used on engines built to a very high state of tune without causing problems.

The standard Rover timing gears are "adequate" under most road applications, being a Morse type silent chain with only a nylon toothed alloy camshaft sprocket. As a first step this can be replaced with steel but special steel sets with Duplex chain are available from such manufacturers as Cloyes. Auto Power Services can supply a heavy duty steel gear set with Duplex chain which includes a nylon thrust button on the bolt that fixes the timing gear on the end of the camshaft. This thrust button acts against the inside of the front cover and restricts 'end float' – the forward movement of the camshaft in the block.

177

Make	Number	Timing	Period	Valve lift	Lifters	Class	Comments
Oselli	RV8255	22/62/62/22	264°	.421"	Hyd.	Mild Road	Extra low and mid end power. Good for towing/load carrying.
Oselli	RV8271	28/64/64/28	272°	.439"	Hyd.	Road	Improves mid and top end power. Good flexibility.
Oselli	RV8214	31/73/80/34	284/294°	.469"/.494"	Hyd.	Road	Good all round improvement.
Oselli	RV8286	44/72/72/44	296°	.439"	Hyd.	Road	Excellent road cam. Ideal for fuel injected engines.
Oselli	RV8480	36/76/76/36	292°	.480"	Hyd.	Fast Road	Extra mid and top end power. Ultimate for auto-transmission.
Oselli	RV8502	37/77/77/37	294°	.495"	Hyd.	Road/Rally	Slightly lumpy tickover. Good power 2000 rpm upwards.
Oselli	RV8224	36/78/85/39	294/304°	.494"/.520"	Hyd.	Road/Rally	Extended top end power with up to 7000 rpm
Oselli	RV 84	35/71/71/35	286°	.516"	Hyd.	Rally	Good all round competition cam. Power band 2500-7000 rpm
Oselli	RV8481	42/82/82/42	304°	.496 "	Hyd.	Rally	Poor low end tractability. Power band 3000-7000 rpm
Oselli	RV8234	38/80/87/41	298/308°	.520"/.542"	Hyd.	Rally	Poor idle and low end but excellent power over 3500 rpm

Make	Number	Timing	Period	Valve lift	Lifters	Class	Comments
Oselli	RV8500	46/82/82/46	308°	.542″	Hyd .	Race	Ultimate hyd. camshaft. Power band 4000-7000 rpm
Oselli	RV8900	42/78/78/42	300°	.500″	Solid	Rally	Poor tickover. Excellent mid and top range power.
Oselli	RV8100	47/83/83/47	310°	.530″	Solid	Race	Maximum power for full race spec. engine. High rpm.
Kent	H180	28/64/64/28	272°	.439″	Hyd.	Mild Road	Good for automatics Power band 1000-4500 rpm
Kent	H200	20/64/69/25	264°	.435″/.460″	Hyd	Mild Road	For pre-SD1. Also good for automatics.
Kent	H214	31/73/80/34	284°	.469″/.494″	Hyd.	Fast Road	Very flexible. Power from 1500-5000 rpm. Good road camshaft.
Kent	H224	36/78/85/39	294°	.494/.520″	Hyd.	Road Rally	Slight loss of flexibility. Power comes in 2000-5500 rpm.
Kent	H234	38/80/87/41	298°	.520″/.542″	Hyd.	Rally	Poor low end, but improves mid and top end power.
Kent	GPA	44/76/76/44	300°	.390″	Hyd.	Rally	Same valve lift as standard engine (.390″)
Kent	M238	42/78/78/42	300°	.512″	Solid	Rally	Higher rpm use. Power band from 2750-7000 rpm.
Kent	M248	48/82/84/46	310°	.533″	Solid	Rally/Race	High rpm camshaft. Power band from 3500-8000 rpm
Kent	M256	42/70/83/39	310°	.546″/.564″	Solid	Race	Ultimate race cam. Full race engine only. Power 4000-8250 rpm.
Piper	HR270	22/62/64/28	264°/272°	.421″/.439″	Hyd	Road	Flexible with good mid and top end improvement.

Make	Number	Timing	Period	Valve lift	Lifters	Class	Comments
Piper	HR270/2	28/64/64/28	272°	.440″	Hyd.	Fast Road	Mk11 of above cam.
Piper	HR285	44/72/72/44	296°	.439″	Hyd.	Fast Road	Ultimate road cam. Tractable but slightly lumpy tickover.
Piper	HR300	36/68/68/36	284°	.440″	Solid	Competition	Accent on mid-range power. Power band 3000-7000 rpm.
Piper	HR320	52/84/84/52	316°	.471″	Solid	Race	Mid and top end power. Excellent circuit race cam.
Crane	H-194	10/54/59/15	244/254°	.400″/.430″	Hyd.	Road	Economy cam only. Not to be used with comp. ratio over 8.75:1
Crane	H-204	15/59/65/21	254/266°	.430″/.456″	Hyd.	Mild Road	Improvement over standard cam. Can be straight swap.
Crane	H-216	21/65/71/27	266/278°	.456″/.480″	Hyd.	Road	Excellent all rounder. Good power increase across rev. range.
Crane	H-224	36/78/85/39	294/304°	.494″/.520″	Hyd.	Fast Road	Slightly lumpy idle. Good for lighter vehicles eg. sports cars.
Crane	H-234	38/80/877/41	298/308°	.520″/.542″	Hyd.	Road/Comp.	Ultimate hyd. cam but compromise in road car.
Crane	F-228	38/72/74/36	290°	.491″	Solid	Road	Particularly suitable for turbo or supercharging.
Crane	F-238	42/78/78/42	300°	.512″	Solid	Road/Comp.	Wide power band. Does not need high rpm.
Crane	F-248	48/82/84/46	310°	.533″	Solid	Rally	Wide power band. Works well with Holley 4-barrel carb.
Crane	F-256	42/70/83/39	292/302°	.546″/.564″	Solid	Competition	Good mid and top end power.

Comment	Number	Timing	Period	Valve lift	Lifters	Class	Comments
Crane	F-266	47/75/88/44	302/312°	.564"/.584"	Solid	Competition	Out and out power. Engine must be capable of high rpm.
Crane	F-276	52/80/93/49	312/322°	.584"/.602"	Solid	Competition	Radical race engines only. The ultimate.
JE Motors	JE101	20/65/25/20	265/225°	.430"	Hyd.	Road	
JE Motors	JE102	43/79/79/43	302°	.500"	Hyd.	Fast Road	Good power from 3000-6500 rpm. Peak torque 5000 rpm
Holbay	111R	39/73/73/39	292°	.429"	Hyd.	Fast Road	The Tornado
Holbay	125LHC	40/84/89/45	304/314°	.520"/.541"	Hyd.	Competition	Designed for maximum performance within rpm limits of hyd. lifters.
Holbay	K3A	58/88/74/50	326/304°	.432"	Solid	Competition	High torque design.
Holbay	751R	63/95/95/63	338°	.451"	Solid	Competition	Maximum bhp at higher rpm.
Rover	Standard	30/75/68/37	285°	.390"/.385"	Hyd.	Production	3.5-litre (SD1)
Rover	Standard	32/73/70/35	285°	.390"	Hyd.	Production	3.9-litre (designation ETC 8686)
Rover	Standard	28/77/66/39	285°	.390"	Hyd.	Production	4.0-litre (designation ERR 3720)
Rover	Standard	14/70/64/20	264°	.416"	Hyd.	Production	4.6-litre (designation ERR 5250)

ROVER V8

ENGINE LUBRICATION

There is nothing remarkable about the standard Rover V8 lubrication system and if certain precautions are taken to ensure it always has plenty of clean oil to pump will prove sufficient to preserve an engine up to 7000 rpm, assuming of course that the rest of the engine is up to it! It is of course wet sump, with oil pumped around the internals of the engine by a gear pump which feeds oil under pressure to the crankshaft and camshaft bearings, hydraulic tappets, the bearings on the rocker shafts and the skew gear (distributor drive) on the camshaft nose. The gudgeon pin, timing chain and cylinder walls are all splash fed. The standard oil pressure is 35 lbs/in², nominal at 2400 rpm.

The lubrication system was improved for the SD1 engine by improving the skew gear drive to the oil pump and more rigidly supporting the pump shaft to avoid binding. Sump baffling was improved in anticipation of higher cornering forces and the oil capacity raised.

The oil pump gears are driven off the end of the distributor shaft which is itself driven by a pair of skew gears, one on the distributor shaft and one on the end of the camshaft. Any attempt to uprate the oil pump by increasing its volume or oil pressure increases the load on these gears. It follows that anyone attempting to do either of these things is intending to use the engine in some kind of higher rpm performance application and at anything over 5500 rpm the wear rate on the skew gears is alarming. It has been described as the 'Achilles heel' of the engine and under certain circumstances it is. Sets of replacement gears are available, made from much harder material (J E Motors do a set in EN36B nitrided material as used on the Group A Rovers) but even these will wear under the circumstances described above. J E Motors have found that an external oil feed, taken from the top of the oil filter mounting to a hole drilled and tapped in the front cover, squirting oil directly on to the gears is a great help and an easy modification to carry out.

Group A Rover Vitesse racing engines were prevented from using dry-sump systems by the regulations but raced successfully with the standard oil pump with the relief valve altered to 60 psi. They also had the oil supply to the top end of the engine (the valve gear) restricted by as much as 80% because even after careful block preparation to enlarge all the drain-back

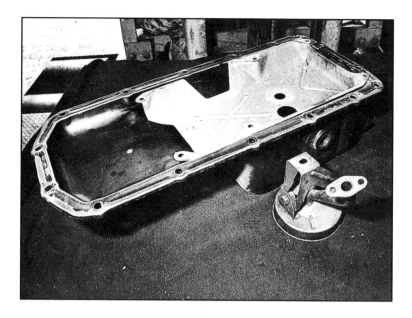

areas the engine still has a tendency to retain oil in the vicinity of the valve gear in competition conditions, to the detriment of the bearings. In these circumstances the only alternative is to fit a large capacity sump. The standard steel pressing can be cut, reshaped with additional fabricated 'wings' and suitably baffled depending on the space available or Auto Power Services can supply large capacity sumps up to 16 pints for various applications. If you can locate one and are prepared to pay, there are also some Group A sumps still available which probably represent state of the art wet sump lubrication.

The Rover V8 does not like modern lightweight oils, in fact 5W – 50 oil could, under certain circumstances be detrimental to the engine. Thin oil cannot be

Standard Rover SD1 sump, showing baffle and oil pick-up.

Modified and baffled Range Rover sump. In the right foreground is a modified oil pickup with additional locating stay.

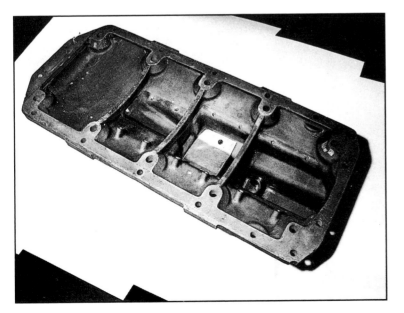

The ultimate Group A wet sump for the racing Rover Vitesse.

A genuine 'Works' cast alloy dry sump pan for the Rover V8.

Increasing or uprating the oil pump volume simply increases the load on those vital skew gears although it is worthwhile uprating the pump on the pre-SD1 engines with an uprating kit.

The ultimate lubrication for the Rover V8, as with any competition engine, is a dry-sump system, although B/L Motorsport found that even this was not without its problems. They eventually had to resort to a twin scavenge pump and a windage tray to make their system completely effective. The V8 engineers at Rover, Solihull evaluated windage trays in the light of information fed back to them from the TR7 V8 rally programme but found nothing to be gained by using them on a production engine. A good dry-sump system will actually add horsepower to a competition engine, as well as eliminating the problem of distributor drive gear wear.

Auto Power Services offer a complete dry-sump lubrication kit, with mild steel sump, pump and tank but the cost of such a system makes it a serious competition option only. Also available are cast alloy sumps as used on the works dry-sump systems, which add considerable rigidity to the lower half of the block. Most Rover specialists can supply all the necessary parts for converting a Rover V8 to dry-sump, J E Motors have been manufacturing their own alloy sumps for some time, or alternatively your engine can be taken along and converted for you.

pumped in volume in the same way as heavier oils, although the pressure will be maintained. For competition purposes try to use straight SAE 30 or 40 oil although *the* oil for the Rover V8 under serious competition stress is Motul V300. It is not cheap but its reputation amongst Rover V8 engine builders speaks for itself. The oil temperature is not critical, but ideally should be kept about 10° hotter than the water temperature which needs to be around 80–85°C. As the water temperature rises above that, the power output falls off alarmingly.

The standard oil pressure is perfectly adequate for most applications unless the engine is to be revved beyond 7000 rpm and if hydraulic lifters are being retained anything higher will pump up the lifters.

CARBURATION

Two popular misconceptions regarding induction systems for the Rover V8 should be dispelled immediately. One is that the standard twin SU carburettor and Rover manifold are no good for a performance engine. Perhaps for some the sight of a pair of good old SUs on a well prepared engine does not have the same visual impact as other, more sophisticated systems but they should not be dismissed so easily. They can be tuned to a certain extent and they can provide good power and torque on an engine which has received a camshaft change and other tuning. Even the humble Stromberg is acceptable for a mildly tuned road engine but the lack of a good range of needles makes it much less useful than the SU.

The second fallacy concerns the Holley 4-barrel carburettor, which admittedly

ROVER V8

The standard pair of SU carburettors can be used on a mildly tuned engine and made to look good too.

looks great, has a very low profile even with an air cleaner which helps when under bonnet clearance is a problem and is relatively easy to install and set up. It has been suggested that people who have problems with the Holley just do not understand how to 'tune' them and to a certain extent this is true, but the general concensus is that the Holley is indeed a good instrument generally, but on the Rover V8 it gives poor mixture distribution at low rpm and suffers too many flat spots over a wider rpm range. This is really more a problem of poor manifolds than bad carburettor design but its popularity far exceeds its suitability for road use. It is however an excellent budget setup for competition use, with the right manifold and can be tuned effectively within its limitations. More on this later.

So, the standard pair of SU carburettors on the Rover manifold can be used in combination with a fairly mild camshaft and other budget tuning to increase the power and torque of the engine without spending a fortune. The biggest restriction with SUs is the standard BL-type air cleaners which must be replaced with a good pair of free flow filters such as those made by K & N. Tuning with new needles (perhaps BAF or BCA) and springs, depending on the other modifications carried out, will be adequate for nearly 200 bhp, when used in conjunction with a good 'road' camshaft and modestly reworked cylinder heads. Also they help retain good fuel

The Holley 4160 – 390 cfm 4-barrel carburettor, probably the most widely used carb for Rover V8 tuning.

economy, a point not to be overlooked when running a V8 engine. The 2" SU carburettor works even better and a pair from a Rover 2000TC or Jaguar, with some minor modifications will bolt straight on to the Rover manifold. Rovertec in Leicester will carry out the work for a reasonable fee.

The Holley 4-barrel is available in a variety of sizes for the Rover V8, ranging from 390 cfm (cubic feet per minute) to 600 cfm. They have two of the four barrels (or venturi) opening via a mechanical linkage from the accelerator – the primary throttles – with the other two being actuated by inlet manifold vacuum – the secondary throttles – although it is possible to

The Offenhauser 360° manifold for the Rover V8. Actually a Buick/Oldsmobile design it can mount a Holley 4-barrel or pair of Webers with an adaptor.

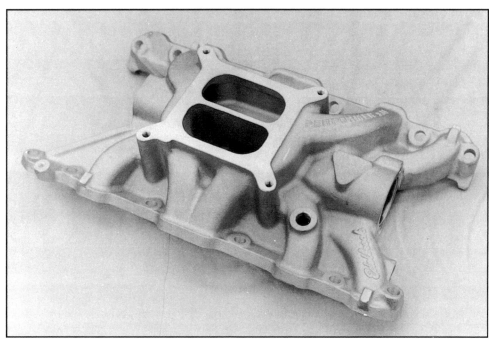

The superb Edelbrock Performer manifold improves upper rpm power.

have both linked and operating mechanically but this is really only done for competition applications. Some Holleys have accelerator pumps on the primaries and secondaries and these are known as 'double pumpers'.

Since the Holley carburettor is such a popular choice for the Rover engine it might be worth while just clarifying how they should be set up and what can be done to 'tune' them to individual engines. The Holley is a very straightforward instrument but being from America (where it is

VERY popular) it is not fully understood by many. The size of carburettor you need for your engine is calculated thus: multiply the cubic inches of the engine by the maximum rpm the engine is likely to operate at (be honest!) by 0.85. The figure 0.85 represents the theoretical thermal efficiency of the engine and you can go up to 0.90 if the engine is built to racing standards. Divide the resultant figure by 3456 and you will arrive at the cfm rating of the required carburettor. A more or less standard Rover V8 already has more than adequate flow with a 390 cfm Holley 4160 series (Model 8007), which is the smallest 4-barrel in the range and probably the most popular Holley carburettor used on the Rover V8. The 350 cfm Holley is a two barrel and has poor mixture distribution with the available manifolds. Offenhauser make a manifold for the Buick version of the engine which mounts two 2-barrel Rochester carburettors but this manifold has never been made available in the UK and the carbs would not be easy to find.

Having selected the right Holley carburettor it should be fed with clean fuel at a pressure of between 4.5 and 7 psi and this should be checked. Make sure it is mounted without vacuum leaks and that all unused vacuum tubes are capped or plugged. With the engine up to operating temperature and the choke fully open the float level should be set by the external adjustment screw, with the sight plug removed. It is a very simple procedure but very important to get right as it effects the fuel metering of both the main and idle circuits within the carb. The tickover speed can then be set with the external stop. Next, the idle mixture must be set with the two screws on the sides of the metering blocks, which are sandwiched between the float chamber and the carb body. They should be adjusted, more or less equally, to obtain the highest possible tickover speed or manifold vacuum reading, after

which the tickover should be reset by the external screw. If the idle mixture screws seem to have little effect on engine rpm when turned there is either a vacuum leak somewhere or the primary throttles are having to be set too far open to get any tickover. If this is the case you will have to remove the carb and from underneath, adjust the secondary throttle so that it allows slightly more airflow. Try to adjust the secondaries so that the fuel transfer slots, cut in the body of the carb, are just visible. Eliminating any 'bogs' or hesitation during hard acceleration is the next step and for this it may be necessary to alter the diaphragm spring on the vacuum

The novel and effective 'Boxer' inlet manifold – more power and torque throughout the rev range.

Cast alloy inlet manifold to mount a pair of downdraught Dellorto carburettors. One manifold is needed for each cylinder head.

secondaries and the size of the accelerator pump squirters. Try using the next heavier spring (they are colour coded) until the hesitation clears up, then move on to the pump squirters. Incidentally, if the engine is generally not responding sharply enough to full throttle acceleration (but not actually bogging), try a slightly lighter spring. The pump squirters are numbered according to the size of their nozzles eg. No. 26 is an 0.026″ diameter nozzle. Simply increase the nozzle size, one step at a time until the hesitation clears up but try to stick with the smallest you can.

The other areas for tuning are the main circuits and power circuits but in general these should not need adjustment. Certainly the main circuits, which are controlled by jets or plates depending on the model, are best left alone. The power circuits are controlled by valves which are rated according to the manifold vacuum level maintained during tickover and can be changed to improve acceleration from tickover (or 'off-idle') but generally should be left alone. Set up properly, with a little care, and fitted with a good unrestrictive air cleaner the Holley 4-barrel can work well on a Rover V8, especially as a budget semi-competition or competition induction system.

The choice of manifolds for the Holley is rather restricted. There are two main types – the dual plane and single plane.

To begin with we will discuss the single plane and the simplest manifold for a Holley 4-barrel is the converted standard Rover item as offered by Auto Power Services. This is really a low-cost system which involves machining off the pent roof mounting for the two SUs, opening out the orifice and welding on a Holley mounting flange. The Huffaker manifold was a very popular performance manifold which uses a mild interpretation of the tunnel ram principle of raising the carburettor and having longer, curved manifold runners into the ports. It is a simple single plane (or common chamber/runner) manifold so its internal design, with one large plenum chamber beneath the carburettor supplying all the manifold runners without any baffling does make it an out-and-out competition manifold. It does work well with the Holley or even a pair of sidedraught carburettors on a 'Repco' type adaptor but has no thermostat housing or water heating and installation on the Rover would require the fabrication of some cooling system plumbing. It was used with a Holley 350 cfm 2-barrel carb on some Group 1 racing Rover SD1s in the early 1980s. There are also 'dual-plane' inlet manifolds which take the Holley which are a more practical proposition for road use, although it also makes an excellent budget competition manifold. They are divided internally so that one side of the carburettor supplies

Close-up of a Dellorto 45 mm downdraught carburettor. Equally at home on road or race engine.

Full house – quadruple down-draught Dellorto carburettors mounted on a Rover V8.

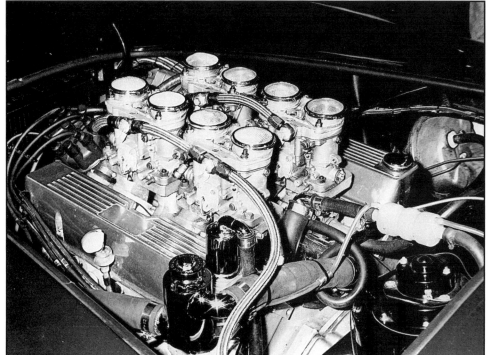

This J E Motors 3.9-litre Rover V8, with four Dellorto carburettors produces 256 bhp at 6000 rpm with torque of 251 lb/ft at 4500 rpm. It is installed in a 'BRA 289' Cobra replica.

one side of the engine, and the two sides of the manifold are not inter-connected, which is supposed to increase low and mid range throttle response. They also have internally cast water passages, although being based on a Buick design some slight work is required to fit them to the Rover engine.

The final option with the Holley is the Offenhauser/John Woolfe Racing Dual Port Manifold which is the ultimate development for road use. It is effectively two manifolds in one alloy casting, with the inside of the manifold divided horizontally with the primary mixture being fed into the bottom half of the manifold runners

heater hose clearance channel underneath, correctly positioned vacuum takeoff point and is a low profile design for better under bonnet clearance.

There is one other option for these manifolds which was used on the works Triumph TR7 V8s for a time and was always offered on BL Motorsport 'customer' engines. That is the Repco type cast adapter which bolts to the Holley flange and mounts a pair of sidedraught Weber carburettors. It is still used today but the fuel consumption is actually worse than using four correctly set up downdraught Weber/Dellortos because of the poor mixture distribution of the manifold. The

A rallycross TR7 V8 engine with four side-draught Weber carburettors on U-shaped steel manifolds.*(Bill Mantovani).*

and the secondary being fed into the top half. This means high mixture velocity on low rpm operation, through the bottom half of the manifold and when full acceleration is called for the secondary throttles open, supply mixture to the upper half of the manifold, giving maximum flow. In theory the engine gets the right mixture volume/velocity for its needs at all throttle openings. This manifold is very much for normal road use and with a good camshaft and correctly set up Holley 380 cfm 4-barrel will give a very healthy increase in horsepower and torque. It is also a direct bolt-on replacement for the Rover V8, not an adapted Buick component, having the correct water temperature sender outlet,

Works rally cars always had a problem with fuel condensing in the manifold under certain circumstances, causing the plugs to soot up, so this set-up is very much a compromise.

Once we move on from the SUs and Holleys we enter the realm of more costly induction systems. Although expensive, a good quadruple set of downdraught or sidedraught Weber or Dellorto carburettors probably represents the best value for money in terms of bhp per £ spent. Apart from the cost, these quadruple downdraughts are notorious for requiring frequent tuning. This is something of a fallacy, because although you do need eight vacuum gauges to set them up

189

ROVER V8

properly they are reliable and do not need retuning any more than any other carburettor. The physical height of downdraughts can cause underbonnet clearance problems in some applications (the TR7 V8 for example) and these problems are also accentuated by the need for a good air filter system, which can add considerable height. It is possible to mount four sidedraught Webers on steel U-shaped manifolds like those supplied by Janspeed, but they are still mounted quite high and access to the valve gear for servicing is restricted. There is also the option of sidedraughts mounted on cross-over manifolds which gives the fuel/air mixture a straighter shot at the inlet ports but the 'U' shaped manifolds are more popular, having been proved in competition by the Works rally cars.

FUEL INJECTION

The standard Rover Vitesse type fuel injected engine is an expensive proposition for the enthusiast, being used in production first in the Rover Vitesse, then the Rover SD1 Vanden Plas and now the Range Rover EFi and Vogue models. The availability of secondhand engines is fairly limited, but as the years go by this situa-

tion will change and more recently the unit is being used in an increasing number of specialist vehicles such as the Morgan and TVR sports cars. The performance potential of the unit is thus becoming of greater interest.

In production saloon racing, which has more restrictive regulations than the frequently referred to Group A, the best Rover Vitesse engines were squeezing out 218 bhp but this did not even allow a change of compression ratio. A single throttle plenum (ie. the normally available type) was good enough to fuel the 300 bhp + Group A racing engines in the Rover Vitesses. The twin-plenum injection system used on the 1986 Group A racing Rover Vitesses were even better, these racing engines producing well over 300 bhp, but it was really too much of a compromise on a road engine, actually giving too much flow at lower rpm. This system is also extremely rare, there probably being only about 200 in existence, and thus very expensive. There is an injection system available from the USA, made by Hilborn but again the cost is prohibitive and unlike other injection systems available (like the standard Rover system) was designed for the Buick/Oldsmobile engine and is totally unsuitable for road use. Besides, such power gains can be achieved without resorting to such an 'odd ball' route.

A standard Rover Vitesse fuel-injected V8 in the engine bay of a Marcos Mantula V8.

The plenum chamber base plates of a twin throttle plenum (left) and single throttle plenum (right).

From a practical point of view the Rover Vitesse/Range Rover EFi fuel injection system is probably the best option. The Lucas 'L' system owes much to the well tried Bosch L Jetronic, to which it bears some resemblance, using a similar flap type airflow meter as the main sensor. The ECU (Engine Control Unit) however, is more closely related to the Lucas 6CU 'P' system used until recently on the Jaguar V12 HE. The Bosch airflow meter is quite simple although many of its functions are rather subtle and not immediately apparent from observation. It consists of a specially profiled channel containing a pivoted and spring biased flap which is deflected by air passing through to adopt an angular position where the spring force is balanced by the force of air against the flap. The angular position of the flap is converted to a voltage via a sophisticated potentiometer and this voltage signal is converted within the ECU to a digital code, which in combination with a speed signal from the ignition coil is applied to a 'look up table' type of memory which determines the required pulse duration driven by an oscillator or clock. The various correction factors for coolant temperature, air temperature, throttle position and cranking enrichment are added by further analogue circuitry which modulates the clock frequency to extend the pulse as required.

All 'L' type ECUs are identical in appearance, apart from the Lambda sensing emission type, and are more or less interchangeable although there are some differences according to engine specification. Accuracy is greatest at the lower airflow values typical of urban use where economy is most important. A bypass channel with screw adjustment is provided for optimising the idle mixture. Acceleration enrichment is less necessary with airflow measuring systems because increased airflow is detected well before it reaches the engine, by which time the fuelling has increased accordingly. Fuel pressure is governed by a regulator with a vacuum connection off the intake plenum and at full load the pressure will be 2.5 bar (abs) but at idle this will drop to 2 bar. A cold start injection system is provided which operates independently of the main injectors, spraying a fine mist of fuel into the plenum to assist cold start up.

It should be noted that more recently, some Rover V8 engines are being fitted with a Lucas 13CU 'hot wire' mass sensing system but only for certain emission critical areas.

The vast majority of modified engines are equipped with the digital 'L' 4CU system, the 13CU system being too recent for inclusion here. When the Rover V8 EFi is modified to increase power output the injection system must be adapted to provide extra fuel. The first step is to change the standard fuel pump for one with greater capacity, then the simplest method of providing the extra fuel is to increase the fuel pressure to suit the maximum power requirement and adjustable regulators are available from various sources. This approach is not very satisfactory however, because considerable compromise must usually be accepted over much of the operating range and safety margins deteriorate as the pressure increases.

It is also possible to increase the fuelling by fiddling with the sensor signals. For instance, if extra resistance is added to the coolant sensor circuit the ECU will provide extra fuel; thinking the engine is cool. The overall effect on driveability is most unsatisfactory, aggravated by the 'L' system having the unusual characteristic of triggering acceleration fuelling with sharp changes in sensor voltage.

When a significant power increase is planned the standard injectors may be unable to flow the required quantity of fuel because as the engine speed rises the time available for the injection process becomes less. At 6000 rpm for instance, the available injector time is 10 *milliseconds* and if the pulse duration is of the same magnitude the injectors will be continuously open and the fuelling limit will have been reached. On large displacement or high revving versions of the Rover V8 engine it is therefore usual to find that black or green injectors with higher flow rates have been substituted for the standard light grey type. Again, however, the fuelling will be enriched everywhere and if part load performance is not to be compromised the fuelling must be weakened at such times.

An alternative solution is to provide an extra injector or two squirting into the inlet tract, usually onto the throttle plate, so that the contribution is distributed equally to the eight cylinders. This method can be arranged to function only at full throttle or under boost in the case of forced induction, but the additional complication, increased risk of failure and general difficulty of obtaining smooth progression from a system that is unavoidably of a step change nature is unattractive to most engine tuners.

If satisfactory performance across the whole engine performance spectrum is required then changes to the ECU are necessary. The main fuel memory chip in the ECU is custom-made and can neither be replaced with an alternative nor reprogrammed. Fortunately the analogue circuitry can be recalibrated or even redesigned to 'bend' the fuel programme when necessary.

A further consideration is the flow restriction caused by the Bosch airflow meter. The power gain possible by removing this restriction from the standard Rover EFi engine is about 8 to 10 bhp but larger displacement versions of the engine can gain twice this amount. A simple solution adopted by some has been to fit the larger airflow meter from the Jaguar V12 but this is only a partial solution involving a number of compromises. Obviously, to remove the airflow meter entirely is not a simple matter. Until recently, the only answer when omitting the airflow meter was to replace the ECU with a programmable alternative but these are usually very expensive. However, through J E Motors it is now possible to obtain a relatively inexpensive ECU conversion to sense engine load from inlet manifold pressure thereby eliminating the restriction of the airflow meter. It is available with adjustment via several micrometer dials or to a fixed specification. When first tested on a Sprintex supercharged 3.5-litre Range Rover a power gain of 18 bhp was achieved. Another alternative is becoming available. Lucas, at the instigation of, and exclusively for, J E Motors, have developed a programmable system which uses throttle angle

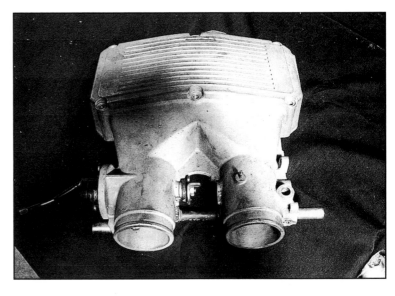

and engine speed as main parameters on a 16 x 16 site matrix with added correction for air temperature and barometric pressure. This is designated 14CU and is based on the hardware for the 13CU system. A portable PC computer is used with a development aid to map the engine fuelling requirements from dynamomometer tests and final road testing, the resulting data being burnt into a EPROM memory chip for installation inside the ECU. Such a fuel programme can easily be stored and reproduced for other engines of the same specification. For security reasons the programme will partially corrupt if an unauthorised attempt is subsequently made to copy it from the ECU.

The special twin throttle plenum chamber developed specifically for Group A racing – known as the 'twin plenum injection' Vitesse.

EXHAUST SYSTEMS

The SD1 engine was blessed upon its introduction in 1976 with a pair of very efficient cast iron exhaust manifolds, with dual outlets for each bank of cylinders phased thus: left hand 1 + 5, 3 + 7 right hand 2 + 4, 6 + 8.

Exhaust systems are very difficult to appraise objectively and opinions differ widely. One fact however is inescapable and that is that the majority of systems depend more on the limitations imposed by the vehicle than on producing an optimum system for the engine and the requirements of the vehicle. It is not so much a question of what exhaust system you would like, so much as what will realistically fit.

There are one or two principles

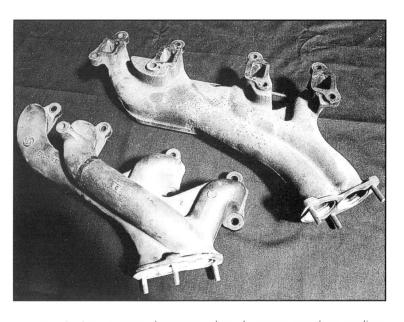

Standard Rover SD1 cast exhaust manifolds? Actually a pair of Group A items, painstakingly ground out inside for extra gas flow.

Mallory high performance distributors are available for pre-SD1 and SD1-type Rover V8 engines.

Group A Rover Vitesse leading into 2″ diameter primary outlets and via a Y piece into a 3″ bore tail pipe. He found that the length of the primary pipes was critical to the characteristics of the engine. The pipe size after the manifolds seems about right for any tuned Rover V8 at 2″ and if the system then goes into a single outlet the diameter can vary depending on requirements from 2.5 to 3″.

Tubular manifolds are available from more than one source for just about every production vehicle that uses or has used the Rover V8, from Range Rover to Morgan Plus 8. They are expensive and the power to be gained from fitting them to an otherwise standard engine is no more than 15–20 bhp. Cast manifolds are quite adequate for a mildly tuned road engine up to about 200 bhp, but once an engine is tuned beyond that tubular manifolds will probably be needed to yield the full benefit of further tuning.

however, that do seem worth recording. The manifold design if tubular, needs to be made from equal lengths of pipe although the limitations of the engine bay do not always make this practical and the bore size of the exhaust system is more critical than its length. Race car systems have used 4-into-1 and 4–2–1 designs and single pipe systems are definitely the favoured set-up currently. But where twin systems have been used the positioning of the balance pipe has been found to change the point in the rpm range at which peak torque occurs by as much as 1000 rpm. This alteration of the engine's torque characteristics by the exhaust system is borne out by Dennis Leech, long time Rover V8 racer, who used 'standard' SD1-type cast manifolds on his black

IGNITION SYSTEM

The pre-SD1 engine was fitted with a Lucas single contact breaker ignition system (their first for an 8-cylinder engine) but when engine peak rpm was raised to 6000rpm for the SD1 it was deemed unable to cope and the solution of using a twin contact breaker system was rejected because of possible service problems. Lucas again came to the rescue with an electronic system using a proximity switch make and break, with an amplifier incorporated into the distributor.

The early ignition systems (pre-SD1) suffer from above-average spindle wear, points bounce and poor dwell angles. The answer was to fit a Lumenition electronic kit which was good but fickle in operation. The SD1 electronic system on the other hand is excellent but prone to misfiring and deterioration of the system through heat from the engine. The system used on the Rover Vitesse is probably the best – it has an ignition amplifier underneath the coil. However the latest specification injection engines used on the Range Rover now have the ignition amplifier on the side of the distributor where once again it can fail due to overheating.

It must be stressed that the above comments apply to exceptional cases, for instance when the engine is being pushed hard or has been modified. The standard

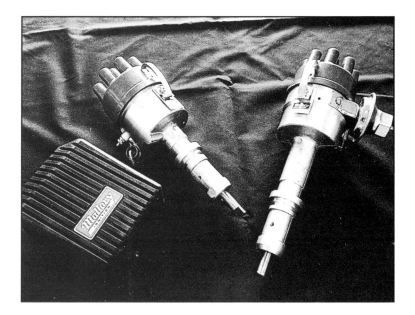

193

ROVER V8

Rover ignition system, particularly the electronic system produced after 1976, is very good, even down to the plug leads. Do not swap ignition components between systems either, try to stick to one specification.

The standard ignition system has been retained in many competition engines and found to be adequate but there are certain situations where some uprating is necessary. Auto Power Services of Daventry have an uprated distributor using Chrysler V8 points and John Woolfe Racing in Bedford collaborated with Mallory, the performance ignition company of Carson City, Nevada, on the production of Buick-based distributors for many Rover V8 applications. It must be stressed that this did not simply involve adapting Buick/Oldsmobile 215 parts although these were used as a base. JWR and Mallory have produced a range of dual point and breakerless electronic ignition systems with adjustable advance, specifically for Rover V8 engines. There is even a full magneto system available too.

INCREASING THE CAPACITY

Increasing the capacity of the Rover V8 has become the subject of intense interest amongst specialist engine builders, and Land Rover themselves have made a considerable contribution to the possibilities with the 3.9, 4.2, 4.0 and 4.6-litre production versions.

Still the most popular capacity boost for the 3.5-litre engine is the 3.9-litre 'conversion', which involves replacing the cast iron cylinder liners of the standard engine and boring the cylinders to 94 mm diameter. Depending on the exact pistons/bore size being used, the capacity comes out at around 3950 cc.

The bigger bore size decreases the shrouding effect that the cylinder walls have on the valves, giving better engine breathing, and the increase in capacity gives a healthy power boost without involving an increase in engine operating rpm. However, if you already have a 3.9-litre Rover V8 and want more, read on.

When Land Rover began producing their own 3.9-litre engine in 1989, they too used a 94 mm bore for a capacity of 3958 cc. The cylinder block of this engine has slightly more aluminium material surrounding the liner, so will accommodate a bore of 94.5 mm and can even be stretched to an absolute maximum of 96 mm.

With the bore limits thus set, the stroke then became the focus of attention and in 1992 Land Rover introduced a 4.2-litre Rover V8, using a 76 mm stroke cast iron crankshaft increasing the engine's capacity to 4292 cc. Suddenly the enthusiast had a factory produced crank, which with standard length rods would bolt straight into the 3.5 or 3.9-litre block.

The factory 94 mm bore pistons come in two different compression heights, one of 48 mm for the 71 mm 'short' stroke crank, and one with of 44 mm for the 76 mm long stroke crankshaft. So, by using a factory 3.9-litre block (94 mm bore), or having a Rover V8 specialist bore the older 3.5-litre block and fit new liners, big capacities are a home workshop job.

So 4.2 litres is 'easy' using factory parts, but the Rover V8 specialists have plenty more to offer those with the desire to own their own Rover V8 'mountain motor'!

Cranks with a stroke beyond 76 mm had been around for some time. J E Engineering (formerly J E Motors) of Coventry, for instance, had developed cast iron crankshafts of 77 mm and 81 mm from defunct Land Rover tooling intended for the defunct 'Iceberg' V8 diesel engine project. Rovercraft in Maidstone have their own 82 mm cast crankshaft and there were one or two oddball alternatives, such as the 88.9 mm stroke crankshaft from the Leyland Australia 4.4-litre Rover V8, and the Buick 300 crank, which could be made to fit with some work.

Real Steel in Uxbridge have a 'kit'

Different engine capacities and bore/stroke combinations require different height pistons to maintain required compression ratio.

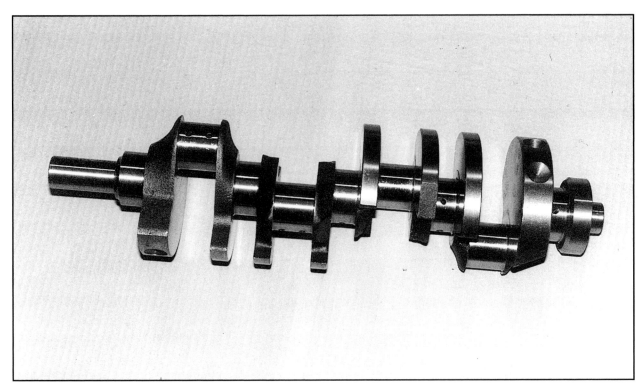

The Real Steel 86 mm stroke crankshaft in cast iron.

available that utilises the standard bore of the 3.5-litre engine and offers the convenience of a bolt-in capacity increase to 4.3 litres! The kit consists of a nodular cast iron crankshaft with a stroke of 86 mm, cast hypereutectic aluminium pistons and 4340 stainless steel connecting rods of 148.6 mm length. The crankshaft is especially interesting in that it is internally balanced, unlike all factory cranks, which are externally balanced, having eight counterweights instead of the usual six. This

makes the crankshaft heavier (22 instead of 17.5 kilos). The specially cast pistons use a Chevy small block size wrist pin and weigh 518 grams compared with a standard factory 88.9 mm piston, which weighs 645 grams. The kit is ideal for adding lots more mid-rpm torque for towing and the like, but has wider potential.

The Land Rover casting for the new 4.6-litre Rover V8 crankshaft is now being machined to produce a whole range of crankshafts for the earlier engines right

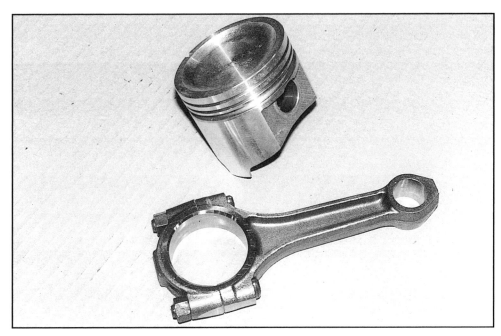

The Real Steel 148 mm stainless steel con rod and 88.9 mm diameter piston – bolt in with the above crank for 4.3 litres!

ROVER V8

up to a 96 mm stroke. The very large capacities do compromise block strength (at higher rpm) and push the breathing limits of the Rover cylinder heads, but the strength problem can be solved by using four-bolt or cross-bolt blocks that have the main bearing caps fastened by two bolts going vertically into the block and two bolts coming horizontally through the block, one from each side of the cap. These blocks were 'issued' by the factory in very small numbers, so were expensive and highly prized. J E Developments and Rovercraft have successfully machined standard Rover V8 blocks to take billet mains caps with four-bolt fixing, which adds enormously to the integrity of the block, especially in hi-output or competition engines.

The factory has again filled the breach with their own cross-bolted blocks, which are standard on the new 4.0 and 4.6-litre blocks, and these castings, now being common to all but the 3.5-litre factory engines, can be machined to produce cross-bolted blocks for the earlier engines.

J E Developments in collaboration with Ian Richardson Racing now have a new Rover V8 cylinder block casting, again with four-bolt mains, which can be safely bored to a maximum of 102 mm, which gives a potential for engines of 6.2 litres when combined with the 96 mm cranks available. The race is now on amongst the serious specialists to produce significantly better cylinder heads to enable these bigger engines to yield their full potential.

In conclusion, then, what can we expect from a well built big capacity engine for fast road use? Here are the figures taken from a dynamometer read-out on a 4.9-litre Rover V8 built by Rovertec. The engine uses a 94.5 mm bore and a cast crankshaft with an 86 mm stroke, standard connecting rods, special cylinder heads and quadruple downdraught induction.

Rpm	2000	2500	3000	3500	4000
Bhp	84	102	136	207	261
lb/ft torque	222	222	239	311	343
Rpm	4500	5000	5500	6000	6500
Bhp	289	320	326	342	353
lb/ft torque	353	336	311	300	259

SUPERCHARGING & TURBOCHARGING

As with other methods of engine tuning, there are both advantages and disadvantages to supercharging or turbocharging the Rover V8. In the case of supercharging there is obviously the cost; it certainly is expensive and the 'kits' available do not bolt straight on to the engine, so there is a certain amount of work involved in DIY installations. The better known Roots-type are mounted, via an adaptor, on to the Holley 4-barrel flange of an Offenhauser-type manifold which obviously puts it on top of the engine. With a carburettor (usually a Holley) on top of that the whole device can seriously impede forward visibility! Perhaps it is not quite that bad, unless we are talking about fitting one to a Triumph TR7 V8, but it is a problem. One of the reasons so many Range Rovers have been fitted with this type of supercharger (comparatively speaking) is that there is plenty of room in the engine compartment and possibly those who can afford a Range Rover are more likely to be able to afford a supercharger!

However, supercharging considerably increases power output, depending on the pressure the supercharger is geared to operate at, even though engine power is absorbed just driving the supercharger itself. As long as the engine is healthy the 'blower' can be fitted without extensive engine modifications. As previously stated, most of the established installations mount the supercharger on top of the engine where it is driven by a belt from the front of the crankshaft. The belt also has to be kept in correct tension, which involves mounting some form of tensioning device. Operating pressure is determined by the ratio of pulley drive to crankshaft speed and the engine is protected by a pop-off valve in the inlet manifold. Adjustments to the engine's ignition timing are required, more advance at idle with less at the top end and if higher boost pressures are going to be used then the compression ratio has to be lowered to perhaps 8:1 or 7:1 depending on boost.

With the interest in turbocharging now beginning to wane, considerable strides forward are being made in the design and engineering of superchargers. In Europe there is the 'G' type unit being pioneered in production car use by Volkswagen and in Britain Fleming Dynamics of Glasgow have designed the Sprintex supercharger which is manufactured in the

The American B&M supercharger on a Rover V8. This is a Roots-type blower with extruded aluminium two-lobe rotors. Installed by NCK Racing of Coventry.

The 'Sprintex' supercharger.

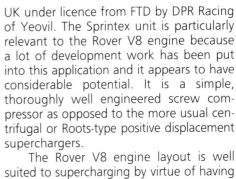

UK under licence from FTD by DPR Racing of Yeovil. The Sprintex unit is particularly relevant to the Rover V8 engine because a lot of development work has been put into this application and it appears to have considerable potential. It is a simple, thoroughly well engineered screw compressor as opposed to the more usual centrifugal or Roots-type positive displacement superchargers.

The Rover V8 engine layout is well suited to supercharging by virtue of having all inlet ports grouped closely together. The Rover Vitesse/Range Rover EFi fuel injected version is particularly convenient and with a plenum chamber drawing air from one side, the supercharger can blow into it via relatively straightforward trunking. Mounting the Sprintex unit is also easier, as it normally sits alongside and slightly above the engine, either flat or on its side, depending on the particular engine compartment involved. The Sprintex supercharger on a Range Rover EFi engine only absorbs 15 bhp to drive it, while producing an additional 75 bhp at the flywheel, yet the maximum boost rarely exceeds 6 psi. Furthermore the power absorption at light throttle is so minimal that any fuel consumption penalty is more than offset by the reduced dependency on low gear ratios to obtain satisfactory performance. The engine is left virtually standard except for the fitting of thicker head gaskets to slightly reduce the compression ratio in order to ensure freedom from detonation at maximum torque. Soon even this will be unnecessary when development of a programmable ignition system is completed. Fuel injection development centered around the ECU and disposing of the restrictive Bosch airflow meter of the Rover V8's injection system. This increases maximum boost pressure and increases power thereby further increasing supercharger efficiency and may possibly form the basis for an even more powerful conversion.

The aim of the Sprintex conversion is the provision of tremendous torque and engine flexibility with no trace of the lag which detracts from so many turbocharger installations. Flooring the accelerator pedal at any speed produces instant response and acceleration. The DPR Sprintex Range Rover, based on an EFi engine, produces 240 bhp at 4750 rpm and 280 lb/ft of torque at 3200 rpm. It will accelerate from 0–60mph in under 8 seconds (the standard Range Rover EFi takes 12.4 seconds). The conversion is also available for carburetted Rover V8s so can be applied to the Land

The 'Sprintex' super-charger fitted on a Rover 350 '350SX' for Haughins, the Northern TVR Centre Ltd. It is a very neat, well engineered installation.

Rover and Rover SD1.

In general, engines can tolerate a 50% increase in power output before serious engine work is required to ensure reliability. An important advantage with supercharging is also that the rpm operating range of the engine does not have to be increased to produce that extra power, so preparing the engine for high rpm use is not necessary.

Turbocharging was very fashionable a few years ago but successful installations now tend to involve microchip technology, which is not only sophisticated but expensive, as are many of the state of the art systems. As a general rule turbocharging has little effect on low rpm power and torque output of the engine because exhaust gas velocity at lower engine speeds is insufficient to drive the compression turbine fast enough to pressurise the induction charge to any appreciable extent. The phenomenon of 'turbo lag' – the delay between pressing the accelerator and getting the engine's response – is an ever-present problem. This situation can be overcome to a certain extent by playing around with the size of the compressor and the design of the overall installation but a compromise will always be required. As the engine rpm rises, so the turbocharger produces boost, forcing the induction charge of fuel and air into the engine at a greater rate than the engine

could normally 'breath' it, thereby releasing additional power and 'urge'. So turbocharging cannot give increased power and torque over as wide an rpm range as supercharging, although it absorbs little engine power itself, being driven from spent or waste exhaust gases.

As with supercharging, systems are expensive and really outside the usual abilities of the DIY mechanic. Underbonnet heat is also a tremendous problem with turbocharging. Twin turbochargers are the obvious choice for a V8 (one to each cylinder bank) but this increases the cost and heat emission. Locating a single turbocharger, without ending up with unequal length exhaust feeds to the turbine is also a problem depending on space limitations within the vehicle involved. Many modern systems also use an intercooler between the compressor and the inlet manifold to cool the induction charge which must therefore also be located close to the engine.

NITROUS OXIDE INJECTION

The use of nitrous oxide injection systems to increase engine power is now virtually outlawed in every type of automobile circuit racing and was recently banned in hillclimbing and sprinting too. This is mainly due to the concern over having a pressurised bottle of the gas on a racing vehicle, rather than its competitive advantage, which can be considerable, but it is still used in many classes of drag racing and can be used on a road vehicle.

The use of nitrous oxide or 'laughing gas' has its origins, at least when applied to engine performance, in the United States where it has been used extensively in drag racing and on road vehicles for over ten years. It is a chemical compound (N_2O), rich in oxygen which in liquid form is injected into the engine, where under combustion it breaks down and releases oxygen to burn with the usual petrol/air mixture. An engine breathes air and uses the oxygen in that air for combustion. Introduce an additional source of oxygen plus some additional fuel to burn with it and the result is considerably greater engine power.

On a typical system, the nitrous oxide is stored, usually in the car boot, in a cylinder under pressure. A solenoid, actuated by a switch, releases nitrous oxide from the cylinder via a small diameter pipe to the engine, where it enters the inlet manifold through nozzles. Another solenoid simultaneously releases an additional fuel supply, via another set of nozzles. The nozzles can be fitted easily by mounting them on a carburettor spacer plate, so that the N_2O enters the inlet manifold in the same place as the usual fuel air mixture. Alternatively a pair of nozzles – one for N_2O, one for additional fuel – can be tapped into each manifold runner, near the port. Some systems on Rover V8 engines have been plumbed in this way, using the space *underneath* the inlet manifold so that all the pipework is out of the way and neatly hidden from view.

The supply of N_2O, once switched on, is at a constant rate, so the engine more or less receives a set amount of additional horsepower, perhaps 50 or 100 bhp depending on the system fitted. It can only be made progressive by using more than one system in stages e.g. three 50 bhp systems, introduced to the engine at specific rpm increments will give 50 bhp, then 100 bhp then 150 bhp. Or so the theory goes!

The use of nitrous oxide injection need not be limited to out and out performance situations. For example, it can also be used to compensate for turbocharger lag and a system capable of delivering perhaps 50 bhp could be installed on a blow-through turbocharged engine, and switched on by a vacuum switch (manifold pressure *low*) and switched off by a pressure switch (boost pressure having built up). In such a situation, a nitrous oxide system could be used on the road quite economically to eliminate turbo lag.

One company with a lot of experience of nitrous oxide systems on Rover V8 engines is TMC (Automotives) Ltd of Doncaster. Trevor Langfield, who runs the company, has successfully campaigned a Ford Escort Mk1 powered by a 3.5-litre Rover V8 in the Real Steel/Street Machine Magazine Rover V8 drag racing championship, using a nitrous oxide system of his own design. On a standard Rover 3.5-litre SD1 saloon his system improved the quarter mile time from 17.8 seconds with a terminal speed of 77 mph to 13.5 seconds and 102 mph. The 'Highpower' systems of which there are a range of five from Stage I Econo-Street' to 'Stage V Eliminator Delta' all use a single 'duo' solenoid valve to control both nitrous oxide flow and fuel flow with a 'duo' jet introducing both nitrous oxide and fuel to the inlet manifold. These 'Highpower' systems offer considerable performance gains and have further development potential.

ENGINE TRANSPLANTS

The Rover V8 engine has been transplanted into an enormous variety of cars. Its light weight, compact dimensions, ample power, and easy availability have made it a firm favourite for replacing all sorts of standard powerplants.

Scimpart of Witcombe near Gloucester specialise in the Reliant Scimitar (GTE/GTC) and they can supply a comprehensive kit of parts to enable the standard cast iron Ford V6 engine to be replaced by a Rover V8. The emphasis is on making the Rover engine fit neatly, to the point of retaining the spare wheel mounting under the bonnet, with very few changes having to be made to the rest of the car. It can retain the standard Reliant suspension, brakes and rear axle ratio. Even in a relatively mild state of tune the Rover engine, being some 100 lbs lighter than the Ford, completely changes the character of the car and of course the Rover engine can be tuned for still more power since the running gear is well up to coping with extra performance. The Datsun 240/260Z sports cars were

199

Datsun 280Z with 3.9-litre Rover V8 competing at Prescott.

ROVER V8

enormously popular in the early 1970s, before they evolved into an overweight, refined and up-market grand tourer. The Americans wasted no time in replacing the big lazy 6-cylinder engine with home grown engines, such as the small-block Chevrolet V8, and for a car designed to take a straight six engine the engine compartment is surprisingly suitable for such a swap. More recently the Rover V8 is proving equally ideal for the usual reasons of light weight, easy availability, economy, power and torque. The substitution of a Rover V8 for the original engine is very straightforward, the Rover engine being some 200 lb lighter than the Datsun unit so there are immediate performance gains to be made. The engine and gearbox mounts have to be altered, new exhaust manifolds made, the propshaft has to be shortened and a larger radiator fitted. The experts in this conversion are The Z Centre of GB at Worplesdon, near Guildford and the result is a big improvement over the original car although it must be said that good examples of the Datsun 240/260Z are appreciating in value and anything that detracts from their originality could affect that. But the Rover V8 does give a big improvement in performance and fitting the engine requires no alternations to the sheet metal of the car. It would not be impossible to convert the car back again and with the original engine rebuilt and stored it would be in fine condition should it be needed!

Probably the best known engine swap involving the Rover V8 is the conversion of the Triumph TR7 to Triumph TR8 specification. The Triumph TR7 was powered by an unique combination of Triumph Dolomite Sprint cylinder block with Dolomite 2-valve cylinder head which gave adequate, if not exciting power for a sports car. The Triumph TR7 V8 referred officially to the rally cars built by BL Motorsport from coupé bodyshells and the Triumph TR8, at least as far as the UK market is concerned, was a Rover V8-powered Triumph TR7 drophead of which only 20 or so pre-production examples were built and sold. Few converted cars are built as true Triumph TR8 replicas. For a start many people have converted coupés (TR8 coupés were sold in North America) and there are one or two aspects of the real TR8, such as the brakes, or more specifically the front discs which are considered inadequate, so converted cars very often have a ventilated disc with 4 piston caliper setup derived from the TR7 V8 rally cars. UK specifica-

tion TR8s also had 152 bhp Rover V8s with twin Zenith/Stromberg 1275CD carburettors, which converters usually ignore and use perhaps as SD1 type engine with any amount of tuning goodies.

Triumph TR7 conversions have become considerably more sophisticated than those early attempts to emulate the TR8. The basic procedure for installing a Rover V8 into a Triumph TR7 is as follows: the car should first of all be a 5-speed model, which has the 77 mm Austin Rover 5-speed gearbox and a slightly narrower version of the Rover SD1 back axle already in place. Early TR7s had a weaker 4-speed gearbox and Dolomite rear axle. The original 4-cylinder engine is removed and the crossmember is modified (genuine TR8 items are now rare) to take a pair of engine mountings, instead of the original one. The radiator is moved forward and downwards on new brackets. A Rover V8 with a Rover SD1 manual bellhousing fitted will then mount on the crossmember.

With the aid of a shortened propshaft, the engine and gearbox are moved back slightly and the gearbox crossmember mounting holes are re-drilled further back. A Jaguar gearchange extension housing will put the gearstick back into its original position if required. The rev counter then has to be modified for eight instead of four cylinders. From this point the options begin to widen. For instance, if twin SU carburettors are retained the front subframe will have to be lowered to get them under the low bonnet, cast SD1 exhaust manifolds can be retained and linked to a specially made exhaust system, or as most people tend to do, tubular manifolds with a compatible exhaust system can be fitted. The standard TR7 final drive ratio of 3.9:1 is really too low for a road car, although the acceleration is terrific! It should be changed for a 3.45:1 or 3.08:1 although a 2.84:1 is available for really relaxed cruising. The front discs need to be at least uprated to TR8 spec which are thicker discs with callipers using larger area pads but for a conversion using a tuned V8 they really should be ventilated discs with 4 piston callipers. There are also subtle but almost essential suspension modifications, although many converters want to uprate the suspension with uprated springs and shock absorbers. The engine is of course open to a whole range of tuning possibilities which can easily push a conversion into the realms of really high performance. As a DIY conversion it is not that simple, but it is made easy by the availability of all the

Transplanting the Rover V8 can produce good competition vehicles too. Richard Painton's rallycross car was probably the most successful TR7 V8 in the sport.

components needed and the excellent value for money such a conversion offers. There are also a number of good companies who will carry out the transformation at a reasonable cost.

The MGB, in roadster and GT guise, is now revered by MG enthusiasts as the last great British sports car, but its B-series 1800 cc 4-cylinder engine was never a performance unit. It was heavy, noisy and rough which to some extent suited the character of the MGB but transplanting the Rover V8 engine recreates all the attributes of the MGB GT V8 and there is the option of creating an MGB V8 Roadster, a choice never made available to the buying public by Leyland.

The Rover V8 is a fairly tight fit, more so in the pre-1974 black bumper era cars, but it can be done by mating the V8 to the all-synchromesh MGB/MGC gearbox via an adaptor plate and MGB GT V8 engine mountings. An MGB GT V8 clutch centre plate is used with an MGC pressure plate. It is perfectly feasible to use the complete engine, bellhousing and 5-speed

gearbox from a Rover SD1, installing the engine on MGB GT V8 front mountings and modifying the MGB gearbox crossmember to accept SD1 gearbox mountings; but a special propshaft has to be made. The radiator, an MGC item, has to be mounted further forward (it already is on the later models) to clear the Rover water pump and there is no room for the engine-driven fan, so an electric fan must be used. Tubular exhaust manifolds are best fitted in conjunction with an MGB GT V8 exhaust system. As with the TR7 to V8 conversion, the rear axle ratio is too low at 3.9:1 and needs to be raised to 3.3:1 or maybe even 3.07:1. Some slight uprating of the brakes and suspension is also advisable. The low under bonnet clearance of the MGB for the induction system is a problem, the standard Rover V8 twin SUs cannot be used without a bonnet bulge so an MGB GT V8 type carburettor adaptor has to be used, or a Holley 4-barrel carburettor on an Offenhauser manifold is low enough. There is an adaptor available to mount a single rearward-facing twin

203

ROVER V8

choke Dellorto carburettor on a Holley mounting flange which solves the problem. One company with a lot of experience in this conversion and fitting the Rover V8 into a variety of vehicles, is the V8 Conversion Company in Orpington, Kent. The origins of the company go back to the Costello V8 conversion on the MGB.

Transplanting the Rover V8 into a car which has the power unit in the mid-engined position ie. ahead of the rear axle line, requires mating it to a gearbox/differential unit or transaxle and no such unit was used in the Austin Rover/Land-Rover vehicle lineup. The Rover V8 can be attached to the VW transmission unit, which has to be turned round for such applications, by means of adaptor kits. If the engine is going to produce in excess of 200 bhp the VW transmission may be too weak to withstand the torque but can be strengthened to a point. The Renault 20, 25 or 30 saloon uses a suitable transaxle because the engine was mounted ahead of the front axle line driving the front wheels. This transaxle is readily available secondhand (as is the VW) and capable of handling more torque but in conjunction with a Rover V8 requires a special bellhousing.

The best, within a reasonable budget, is the Porsche 911 transaxle, probably not so readily available secondhand but capable of handling all the torque a Rover V8 can muster and if not, parts to beef it up are available at a price. The ultimate transaxles are Hewland competition units as used in many cars from single seaters to sports racing cars but they are expensive. ZF transaxles also rank in the 'exotic' category having been used in many high performance mid-engined sports cars such as the De Tomaso Pantera. The other consideration in mid-engined applications is the gearchange linkage which is obviously more involved and one must also give a lot of thought to exhaust manifolds and systems which usually have to be specially designed.

The Rover V8 engine has been trans-

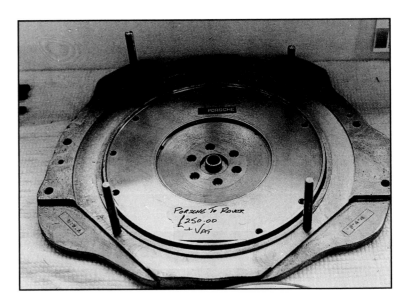

UVA adaptor plate for Rover V8 to Porsche transaxle.

planted into an enormous variety of cars not originally designed to accept it and part of the success of such installations is the engine's light weight which helps retain the original vehicle balance coupled with the engine's compact dimensions. Admittedly it is a little longer than the average 4-cylinder engine, but its weight makes the usual chore of finding suitable front springs and beefier brakes often unnecessary. It has been fitted into Triumph Spitfires, MG Midgets, Triumph Dolomites, Ford Escort Mk3s and Mk4s, Ford Capris, Opel Asconas, Vauxhall Vivas and Chevettes, Morris Marinas, and Vauxhall Ventoras, to name but a few.

It is now possible to have a Rover V8 mated to a Sierra 5-speed gearbox by Auto Power Services of Daventry, which opens up one intriguing possibility. Ford sold a fair number of mundane Sierra 1.6L 2-door saloons before withdrawing the 2-door from the UK market. The same bodyshell is now used on the Sierra Cosworth, so with the right Cosworth panels, spoilers, wheels and tyres a humble 1.6L could, with a tuned Rover V8 under the bonnet be transformed at a very reasonable price into a more than interesting, high performance hybrid.

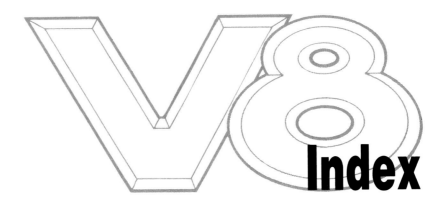

Index

USEFUL ADDRESSES

The following addresses and telephone/fax numbers were believed to be correct at the time of going to press. However, as these are subject to change, particularly area dialling codes, no guarantee can be given for their continued accuracy.

D.J. Ellis Ltd
Unit 3, Exis Court
Veasey Close
Attleborough Field Industrial Estate
Nuneaton
Warwickshire CV11 6RT
Tel: 02476 352888
www.djev8.com
Rover V8 engine specialists. Road and competition engines, machining facilities, performance parts, camshafts, cylinder heads, dyno facilities, flow bench testing.

Janspeed Engineering
Castle Road
Salisbury
Wiltshire SP1 3SQ
Tel: 01722 321844
Fax: 01722 412308
www.janspeed.com
A range of exhaust systems suited to Rover V8 engined vehicles.

J.E. Developments
Claybrooke Mill
Claybrooke Magna
Nr. Lutterworth
Leicestershire LE17 5DB
Tel/Fax: 01455 202909
Rover V8 specialists. Road & Race engine builders, machining facilities, dyno facilities, Efi specialist including mapping, large capacity blocks, long stroke crankshafts, cylinder heads, baffled sumps, specialist parts.

J.E. Engineering
Siskin Drive
Coventry CV3 4FJ
Tel: 02476 305018
Fax: 02476 305913
LPG conversions and supercharged Range Rover conversions.

Kent Cams Ltd
Units 1-7, Military Road
Shorncliffe Industrial Estate
Folkestone
Kent CT20 3SP
Tel: 01303 248666
Fax: 01303 252508
www.kentcams.com
Camshafts and vernier timing gear kit with roller chain.

Oselli Engineering
Ferry Hinksey Road
Oxford OX2 OBY
Tel: 01865 200564
Fax: 01865 791656
www.oselli.com
Lead free conversion for Rover V8

Piper Cams Ltd
St. John's Court
Ashford Business Park
Sevington
Ashford
Kents TN24 0SJ
Tel: 01233 500200
Fax: 01233 500300
www.pipercams.co.uk
Rover V8 camshafts, duplex timing gear with vernier pulley.

Progress Engineering
Unit 1
Progress Estate
Parkwood
Maidstone, Kent
Tel: 01622 687070
Fax: 01622 692273
Formerley Rovercraft. Rover V8 specialists, rolling road and dyno facilities, engine rebuild and performance parts, Efi tuning and mapping, machining (including balancing) cylinder head porting.

Real Steel
Unit 9
Tomo Industrial Estate
Packet Boat Lane
Cowley, Uxbridge
Middlesex UB8 2JP
Tel: 01895 440505
Fax: 01895 422047
Their inventory has a very wide range of Rover V8 engine parts including 4.3 and 4.8 litre stroker kits, performance parts and cylinder heads. In house dyno facility.

Rimmer Bros Ltd
Triumph House
Sleaford Road
Bracebridge Heath
Lincoln LN4 2NA
Tel: 01522 568000
Fax: 01522 567600
www.rimmerbros.co.uk
Extensive Rover V8 Engine Catalogue offering new factory "full" engines, short engines, rebuild parts, performance parts, cylinder heads.

RPi Engineering International Ltd
Wayside Garage
Holt Road, Horsford
Norwich NR10 3EE
Tel: 01603 891209
Fax: 01603 890330
www.v8engines.com
Rover V8 specialists, engine building, performance and rebuild parts, engine dress up parts including pressed steel chrome rocker covers.

S & S Preparations
640 Newchurch Road
Stacksteads
Bacup
Lancashire OL13 0NH
Tel: 01706 874874
Fax: 01706 873873
www.ss-preparations.co.uk
Specialists in TR7 V8 conversions. Engine building, rebuild parts and performance parts.

Turbo Technics
2 Sketty Close
Brackmills
Northampton NN4 7PL
Tel: 01604 705050
Fax: 01604 769668
www.turbotechnics.com
Turbocharger specialists with considerable experience of Rover V8 engines.

V8 Developments
Cobwebs Farm
Swale Bank
Gosberton Westhorpe
Spalding
Lincolnshire PE11 4LG
Tel: 01775 750000
Fax: 01775 750005
www.v8developments.co.uk
Rover V8 specialists. Road and comptition engine building, parts, Efi expertise, dyno facilities.

Wilcat Engineering
The Old Creamery
Rhydymain Dolgellau
Gwynedd LL40 2AY
Tel: 01341 45200
www.roverv8engine.co.uk
Specialist parts for Rover V8. Big capacity blocks, cranks, cylinder heads and inlet manifolds.